CONTINENT BY DEFAULT

CONTINENT BY DEFAULT

*The European Union and the
Demise of Regional Order*

ANNE MARIE LE GLOANNEC

CORNELL UNIVERSITY PRESS
ITHACA AND LONDON

First published 2017 by Cornell University Press

Printed in the United States of America

Library of Congress Cataloging-in-Publication Data
Names: Le Gloannec, Anne-Marie, author.
Title: Continent by default : the European Union and the demise of
    regional order / Anne Marie Le Gloannec.
Description: Ithaca : Cornell University Press, 2017. | Includes
    bibliographical references and index.
Identifiers: LCCN 2017041693 (print) | LCCN 2017042208 (ebook) |
    ISBN 9781501716683 (pdf) | ISBN 9781501716676 (epub/mobi) |
    ISBN 9781501716669 | ISBN 9781501716669 (cloth : alk. paper)
Subjects: LCSH: European Union. | Europe—Foreign relations. |
    European cooperation.
Classification: LCC JN30 (ebook) | LCC JN30 .L336 2017 (print) |
    DDC 341.242/2—dc23
LC record available at https://lccn.loc.gov/2017041693

Cornell University Press strives to use environmentally responsible suppliers and materials to the fullest extent possible in the publishing of its books. Such materials include vegetable-based, low-VOC inks and acid-free papers that are recycled, totally chlorine-free, or partly composed of nonwood fibers. For further information, visit our website at cornellpress.cornell.edu.

CONTENTS

Abbreviations

AC	Arctic Council
ACP	African, Caribbean, and Pacific countries
AKP	Adalet ve Kalkınma Partisi (Justice and Development Party)
BEAC	Barents Euro-Arctic Council
BiH	Bosnia i Herzegovina
BSEC	Black Sea Economic Cooperation
CBC	Cross Border Cooperation
CBSS	Council of the Baltic Sea States
CEECs	Central and Eastern European Countries
CEFTA	Central European Free Trade Agreement
CEI	Central European Initiative
CFE	Treaty on Conventional Armed Forces in Europe
CFSP	Common Foreign and Security Policy
CHP	Cumhuriyet Halk Partisi (Republican People's Party)
CIS	Commonwealth of Independent States
CMEA (Comecon)	Council for Mutual Economic Assistance

CSCE	Commission on Security and Cooperation in Europe
CSCM	Conference on Security and Co-operation in the Mediterranean
CSDP	Common Security and Defence Policy (= also ESDP, European Security and Defence Policy, 1999–2008)
CSTO	Collective Security Treaty Organization
DCFTA	Deep and Comprehensive Free Trade Agreement
DG	Directorate-General
EAEC (Euratom)	European Atomic Energy Community
EaP	Eastern Partnership
EASO	European Asylum Support Office
EAW	European Arrest Warrant
EBRD	European Bank for Reconstruction and Development
EC	European Community
ECHO	European Commission Humanitarian Office, later European Commission Humanitarian Aid and Civil Protection department, formerly the European Community Humanitarian Aid Office
ECSC	European Coal and Steel Community
ECT	Energy Charter Treaty
ECtHR	European Court of Human Rights
EEA	European Economic Area
EEAS	European External Action Service
EEC	European Economic Communities/Community
EFTA	European Free Trade Association
EIB	European Investment Bank
EIDHR	European Initiative for Democracy and Human Rights
EMAAs	Euro-Mediterranean Association Agreements
EMP (EUROMED)	Euro-Mediterranean Partnership
EMU	Economic and Monetary Union
EnCT	Energy Community Treaty
ENP	European Neighbourhood Policy
EP	European Parliament
EPC	European Political Cooperation

ERDF	European Regional Development Fund
ERF	European Refugee Fund
ESA	European Space Agency
ESDP	European Security and Defence Policy
ESF	European Social Fund
ESI	European Stability Initiative
ESS	European Security Strategy
EU	European Union
EUBSS	European Union Black Sea Synergy
EUFOR	European Union Force
EUISS	European Union Institute for Security Studies
EUMM	European Union Monitoring Mission
EUNIDA	European Network of Implementing Development Agencies
EUPOL COPPS	European Union Co-ordinating Office for Palestinian Police Support
EurAsEC	Eurasian Economic Community
EUROJUST	European Unit of Judicial Cooperation
EUROPOL	EU Agency for Law Enforcement Cooperation
EUSBSR	EU Strategy for the Baltic Sea Region
EUSR	European Union Special Representative
FRG	Federal Republic of Germany
FRTD	Facilitated Rail Transit Documents
FSB	Federal Security Service of the Russian Federation
FTA	Free trade area
FTD	Facilitated Transit Documents
GAC	General Affairs Council, superseded by GAERC (General Affairs and External Relations Council)
GCC	Gulf Cooperation Council
GDR	German Democratic Republic
GSP	Generalized System of Preferences
GTS	Ground Transportation System
GUAM	Georgia, Ukraine, Azerbaijan, Moldova
IAM	Incident Assessment Mechanism
IBM	Integrated Border Management
ICC	International Criminal Court
ICJ	International Court of Justice

IDPs	Internally displaced persons
IEA	International Energy Agency
IFI	International Fund for Ireland
INOGATE	Interstate Oil and Gas Transportation to Europe
IRA	Irish Republican Army
ISIL	Islamic State in Iraq and the Levant
JCC	Joint Control Commission
JNA	Jugoslovenska narodna armija (Yugoslav National Army)
LNG	Liquefied Natural Gas
MAP	Membership Action Plan
MEDA	Mesures d'accompagnement financières et techniques
MEP	Member of the European Parliament
MFN	Most favored nation
MIC	Monitoring and Information Centre
NC	Nordic Council
ND	Northern Dimension
NFZ	No-fly zone
NGO	Non-governmental organization
NIS	Naftna Industrija Srbije
NSC	National Security Council
OCHA	Office for the Coordination of Humanitarian Affairs of the United Nations Secretariat
ODED	Office of the Deputy Executive Director
OECD	Organization for Economic Co-operation and Development
OEEC	Organization for European Economic Co-operation
OIC	Organisation of Islamic Cooperation
OSCE	Organization for Security and Co-operation in Europe
PA	Palestinian National Authority
PCA	Partnership and Cooperation Agreement
PEGASE	Mécanisme palestino-européen de gestion de l'aide socio-économique
PHARE	Poland and Hungary: Assistance for Restructuring their Economies
PKK	Partiya Karkerên Kurdistan (Kurdistan Workers' Party)

PLO	Palestine Liberation Organization
PNA	Palestinian National Authority
PSC	Political and Security Committee
QMV	Qualified majority voting
REDWG	Regional Economic Development Working Group
RoC	Republic of Cyprus
SEA	Single European Act
SEECP	South-East Europe Cooperation Process
SFOR	Stabilization Force
SME	Small and Medium Enterprises
SRSG	Special Representative of the Secretary-General of the United Nations
TACIS	Technical Aid to the Commonwealth of Independent States
TANAP	Trans-Anatolian Natural Gas Pipeline Project
TAP	Trans-Adriatic Pipeline
TCA	Trade and Cooperation Agreement
TIM	Temporary International Mechanism
TNC	Transitional National Council
TPA	Third party access
TRACECA	Transport Corridor Europe-Caucasus-Asia
TRNC	Turkish Republic of Northern Cyprus
UAE	United Arab Emirates
UfM	Union for the Mediterranean
UN	United Nations
UNHCR	United Nations High Commissioner for Refugees
UNIFIL	United Nations Interim Force in Lebanon
UNMIK	United Nations Interim Administration Mission in Kosovo
UNO	United Nations Organization
UNOMIG	United Nations Observer Mission in Georgia
UNPREDEP	United Nations Preventive Deployment Force
UNPROFOR	United Nations Protection Force
UNRWA	United Nations Relief and Works Agency
UNSC	United Nations Security Council
WEU	Western European Union
WMDs	Weapons of mass destruction

Continent by Default

INTRODUCTION

Geopolitics without Power Politics

> When I look for the most appropriate way to define the world I grew
> up in, before World War One, what most poignantly comes to my
> mind is "the golden age of security." In our almost thousand-
> year-old Austrian monarchy, everything seemed to be built to last and
> the state itself was the warrantor of permanence. . . . No one believed
> in barbarian relapses such as wars between the peoples of Europe. . . .
> [Our fathers] genuinely thought that demarcations and divergences
> between nations and creeds would gradually vanish to make the
> way for what is common to all of us human beings, and to confer on
> mankind as a whole the most precious of goods, peace and security.
>
> —STEFAN ZWEIG, *Die Welt von Gestern*

Soon after its creation, in 1957, the European Community (EC) stum-
bled into a role: that of organizing the continent.[1] Paradoxically, the EC
was not conceived as a foreign policy actor. Hardly any provision of the
Rome Treaty, which founded the EC, could be construed as paving the way
for a foreign policy role.[2] The ambition of the EC lay elsewhere: it was to
establish peace and security in Europe. After two horrendously devastat-
ing wars in which Europe twice committed suicide, dragging down parts
of the world in its fall and destroying the very foundations of its power
and culture, the EC would not and could not play any more the role that
it had seized and held for a few centuries: that of devising the world.

For several centuries, Europe had spread out all over the world. It had
exported its peoples, though often unwillingly, and its goods and ideas,
from the invention of the state and of the steam engine to the diffusion

of nationalism; it had waged wars and subjugated foreign populations. It had devised the world, for better and for worse, invented states and borders, and imposed its languages and its language of law, international organizations, norms, and mores. Two world wars and a doomed interwar era of weak states and terrifying hubris destroyed the very culture and civilizational values to which the continent aspired, the unique role it played in the world (for a relatively short period of time), and the relative security and peace it enjoyed for the greater part of the nineteenth century while engaging in skirmishes in other parts of the world. Had it not been for the colonial wars that some European countries fought to preserve and eventually discard their empires, had it not been for the partition of the Old Continent and the occupation of its eastern half by the Soviet Union and the Red Army, posing a threat at the Iron Curtain, Europe might have fallen into irrelevance. After a tragic half century, it withdrew. It became a potential theater of war between the two superpowers, an object not an actor of international relations, which, west of the continent, imported its security from the United States and, in the east, was suppressed by an iron rule. It was in the eye of the storm, at the center of power politics, yet the Cold War was mainly fought between the United States and the Soviet Union.

Exhausted and drained, Europe—Western Europe, that is—simply aspired to create the conditions in which its citizens would at last live in peace and prosperity, and to recapture the "world of yesterday," the world of security that Stefan Zweig embraced in the first pages of his autobiography and in the first decades of his life, as the nineteenth century was drawing to a close, a world of complacent security and peace on the Old Continent. While a few, principally in Paris and in London, still harbored grand designs, and while some of the founding fathers dreamed of a continent whole and united, for most the Communities that were created in the 1950s were to be a haven, a sanctuary, a counterpoise to or even an antidote for the traumas of the twentieth century: fascism, Nazism, communism, world wars, the loss of empires, Dutch, Belgian, Portuguese, British, and French, and the "kidnapping" of Central and Eastern Europe by the Soviet Union, as the Czech author Milan Kundera put it. The point was to reconcile former enemies, ban wars from intra-European relations, and become a refuge for bygone empires and lost ambitions. Some still yearned for world influence. Yet as a whole, Europe and the Communities forsook power.

How then could Europe establish peace and prosperity without a foreign policy? And could it do so without falling prey to its past demons? The Communities were devised not to tame wars, but to bar them. In contrast to nineteenth-century Europe, which drowned in the fury of World War I, peace was meant to last. The Communities were to engineer a new order on the continent, to invent a new pattern of international relations in Europe, a new way for states and societies to interact. They were to "domesticate" international relations in Europe. Grasping the very essence of this endeavor, François Duchêne, the British author who coined this expression, wrote in 1972 that "the European Community's interest as a civilian group of countries long on economic power and relatively short on armed force is as far as possible to domesticate relations between states. . . . This means trying to bring to international problems the sense of common responsibility and structures of contractual politics which have been in the past associated exclusively with 'home' and not 'foreign', that is alien, affairs" (1972: 12–20).

Pooling resources, coal and steel in the European Coal and Steel Community (ECSC), nuclear energy in the European Atomic Energy Community (EAEC, Euratom), inventing common policies in the EC, and devising and implementing laws common to all members were instrumental to this process of domestication, of peace through trust. Yet the Communities were not insulated. Postwar Europe was after all a dangerous world, torn between East and West, between Soviet occupation and an empire by invitation, as Geir Lundestad put it. The EC was enclosed by authoritarian regimes in the South, which started crumbling in the early 1970s, and by Soviet-dominated territories in the East, until 1989–1991. Moscow made forays into the West. Inbred terrorism brewed in Germany, Italy, and France, in Spain and in the United Kingdom. Certainly, the Western Europeans relied upon the United States to protect them. Yet as a peace project, the EC needed a secure environment. It needed to influence and, if necessary, to transform its environs. Deprived of foreign policy instruments, having discarded in 1954 the opportunity to set up a European army, how could the EC pacify the continent; more specifically, how could it organize it, as the subtitle of this book suggests?[3] How could an area of peace prosper in uncertain times and surroundings? It had to devise instruments and policies in lieu of foreign policy. It had to become a regional security actor, albeit in a very unconventional way.

The Community essentially exported its methods of pooling and sharing to build trust and reconciliation: from Northern Ireland to Georgia, it would try to pacify by example. And it expanded its area of peace and prosperity. In the beginning, however, enlargement was not conceived as a method to secure the surroundings. It was limited in aim and scope. The EC was to encompass similar states, democratic and prosperous, which was ironical, since the United Kingdom, Ireland, and Denmark were left out and joined only in 1973 after the departure of General de Gaulle, the French president who had twice vetoed the United Kingdom's application. There was not even any agreement as to whether the EC should expand and embrace the continent. In the 1940s and 1950s, some of the founding fathers cherished a grand vision of Europe one and whole, but many more found comfort in a small Europe confined to the western part of the continent, a small Europe bearing a Christian Democratic imprint—and a small Europe it was to stay as long as the Iron Curtain divided the continent.

Starting with the fall of authoritarian regimes in Portugal, Spain, and Greece in the 1970s, and later with the demise of communism at the turn of the 1990s, enlargement became the first, most significant, and most extraordinary tool in the hands of the European Community(EC)/European Union (EU) to stabilize and organize the continent. To help newcomers through the maze of democratic and economic reforms and to engineer stability on the continent, the Community and later the Union came to rely on formidable resources, a combination of attraction and imposition, which European politicians and institutions incrementally turned into instruments they learned to wield. To the new democracies in southern and eastern Europe, to all those that decades of authoritarianism and dictatorship, deprivation and false promises, had exhausted, the EC/EU constituted a pole of stability, prosperity, and liberty, a model to adopt instead of groping for untried experiments, and a market to join lest their economies collapse without access to the large Common Market and to investors. Application for membership thus gave the Union a formidable capacity to lever its attraction.

One of the most vexing quandaries for governments and political scientists pertains to the convertibility of resources into effective power. In spite of holding resources, governments may hardly be able to influence other governments' and actors' behavior. With enlargement, however, the EU has been in the position to exact reforms, to specify directions and road maps, with financial support and technical help. It thus contributed to the transformation, the "Europeanization," of institutions, economies, and societies on the continent. Yet enlargement was not a "given." The EU turned it into a powerful instrument and reinterpreted texts and tools from the 1960s to apply them within a new context. It reinvented criteria that had been enunciated much earlier to filter candidate countries and help them join the EU. In this regard, the EU was extraordinarily creative. It gradually rose to the challenge and invented incrementally and almost haphazardly, unwittingly and sometimes reluctantly, a strategy almost *wider Willen,* a default drive more than a master plan that, however, coexisted with innovation.[4]

The European Union also displayed creativity when it devised, for the countries that were to become its new neighbors after the 2004 enlargement, a new policy, the European Neighbourhood Policy (ENP).[5] It was not prescient, since it was obvious that the new EU would have new neighbors. But the EU displayed foresight, though in many other cases, such as the refugee crisis a decade later, it failed to anticipate foreseeable events. The ENP merged with another proactive policy, toward the Mediterranean, which the EC had invented in the 1970s. It borrowed some characteristics from other policies and programs that the EU had formerly implemented. It was an outgrowth of the EC/EU, which projects its laws and norms, policies and programs, on its periphery. Yet it intentionally devised a strategy—even if the ENP eventually fell well short of expectations and intentions. In other ways too, the Union scrambled to endow itself with foreign policy instruments. After the Community formally became the Union in 1993, it acquired some of the tools of traditional foreign policy actors, mediated, intervened, and sent some military missions.

From Hubris to Crisis

Hence, from the very inception of the Communities, geopolitics, if not power politics, was never far away. It was at the heart of the project, since the Communities and the EU were about reinventing international relations on the continent. Implicitly or not, enlargement was most of the time about stabilizing neighbors and securing peace. When Greece applied to join the Community, in the 1970s, the Commission of the European Communities, though favorable to its membership to anchor democracy, expressed concerns lest it be interpreted as a rebuke to Greece's archfoe, Turkey, and rattle the eastern Mediterranean. When Poland and other Central European countries were taken in, in the first decade of the new millennium, some of the main reasons put forth were that their membership would allow the EU to avoid recreating a Berlin Wall at the German-Polish border, and the former Soviet satellites to wrench themselves from Russia's long shadow. To that extent, the EC/EU has always been a geopolitical actor.

The Communities' and the Union's most extraordinary achievement has been to ease the transition from a war to a new era on two occasions over the last century. On the ruins of World War II, the Communities fostered reconciliation, based on sharing prosperity and sovereignty. At the end of the Cold War, the Union embraced the states that had shaken off Soviet rule. Certainly, the EC/EU benefited from auspicious circumstances, from the presence of the United States, which protected Western Europe and played the role of a formidable equalizer between former enemies, a balancer from across the Atlantic that could prod the Western Europeans into cooperating with one another (Joffe 1984). As the Soviet regime bowed out more or less gracefully, Western liberal institutions, NATO and the EU in particular, were already in place. In a continent in flux, they were poles of stability, just as West Germany was a pole of stability when the German Democratic Republic (GDR) imploded. The western part of Europe and the West gradually came to encompass the East (Ikenberry 2008). Never before had a postwar de facto settlement been so propitiously ushered in—despite bloodshed in Lithuania in 1991, repression in Moscow in 1993, Soviet and Russian forays into the Caucasus and Moldova, and the Yugoslav wars.

This was a tremendous accomplishment that none of the heralds and pioneers of European unity would have ever dreamed of, from Jiři Podiebrad, king of Bohemia, in the fifteenth century, who conceived the first European *universitas*, in which states would have shared a common currency and a common army, to Gottfried Leibniz, Immanuel Kant, and Charles-Irénée Castel, abbé de Saint-Pierre in the eighteenth century, to Victor Hugo in the nineteenth, to Aristide Briand and Gustav Stresemann, who were jointly awarded the Nobel Peace Prize in 1926 (Faye 1992).[6] The Nobel committee in Oslo crowned this achievement when it awarded the Peace Prize in 1998 to John Hume and David Trimble, leaders, respectively, of the Catholic and Protestant communities in the tumultuous province of Northern Ireland who conscientiously emulated the European method of reconciliation; and, in 2012, to the Union as a whole, for having pacified the greater part of the continent. In both cases, though much less so when the Nobel Peace Prize was awarded to the Union, a kind of hubris was floating in the air.

In Europe, the economic crisis that struck the United States when the subprime market collapsed in 2007 turned into a monetary, budgetary, and financial predicament, the so-called Euro-crisis, which became the first of a series of crises that chipped away at the substance of the EU. Some of these crises are geopolitical by nature. A decade after the formidable enlargement of the European Union by twelve new members, some of which had been part of the USSR, a decade after the invention of the so-called Neighbourhood Policy, which was designed to engage and help Europe's periphery, a decade after the St. Petersburg summit, which was to create a common house embracing both the EU and Russia, and a decade after the start of membership negotiations with Turkey, Europe's surroundings are ablaze, from Libya to Syria and Iraq. Russia is waging a covert war in Ukraine, trampling on international covenants, including agreements that the Soviet leaders had underwritten. Borders that European states drew or that the European order condoned have been torn down, from the Middle East to Ukraine. European, Western norms are ignored at best and reviled at worst, and terrorism strikes at the very heart of the Union.

Other crises have security bearings. While refugees flee their countries for security reasons and have the right to cross borders illegally, their massive arrival in Europe as of 2014–2015 exposed one of the main weaknesses of the EU and its member states: the absence of common refugee, migrant, and border policies—a major security lapse. The United Kingdom did not join the EC for security reasons, but Brexit (i.e., Britain's exit), the unprecedented exit from the Union of a country that was, to some extent, economically vibrant and politically influential inside and outside Europe, has shattered the foundations of the multinational construct and questions its irreversibility—besides leaving the United Kingdom in an economic, political, and legal void. It has thrown the EU into an existential crisis. One might also argue that the rollback of democracy in some of the new member states and the rise of populism in new and old members alike also threaten the raison d'être and the very existence of the EU.

Continent by Default, however, is not about all the crises that corrode the EU's substance. Some of these crises are multidimensional. The rise of populism in our Western societies, including the United States, is linked to the weakening of the working and middle classes, to the globalization of world markets and fierce competition, the leveling down of wages and working conditions, outdated modes of political representations and the alienation of citizens from professional political establishments. Dysfunctions in the decision-making system do not characterize the EU alone; they also hamper the proper functioning of other governments, including the American government. Terrorism too is a worldwide phenomenon. The interaction between transnational networks and local franchises, and between a European inside and the outside, raises questions as to its very nature—summarized by the French debate between Olivier Roy, who points at the spread of nihilism with a jihadist face, and Gilles Kepel, who contends that Islam bears the seeds of jihad. And it also raises many practical questions as to the study of national responses and inter-governmental cooperation. By its scope, it escapes the ambit of a book that aims at concision.

An oblique light will be cast on the monetary, budgetary, and economic crisis. Too often, the EU ignored or glossed over the specificities and cultures of individual countries. At the turn of the millennium in particular, despite warnings issued by experts or by the candidates themselves, it was assumed that the same procedures would produce similar results in various countries, and that candidates and later new members, or neighboring states, would apply EU rules in similar ways. The illiberal turn in Hungary and Poland proved the EU wrong. This approach in terms of political culture partly accounts for the behavior of Greece and policies in the EU and the Eurozone. Similarly, the incompletion of the Schengen Area, where internal borders have been discarded and external borders are not controlled tightly enough, echoes the incompletion of the Economic and Monetary Union (EMU).

Though the conjunction of multiple severe crises may eventually relegate the Union to oblivion, *Continent by Default* focuses on the EU's role as a geopolitical actor and provides an understanding of what went wrong as it tried to ensure security on the continent and its surroundings.

The EU did not gloss over political cultures alone. It also crafted policies that were and are essentially bureaucratic, lacking the insight and foresight, in short the strategic thinking, that only national governments have. The Commission put many proposals on the table, some of which qualified as "monuments of bureaucratic boredom," as Lilia Shevtsova

(2010) scathingly wrote, or it formulated policies that member states too often disregarded in the name of national sovereignty.[7] Only individual governments harbor the will to defend interests that remain national, if not parochial. Yet what should have been European interests clashed with national interests.[8] Relations with Tunisia, the war in Libya, and, for too long, the absence of a coherent Russia policy, all encapsulate a lack of cohesion between member states and coherence in the pursuit of interests. However, even national governments lack foresight: they ignored the warning signs that announced the dissolution of Yugoslavia in the 1980s. They have glossed over the rising number of refugees who have arrived on European shores in the 2010s, and have preferred to delegate the control of refugees and migrants to their periphery, shying away from inventing strong common policies.

Facing the EU, formidable challengers have risen almost from the ashes. For centuries, the continent was dominated by three poles, the three Romes, in a way: in the West, a constellation of states and empires, from Sweden to Portugal, from the Habsburg to the British Empire, sometimes extending as far as Poland and Lithuania, and to the southeast and east, the Ottoman and Russian Empires, whose sultans and czars sometimes turned to the "West," that is, Europe, to adopt or adapt its ideas and recipes, and sometimes to challenge them.[9] Turkey and Russia still vibrate with echoes of the past. However differently, neither Turkey nor Russia has completed its long transition from empire into state, and both defy the Union in different ways. While the EU still attracts Turkish secular urbanites, successive governments may have at best misunderstood the significance of membership, which is about sharing sovereignty, while the increasingly patriarchal and patrimonial regime of Recep Tayyip Erdoğan has succumbed to the delusions of solipsist authoritarianism. The challenge posed by Vladimir Putin's iron rule is even more daunting: sketching a counter-EU, ranting about Western decadence and aggressiveness, and steadily swallowing up territories, the master of the Kremlin threatens both the borders of the EU and EU principles. Yet both turn what they deem Western hostility, supposedly compounded by humiliation, into a narrative governing their policies toward the West and the EU.

This book is a study of the European Union's continental or regional role and policy, mostly incidental and incremental, which came about under the pressure of circumstances, as is often the case in international affairs. It frames the EU as a reluctant geopolitical actor, falling short of power politics. It is an actor that, for the most part, used its makeup, its institutions, laws, and policies, to establish a more or less encompassing continental order, through enlargement, and, later, through programs and projects that aimed at transforming neighbors, in a most extraordinary way. Conversely its makeup, particularly its fractured and composite nature, and the daunting challenges it addresses, impair the resources that are at the EU's disposal, from attraction to imposition, from nondeliberate to deliberate power. Its makeup determines the limits the EU encounters, limits that are inherent in the Union's DNA, and those that pertain to the geography of its influence.

Building upon a vast amount of secondary literature and often excellent think-tank analyses as well as on documents emanating from the Commission of the European Communities and the Council of Europe, this book also relies upon interviews carried out in various EU capital cities.

Enlargement went on by default and later by design: its successes and setbacks are the focus of chapters 1 and 2. The EU's often botched attempts to pacify its surroundings and lock them into its policies are considered in chapters 3 and 4. Chapter 5 takes a fresh look at the so-called refugee crisis and the series of decisions, collective or individual, outside and inside the Union, at the national and the EU levels, that showcase the particular weaknesses of the European construct. Chapter 6 is devoted to relations between the EU and Russia. A note on overlaps in coverage: it is difficult to neatly discuss under a single heading such cases as Ukraine, Georgia, and Cyprus. Ukraine was always supposed to be the main target of the EU's neighborhood policy. Yet, the events that led to the war in eastern Ukraine and the Berlin-led effort to deescalate the conflict, if not solve it, will be delved into in chapter 6 as a strategic issue that pits various European countries against Russia. Not all the countries of the neighborhood have been thoroughly analyzed; I have chosen examples according to their relevance. I remind readers how difficult it is to ponder current events *sine ira et studio,* without ire and passion, and not be dragged into the prevalent doom and gloom engulfing things European or Western. Hubris had taken over the EU at the turn of the millennium: the Union was to be a superpower. Now, some forecast its demise. However, too many variables, too many contradictory trends, shape present and future. The EU may rebound. A blessing in disguise of both crisis and incoherence may lie in the diversity of the actors and actions involved, which enrich the Europeans' repertoire and outreach, and in a renewed awareness that the Union has to recoup and rebuild its influence if it wants to withstand the rollback of democracy and liberal institutions. Amid fluctuation and fragmentation, one thing is nonetheless certain: this book ends with the close of an era. Russia's subversion of Ukraine in 2014, the unprecedented arrival of over a million refugees in Europe in 2015, the United Kingdom's exit from the EU in 2016, and the arrival to power of authoritarian governments on the continent and in its surroundings mark the end of an order that the Union strove to establish.

1

In the Beginning Was Enlargement

Central Europe cannot . . . then be defined and determined by
political frontiers (which are inauthentic, always imposed by
invasions, conquests, and occupations), but by the great common
situations that reassemble peoples, regroup them in ever new ways
along the imaginary and ever-changing boundaries that mark a realm
inhabited by the same memories, the same problems and conflicts,
the same common tradition.

—Milan Kundera, "The Tragedy of Central Europe"

No sooner was the Rome Treaty signed and ratified than neighboring
governments knocked on the door of the newborn community. While all
along distrusting the endeavor and skeptical of its success, the British government nonetheless turned to the incipient European Economic Community (EEC) and in 1958 offered to conclude a free trade agreement. The
United Kingdom (UK) applied to join in 1961, and, together with Ireland and Denmark, it became a member in 1973. This was the first of
a series of enlargements. The history of the Community is the history of
enlargement. Paradoxically though, the European Community (EC), later
the European Union (EU), hardly ever took the initiative to enlarge. It was
not a policy. This was not *its* policy. The EU did not have any proactive
policy of enlargement till the turn of the millennium. Throughout most of
its existence, applications have been mostly considered with concern and
even disquietude, at least on the part of certain member states. Rather

than a sect of proselytes, the EC/EU is more akin to a club, to which it has often been compared, where potential new members have to show their credentials in order to join.

What explained the drive of the neighbors? Why did they want to join the EC/EU? What benefits did they hope to reap? And what response did they receive? If enlargement was a possibility from the beginning, it changed in nature over the decades, from a promise to include like-minded democracies and market economies to an incremental and almost haphazard strategy designed to embed democracy, the rule of law, and the rights of minorities, to prop up market economies, and to stabilize neighboring countries in transition—in other words, to organize the continent. The neighbors' reasons for wanting to join the long-attractive and powerful Community and Union, the change in the meanings, aims, and significance of enlargement, and the creation of instruments to further the aims of enlargement will be examined in this chapter. The limits inherent in an improvised policy will be considered in the next.

Pressures from the Neighborhood

While past empires often sought to expand their frontiers, and conquer neighboring countries, the pressure to enlarge the Community or Union never originated from its midst. Rather, pressure arose from its environs. The Community's or the Union's neighbors sought to join it, and new neighbors followed suit relentlessly.

In the beginning, neighbors sought or obtained only association, a procedure less constraining than membership, which implied shared laws and policies. The British government first toyed with the idea of a free trade agreement. In 1959, Greece and Turkey applied for associate membership, although the agreements signed with Greece in 1961 and with Turkey two years later gave these two countries the prospect of becoming full members.[1] In 1961, the UK applied to join the EEC, prompting Ireland, Denmark, and Norway to follow suit—though de Gaulle's veto delayed applications and negotiations—while Sweden, Finland, Austria, Switzerland, and Spain sought associate membership. This triggered the first of several waves of enlargements, with the UK, Ireland, and Denmark joining the original six members in 1973, followed by a second wave in 1981–1986 including Greece, and later Portugal and Spain, and a third wave in 1995, with Austria, Finland, and Sweden as new members. The latest, fourth round saw Union membership leaping from fifteen to twenty-seven, between 2004 and 2007, and to twenty-eight members in 2013.[2] Very few among the neighbors resisted or opposed joining; Norway, Switzerland, and Liechtenstein are notable exceptions. Most neighboring countries wanted to join, and there were many reasons, material and intangible, economic, political, and cultural, none of which alone could explain the call for enlargement (Schimmelfennig and Sedelmeier 2005b).

A Myth and Its Facets

The EC/EU, or rather "Europe," provided a myth that exerted a powerful spell over most of its neighbors. At first glance, the EU may not resonate as a myth, mired as it currently is in financial turmoil, economic sluggishness, demographic and geopolitical woes, and dwarfed by the rising power of Asia and the emergence of other models of development. The United States, though weakened compared to its status as the sole superpower at the turn of the millennium, still captured the imagination and minds of young people, by offering a powerful narrative of freedom and the pursuit of happiness. Reduced to a bureaucratic acronym, the EU seemed to offer laws and regulations rather than the promise of shaping one's destiny. Yet it has long been synonymous with peace and stability, the reason the Community was created in the first place, and for decades it also provided prosperity, although this has not been turned into a powerful narrative by successive generations in power—if it is still even possible to produce a narrative in a fragmented and globalized world. It may be too late to work on a narrative, as decision makers are engrossed in the travails of stabilizing the Eurozone, fighting terrorism inside and outside Europe, and facing Russia's hybrid war in the East, and Euroskepticism and populism are gripping citizens, who are turning their back on an EU that can no longer deliver prosperity and security.

One should not forget, however, that for a while the EC/EU offered Southern, Central, and Eastern European elites and citizens a resonating myth. The EC/EU *was* Europe, and Europe meant the West, a symbol of modernity and modernization, of freedom and democracy. It exerted attraction. There is nothing new about attraction. Empires and world cities alike have always exerted a powerful attraction on their peripheries. The populations of subjugated provinces have been attracted by the metropolis and its glory, by its lifestyle and the promises it held, material and intangible. Rome and Constantinople, Tenochtitlan and Cuzco, Madrid, Vienna, London, or Paris, and, of course, the New World and maybe the new Asian world, all offered—and offer—the promise of a better life at the price of acculturation and sometimes submission. In this respect, the EU has been attractive for a long time, offering a solid infrastructure, good education and health, and being on the whole democratic, relatively transparent, probably less corrupt, and certainly less arbitrary than other regions in the world, in spite of its limited access to immigrants, and in spite of robust anti-immigration and xenophobic parties in European societies.

Since the early days of the Community, people in neighboring countries who do not enjoy the same liberties and standards as people inside the EC/EU have been attracted. Various transnational channels conveyed this appeal. Immigration, for instance, played a role, spreading habits and ideas in a Spanish, Portuguese, Greek, Polish, or Yugoslav diaspora in France, Germany, or Austria, ranging from members of the lower middle class, who had come to seek a better living, to dissenters, who had fled repression. Tourism opened up countries and societies, such as Franco's Spain and Tito's Yugoslavia in the 1960s and later. However, while there is nothing new about attracting individuals, attracting countries is another story, though individuals played a role in funneling ideas and aspirations back to their countries of origin. Certainly, in the past, provinces joined empires or states, and federations emerged. Yet the way in which the EC/EU has come to absorb not immigrants but new states is remarkable.

To those who fled their countries and to those who remained, the EC/EU offered an alternative to exhausted myths and vanishing empires; it offered a new home to those who sought refuge from the defunct Soviet empire. The European dissidents from Central Europe, more than Eastern Europeans, brought down communist regimes in the name of Europe. The "return to Europe," the Europe to which they felt attached, as Milan Kundera forcefully reminded us in the early 1980s, was a driving force. Central European intellectuals claimed to have nourished European culture and to have been nourished by it. Europe's identity rested upon its culture, "which became the expression of the supreme values by which European humanity understood itself, defined itself, identified itself as European" (Kundera 1983, 1984). In many ways, "going back to Europe" was, for Central Europeans and for Southern Europeans as well, part of a historical process, a break with the recent past and the completion of a longer-term evolution. The liberals who fought against Franco's domination invoked their *Europeismo*. For many, south and east of Europe, being European was a matter of fact: *Wir sind Europa*—We Are Europe— became the motto of the Austrian government when campaigning to join the Union. In other words, Europe belonged to all Europeans, and all were legitimately entitled to partake in the European construction. Borders that were perceived to be artificial and unjust, running through territories formerly belonging to the same cultural areas and organic economic units, were to be erased. If not a myth to all those who brought down communism, the return to Europe was at least a return to a normalcy that had been forcefully and arbitrarily interrupted.

In other words, the EC/EU served as a means to escape spent models. Some of the economies in the countries abutting the EC/EU were losing steam, and this led their leaders to look for new impulses and ideas. Portugal and Spain started knocking on the door of the Community well before the fall of their respective authoritarian regimes, when it dawned on their elites that they had outlived their time. In the 1960s, Franco tried to open up the Spanish economy to foreign investors and industrialists but needed the EC's support lest the gap between Spain and Europe deepen (Tsoukalis 1981: 76). Though more internationalized, the Portuguese economy was mainly engaged in trading with its by then unruly overseas empire, and it lacked an industrial base, technology, and know-how, though the last government of predemocratic Portugal included modernizers and Europeanists alike (Sampedro and Payno 1983: 132–133). In both cases, a modest degree of modernization and liberalization had the unexpected consequence of further delegitimizing both regimes, which implicitly recognized the superiority of the dominant European model.

Though certainly not looking for new models, the British economy experienced lower growth rates and monetary crises linked to a "stop-and-go policy" of stimulating the economy abruptly followed by a tightening of demand. Even countries that had enjoyed strong economic growth in the past hesitated for a while, before finally choosing to join in a time of crisis: for instance, Sweden in 1992. Of course, Sweden was not Portugal, and though battered, the Swedish model was not to be discarded. Iceland also began to negotiate with the EU after the monetary and economic meltdown of 2008, before withdrawing its candidacy in 2015 (Mattli 1999; Gussarsson 2004). Those who advocated membership in the EU were not always necessarily looking for a new paradigm, but sometimes for an anchor, a support, to rescue their own model, though poorer countries were indeed seeking orientation and guidance, new standards and new blueprints. The latter group included the countries of the southern rim as well as the Central and Eastern European states.

In many respects, there were differences between the Southern European states and the Central and Eastern ones. Not only were the Central and Eastern European Countries (CEECs) trying to gain access to a by then 350-million-consumer-strong market, but they were also looking for technology and credit—as the prior communist regimes had been doing in the 1970s and 1980s—and they were keen to obtain foreign investments and support. On the ruins of a wrecked system, they were also looking for templates, recipes, and advice in a more radical way than the Southern European countries had twenty years earlier. After all, Franco's Spain had started opening up to industrialization in the 1960s, and Greece had preserved many of its institutions and practices during the seven years when the junta ruled (1967–1974). Fifty years of communism, on the other hand, had erased most of these practical ideas. Certainly, some of those who helped to overthrow communism yearned for a "third way," a new model, neither communism nor capitalism. Yet the idea of a third way had an unpleasant historical aftertaste, reminiscent of postwar experiments, which the Soviet regime had rapidly manipulated and destroyed in order to impose communist rule. Most in Central and Eastern Europe did not want to innovate, but rather preferred shortcuts toward democracy, the rule of law, and the market economy. The EU and its member states offered the knowledge and competence they sought, the templates and blueprints they needed, in short, the help required to overcome decades of straying from and trailing behind Western Europe and the Western world.

The countries that shrugged off authoritarian and communist regimes were looking then for new standards, that is, not only standards of living but those very principles that are the hallmarks of democracy and the rule of law, which would serve as guidance toward a better life, just as the Greeks, the Portuguese, and the Spanish had been seeking to replace "habits rooted in the past which are impeding rationalization of the economy . . . [and] also lead to introversion and chaos" (Sampedro and Payno 1983: 207). Standards did not amount to material benefits alone, but also to the political, economic, and moral prerequisites that underpin them, which Europe, and the EU, were supposed to embody—in short, modernization, or more specifically democratic modernization.

The Specter of Isolation

Had these countries surrounding the EC/EU stayed away, they would have suffered from what economists call negative externalities. An emerging common market and even more so a trading block, such as the Single Market, with elaborate standards and rules, spells losses for outsiders who cannot access it. It also results in investment diversion as investors, attracted by the bigger, regulated market, shun the outsiders, especially the smaller ones (e.g., Mattli 1999; Gros and Steinherr 2004). The absence of membership, and the existence of trade barriers of all sorts, hamper trade relations between outsiders and insiders, while institutionalized relations through membership facilitate them by reducing transfer costs, aligning standards and procedures, and increasing trust. Economists speak of the "gravitational pull" of a trade bloc, which attracts neighboring trade partners, gravitation being a function of size and proximity (Gros and Steinherr 2004; Emerson and Noutcheva 2004).

Indeed, it was often "the fear of being excluded from an economically dynamic core" that prompted outsiders in Europe to seek membership in the EC/EU (Gehler 2004: 141). Most applicants dreaded being relegated to an economic backwater if they did not join. At the end of the fifties, the Foreign Office warned the British government against trade diversion, and the European Free Trade Association (EFTA), which the UK had called into existence in 1960 to counter the EC, was not sufficient for London to avoid joining the latter (Ludlow 1997). Before enlargement, Spain, Portugal, and Greece depended on the Community for over 50 percent of their exports (Sampedro and Payno 1983). The Danes, Greeks, and Austrians depended primarily on the German market, while the Irish, Portuguese, and Swedish economies were too tightly intertwined with Britain's economy not to follow the latter's lead when London applied for membership.[3] With the fall of the Berlin Wall and the implosion of the Soviet Union, the CEECs severed their ties to the latter and quickly reoriented their trade to Western Europe, which posted large trade surpluses with them (Gower 1999: 6–7). The completion of the Single Market, due by 1992, enticed a number of countries to join the EU: an unprecedented number of applications were put on the table before the fall of the Wall. While most EFTA members and smaller states south and east of Europe chose to join the EU, only the richer neighbors that had a specific added value to defend, whether an economic niche (fisheries, oil and gas, finance) or a political one (status as a neutral country, a role as an international mediator or facilitator), opted for tailor-made elaborate agreements, multilateral ones, such as the European Economic Area (EEA), or bilateral ones, to adopt the Community's rules and standards and access the Single Market while retaining some independence.[4]

For most, staying outside would also have meant strategic isolation. Without the Community, it was feared that London would lose its significance in the eyes of American administrations, which wanted Britain to bear upon the Community (Kaiser 2004: 17; see chapter 2 below). A founding member of the North Atlantic Treaty Organization (NATO), a member of the Organization for European Economic Co-operation (OEEC), now the Organization for Economic Cooperation and Development (OECD), and a recipient of Marshall aid, Portugal was more internationalized than Spain. Yet it was geopolitically and economically less relevant, and it was losing its grip on its waning empire. Driven out of Africa, it had no place to turn to but Europe. Spain under Franco was isolated, and Greece's military junta was shunned. One of the main concerns that prompted the new democratic government in Athens to apply for membership, in 1975, was what it considered a shifting balance of power in the eastern Mediterranean following the Turkish invasion of northern Cyprus in 1974, and compounding the seven years of isolation that the West had imposed upon the military junta. Resentment vis-à-vis the United States and US-led NATO, both deemed to have favored Ankara instead of Athens, the perceived necessity to counterbalance the United States and Turkey, and the heavy-handed interference of the former and the military intervention of the latter, all led Premier Konstantin Karamanlis to seek support from the Community (Tsoukalis 2002: 41).

Toward the end of the Cold War, the so-called neutrals were also essentially threatened by irrelevance, as the meaning of neutrality between East and West lost its significance. Sensing the winds of change, Austria applied in July 1989, followed by Sweden and Finland just after Austrian and Hungarian authorities had cut down the barbed wire separating their two countries in May that year. Though it had first chosen to join the EEA, Finland also joined the Union in order to flee strategic isolation, after Sweden's choice of Europe (Ojanen 2004).[5] Yet Russia's neighbors were certainly among those that had the strongest urge to escape isolation and seek refuge in the EU as a "community of security," to borrow Karl Deutsch's expression, where belonging to an ever-larger community provides, if not military guarantees, at least the security that an economically powerful, politically divided, but nonetheless important civilian power may need (Deutsch 1957). The aborted military coup in Moscow on 19 August 1991 accelerated the rapprochement between the CEECs and the Community. The so-called European agreements were concluded in December that year. Modeled, to some extent, on the first two Association Agreements with Greece and Turkey, they opened the door to a possible membership in the EU.

Core and Periphery

The influence the EC/EU exercised over most of its periphery reproduced a centuries-old pattern in which Western Europe, with, at its core, a changing constellation of states, from Sweden to Spain, from England to Austria-Hungary, served as a pole of attraction to the south, north, and east of the continent and even beyond. For centuries the Western world, that is to say, Western Europe, was the symbol of renaissance, enlightenment, and modernity, reason and progress—but also of colonization and wars, in particular the two world wars it unleashed, wreaking havoc upon itself and upon the world before it passed the torch to the United States. The relations between the EC/EU and its marches have been best captured by the twin concept of core and periphery, a core and a periphery linked by deeply asymmetrical relations in many areas, economic, political, and cultural (Rokkan and Urwin 1983; Pollard 1981; Seers, Schaffer, and Kiljunen 1979; Buzan and Waever 2003).[6]

"Peripherality" is understood in terms of both geographical proximity and the periphery's dependence upon a center. In the early 1970s, Johan Galtung also included in this analysis what was then called Eastern Europe, underlining the asymmetries and the latter's "quasi-colonial" reliance on the EC (Galtung 1973).[7] The notion of periphery certainly did not apply to all applicants, and when it did apply, it was in differentiated ways. Finland was deemed a semiperiphery. Great Britain could not be said to have been a periphery. Even though West Germany served as a pivot for all of Western Europe, two economic blocs coexisted in that part of the continent: a central and southern bloc around Germany and a northern bloc with both the UK and Germany as a pivot (Wijkman 1990: 96–97).

Dependence is not solely economic, industrial, and technological. It is also cultural and ideological, characterized by one-sided, asymmetrical flows from the outskirts to the center (migration, agricultural goods, and so forth) or by flows from the center to the outskirts (tourism, ideas, models and habits, ways of life and ways of doing things). It includes the ideological and psychological orientation of the populations of the periphery toward the core as a model. It is multidimensional and encompasses control over security, over production, over credit, and, last but not least, over knowledge, beliefs, and ideas. This is what Susan Strange called structural power. Differing from relational power, which is "the power of A to get . . . B to do something they would not otherwise do," "structural power . . . is the power to shape and determine the structures of the global political economy within which other states, their political institutions, their economic enterprises and (not least) their scientists and other professional people have to operate. . . . Structural power, in short, confers the power to decide how things shall be done, the power to shape frameworks within which states relate to each other, relate to people, or relate to corporate enterprises" (Strange 1988: 24–25).

Other political economists and political scientists, before and after Strange, also underlined the many dimensions of structural dominance, in particular the importance of ideological power (Galtung 1973; see also later Barnett and Duvall 2003, 2005). Referring to the power of ideas, Joseph Nye coined the notion of "soft power." Far from the trivialized version of soft power, which equates it with nonmilitary, civilian power, soft power is the power to get "others to want the outcomes you want" instead of merely having them do what you want them to do. Attraction is its main resource (Nye 1990, 2004). Attraction helps to shape the values, frame of mind, interests, and aims of citizens and governments of other countries. It is the product of culture, domestic political values, and foreign policy. Attraction is not directed toward foreign actors, nor does it immediately result from a political decision or a specific polity. Rather, it is the outcome of many long-term domestic policies, decisions, and actions in different areas, which eventually weave a political, economic, and societal fabric appealing to societies and decision makers in other countries. Structural power, and the attraction that is part of structural power, are nondeliberate. Conversely, deliberate power is a form of power that is strategically, that is, purposefully, applied (Guzzini 1993).

"Power as a resource" has to be deliberately leveraged into "power over," as Johan Galtung aptly put it (1973). It has to be activated. Structural power endows the EC/EU with considerable resources over its neighbors, and application for membership gave the EC/EU the capacity to leverage those resources, when and if it wanted or needed to do so, and when and if candidate countries were in a particularly weak position. Obviously, a centuries-old, stable, and relatively prosperous democracy like the UK did not look for models and patterns, but sought access to the Common Market, and influence as a bridge between the United States and the Old Continent. The same held, to some extent, for democratic and prosperous Denmark, Sweden, and Finland, albeit differently. Southern, Central, and Eastern European countries, on the contrary, were more supplicants than applicants. As a consequence, the EC/EU theoretically held greater sway over the latter than over countries such as Great Britain and Sweden. Yet did the EC/EU want to use the power it held over most of its neighbors? The fact that candidates knocked on the door was, more often than not, deemed a source of embarrassment rather than an opportunity to organize the continent.

Embarrassment of Riches

As mentioned above, the EC/EU never looked for candidates. Enlargements were driven from outside. For its founding fathers, however, the European Community potentially embraced the whole continent: "Our Community is neither a small Europe, nor is it a confined Community.

We have not set its limits. Limits have been set by those very countries, which for the time being do not join it. It is up to them to push our borders further away and to progressively abolish the barriers which separate our European countries" (Monnet 1955, my trans.). Monnet and others even went so far as to envision a Community encompassing the southern shore of the Mediterranean or even Africa, a "Eurafrique" as Robert Schuman called it (Schuman 1963: 101). Yet these were the times when France and Belgium, among others, extended their rule over large swaths of Africa. To various intellectuals as well, a Community restricted to a small number of countries was unpalatable, because the economic rationale did not hold. A "common market," where goods and services would freely circulate, should theoretically extend to the whole world (Perroux 1955). There was only one argument that justified the restriction of the Community to a small Europe, and this was the necessity for the latter to defend itself against the Soviet Union (Aron 1951). Echoing the founding fathers, the preamble to the Rome Treaty invited the other peoples of Europe to associate themselves with the Community, and Article 237 stated that "any European state may apply."[8] It was a curt article later complemented by subsequent revisions. The EC, and even later the EU in its first years, did not have an enlargement policy. Enlargement was a source of embarrassment.

Each enlargement caught the EC/EU unprepared. Enlargement confronted it with numerous challenges. The first wave of enlargement "was likely to test severely Community institutions which had only been created in 1958 and were thus barely accustomed to work within a six-member grouping, [potentially] disrupt[ing] patterns of cooperation which had grown up during the EEC's successful first few years of operation" (Ludlow 1997: 2). The second wave of applications took place at a time when the Communities were engaged in a European Political Cooperation (EPC), the first version of a European foreign policy mechanism, and progressing toward the completion of a common market while vainly seeking to invent a monetary union. The third wave occurred in the midst of overhauls. A continental order had to be reinvented on the wreckage of Moscow's domination in the East, at a time when the Community was morphing into a Union. An Economic and Monetary Union (EMU) and a foreign policy were put on the table, the Maastricht Treaty was negotiated, and its ratification was rejected at first by Danish citizens. German reunification was also being hammered out, absorbing the attention of diplomats who settled the agreement with the Soviet Union, and of civil servants who worked out all the dizzying details of East Germany's accession. The travails of the EC/EU and the efforts to "deepen," that is, strengthen, the organization were, in other words, always in the way of enlargement.

Each time, the EC/EU and its member states faced several options: opposition, inertia, dithering, and acceptance. When together with three other states, the UK requested membership, qualified by specific arrangements suited to its needs, the French president, General de Gaulle, rejected the British application, and, by way of consequence, the application of all four countries. Only after de Gaulle's resignation, in 1969, did his successor, Georges Pompidou, agree to negotiations and membership. Indeed, successive French governments recoiled at enlargement, except in one case, Greece (Lequesne 2008). After General de Gaulle's famous double veto, Valéry Giscard d'Estaing, the very president who pushed for Greece's inclusion in the Community, tried his hand at delaying enlargement when, in June 1980, he called for deepening before accepting Spain and Portugal as members. Considering Spain a major agricultural competitor and a source of immigration, the French president required the resolution of pending questions concerning agricultural policy and budget. This dilatory gesture irritated the Spanish, who disparagingly dubbed it "Giscardazo." François Mitterrand followed suit a few years later. Lest the balance of power within the smaller community be altered at the expense of France, which had stood so far at the geographical and political center of Europe, Mitterrand asked for an "inventory" of enlargement. Instead of enlargement, he suggested a Europe-wide confederation, which Václav Havel, the former dissident and president of Czechoslovakia, and later of the Czech Republic, took as an insult (Havel 1991).

Conversely, action was required. In particular, the least prepared applicants of all four waves of candidates, namely the Southern and Eastern European states, had to be brought in to stymie political and economic setbacks, and to prevent economic turmoil, social upheaval, and illegal immigration from disrupting the EC/EU. The EC/EU also had to compensate for negative externalities it unwillingly imposed on outsiders, compounding the dire straits these states and societies were going through. Enlargement was about exporting stability in order to avoid importing instability. It gave—or seemed to give—both applicants and members of the Union a guarantee against unforeseeable rollbacks. It was about propping up economies and entrenching democracy and the rule of law, helping the new democracies to "become like us" by allowing them to "become one of us." It was, of course, a bet on the future.

In 1975, the battle for Portugal between the extreme left wing of the political spectrum and democratic forces was partly decided behind the scenes through heavy international involvement, including the Soviet Union, the United States, a number of European countries, the German government, German parties and party foundations first and foremost, and the Community (see below). When a military coup in Madrid was aborted on 24 February 1981, the Commission and the European Parliament thought it necessary to solemnly condemn any step backward to authoritarianism. Conversely, when Greece submitted its application, the Commission, though favorable to Greece's application, warned against the dire state of Greek-Turkish relations, which risked putting the Community in a bind. Yet Greece joined a few years later, with Portugal and Spain in its wake. Associate agreements of a new type, the so-called European agreements, were signed in December 1991 with Hungary, Poland, and the Czechoslovak Republic, four months after the failed coup in Moscow. In 1993 these were followed by similar agreements with Romania, Bulgaria, and Slovakia, and thereafter by the Baltic states and Slovenia.

Constellations instead of Strategies

Among the member states, Germany was indeed the prime mover of a policy of enlargement. Though there was no powerful and permanent constituency or alliance within the European institutions to push for enlargement, the German government and, more often than not, the Commission constituted the core of a variable grouping. Other actors only intermittently favored enlargement. The Benelux countries, the Dutch in particular, dissatisfied as they were by a common market that turned out to be less liberal than what they had originally hoped for, supported the accession of the UK. When Greece applied, the Commission issued a negative opinion that the Council, swayed by the French president, Valéry Giscard d'Estaing, chose to ignore. Later, a transnational alliance of grand, old social democrats, Willy Brandt, Bruno Kreisky, and Olof Palme, who had adopted the young and charismatic Felipe González and the fledging Spanish democracy as well as the Portuguese reformists, forcefully threw their weight behind the accession of the two southern countries.

The latest wave of enlargement, incorporating the CEECs, saw these fleeting coalitions at work. The Commission intermittently backed enlargement, albeit hesitantly. While in favor of deepening first, Jacques Delors rapidly came to support enlargement, although his successor, Jacques Santer, and his enlargement commissioner, Hans van den Broek, doubted the viability of a large community. Conversely, Jacques Santer's successor, Romano Prodi, turned enlargement into one of his priorities, and crafted strategies to include the Balkans and tie in the EU's neighbors, devising proactive policies for the first time. Various European leaders also advocated enlargement, including, most prominently, Helmut Kohl of Germany, as well as John Major of the UK, the Italian government of Beniamino Andreatta, and Felipe González as a representative of Spain's opposition, and later head of government. Transgovernmental alliances of heads of states and governments, members of the Commission, and some of the rotating presidencies of the European Council helped to make the case for a bigger community. As Karen Smith has underlined, leadership was exercised by different member states at different times (K. Smith 2004: 164; also Sedelmeier and Wallace 2000: 443).

All along, Germany was the key, albeit with some qualifications. Having propped up the social-democratic parties in the Iberian Peninsula, it became the new democracies' advocate. Chancellor Helmut Kohl repeatedly contended that no Berlin Wall should be erected at the German-Polish border. As early as November 1989, in his visionary ten-point plan, which devised a German confederation, the chancellor solemnly declared that "the EC cannot end at the Elbe" (Kohl 1989). At the junction between a prosperous and peaceful Western Europe and an area in transition potentially spelling trouble, Chancellor Kohl, his minister of foreign affairs, Hans-Dietrich Genscher, who resigned in 1991, Volker Rühe, minister of defense (1992–1998), and the president of the Federal Republic of Germany (FRG), Richard von Weizsäcker (1984–1994), to name a few, repeatedly conveyed their faith in enlargement, at least to Germany's immediate neighbors. Characteristically, the process of rapprochement, which was sketched out under German presidency at the European Council in Essen

in December 1994, was described as a "contribution to security and stability." (Council of the European Union 1994).[9]

Bonn primarily supported the accession of three/four countries, namely,
Hungary, Poland, and Czechoslovakia, later divided into the Czech
Republic and Slovakia, favoring them over latecomers (Mertes 2001:16).
These were the countries that had most decisively fought against communism and that successive German governments profusely thanked for
having prompted the demise of communism, thereby allowing Germany's reunification. A kind of legal and political imperative, of moral and
historical duty, loomed large, which governments thought they had to
respect. These countries were also closest to the West. Their anchoring
was important to the EU's stability and primarily to Germany's security—
and their inclusion would serve the German economy well. Yet Germany
also balked at the consequences of enlargement. In the early part of the
new century, Chancellor Schröder called for extended transition periods
before fully abiding by the requirements of the free movement of people
within the EU. Though lobbies actually did not raise their voice against
enlargement, the chancellor wanted to heed the opposition that was looming, at the micro- and meso-levels, against the arrival of newcomers. In
particular, the German chancellor feared backlashes in the eastern Länder
where extreme right parties tried to capitalize on xenophobic feelings,
even though foreigners are mostly absent there. In many respects, Germany was always the key to enlargement, not powerful enough to carry
the case alone but necessary to facilitate it.

In short, several mechanisms were at work: the sometimes forceful role
of the Council or the Commission, the desire on the part of the governments that held the rotating presidency of the European Council to turn
"their presidency" into a success, and the influence of Germany. Peer pressure compounded their impact. Actually more than "peer pressure," it
might rather have been the pressure of time, and the progressive closure
of options as, one small step after another, a series of decisions locked
in member states. Add to this the choice of some governments not to
choose, but rather to go along with a majority that gradually emerged,
the fear of being singled out, blamed, and shamed, or simply the desire
not to be out of step by blocking or vetoing enlargement, especially if
strong objections to membership were, for one reason or another, pushed
aside. This dynamic could work the other way round, as we will see in

the case of Turkey where some EU governments let others lead the opposition to Turkey's candidacy. In any case, free riding and hiding behind strong proponents—or opponents—underlined the fact that enlargement resulted from agreements by default, for lack of palatable alternatives. Legal commitments, compounded or framed by historical, moral, and also security arguments, and a lack of clear strategy seemed to lock in the decision makers and limited their options, creating a default drive. And because of lack of alternatives, the enlargement process conveyed a sense of inevitability.[10]

Certainly, the first enlargement, incorporating the UK, Ireland, and Denmark, did not seem inevitable, as the French president twice posed a veto. This "perversely" disqualified the idea that "it is extremely difficult for any member state to block the entry into the Community of another European and democratic state," as N. Piers Ludlow put it (Ludlow 1997: 250–251). Indeed several factors accounted for the jolts without dismissing the argument that, for a long time, it has indeed been difficult to halt enlargement. The British government did not abide by the rules of the game. It failed to understand that the onus of adaptation is on the applicant, not on the organization it wants to join, a mistake that future applicants will not want to repeat, aside from Turkey, which apparently replicates the British interpretation. Moreover, the British were not convinced or determined enough to join the EC at a high cost, a consideration that also applies to Turkey. Conversely, the fleeting alliance of those supporting Britain's entry was not consistent and forceful enough (Ludlow 1997: 250–251). The most recent negotiations seem also to contradict the notion of inevitability. In the case of Turkey's candidacy, for instance, negotiations have been halted, not only because of Turkey's "Britishness" but also because, as we shall see, the rules of the game changed in the first decade of the new millennium, barring inevitability, building in firebreaks, and repoliticizing the process, and because Ankara has chosen to backtrack and sideline democracy.

Between those two bookmarks, the UK and Turkey, however, enlargement was often perceived as the only option. Yet it was at the same time dilatory, marked by procrastination and even reluctance, both because it was driven from outside and eluded a preconceived strategy, and because, in the absence of a supreme arbiter, some of the decision makers hesitated or dithered. As a result, it took fifteen years for the Central and Eastern

European countries to join after they had shaken off communism. Yet that is fairly quick considering the daunting task they confronted. At the beginning of the 1990s, most in Brussels thought that none of these countries would be ready to start negotiating before the turn of the century. What they failed to give, however, was an early and clear signal, welcoming these countries as part of "us." In December 1991, Poland, Hungary, and Czechoslovakia were promised only a vague "European perspective." They were not embraced, just as the Arab countries were not embraced at the time of the Arab Spring. There was no European discourse because there is no European voice. Reluctance transpired. Procrastination and inevitability were most visible in a queer mixture, depriving the enlargement process of its political edge.

However, what helped the EC/EU devise a gradual, incremental, and certainly imperfect strategy was, first, the extraordinary structural power it held over most of its neighbors; the attraction, both material and immaterial, it exercised over them; and the drive, and even the necessity, for the latter to join. Second, the EC/EU's reluctance to expand, engrossed as it was in internal travails, endowed it with an extraordinary capacity to dictate the terms of engagement, to establish the rules of the game, and to devise the way the continent had to be organized. Countries that yearned for membership had to defer to the EC/EU. Once member states agreed step by step to engage applicants, the EC/EU was in a position to impose conditions, to introduce safeguards, and to guarantee its future by helping newcomers to put their house in order—or so it thought.

The Seeds of Conditionality

Already in the 1960s and 1970s, the EC resorted to conditions even when enlargement was not being discussed or even looming on the horizon. It occasionally applied various pressures to show displeasure, or to coerce or persuade a government into relenting on specific issues. Well before Greece presented its candidacy in 1975 and joined in 1981, the Community, the Commission, and/or member states showed strong disapproval toward unwelcome policies. For example, after a military coup took place in 1967, the EC froze its Association Agreement with Athens, though at "a mild temperature," as Loukas Tsoukalis put it (1981: 31). Conditions also applied to Portugal and Spain. In July 1975, at a time when an intense political battle was threatening to engulf the democratic forces in Portugal, the EC's Council of Ministers agreed to a financial package for the country on the condition that pluralist democracy be upheld (Sampedro and Payno 1983: 135). Negotiations with Spain were suspended in 1975 following the execution of prisoners who belonged to the Basque separatist movement. German politicians also convinced their Spanish counterparts to free Felipe González, the young leader of the forbidden socialist opposition, and grant him a passport.

Not only did EC institutions and member states play a role, but so did transnational networks of parties and trade unions, in particular the Socialist International, the international organization of socialist, social democratic, and labor parties. Three of its most prominent figures, Willy Brandt, Bruno Kreisky, and Olof Palme, relied upon their moral authority, and their political weight and resources, to support the democratization process in Portugal and Spain. In fact, external pressures did not bring down the Greek or the Spanish regime—the Greek junta was responsible for its own demise, having failed to build alliances and fomented an aborted coup in Cyprus, and Franco's liberalization was a desperate attempt to salvage a bankrupt regime (Tsingos 2001; Powell 2001). Yet as the EC member states lent moral and practical support to opposition forces, they underlined how isolated the Greek and the Spanish regimes had become and how little legitimacy they retained. The time of reckoning had come.

In Eastern Europe, as it was called during the Cold War, the EC and its member states and societies exerted a combination of pervasive societal influence and skillful diplomatic pressure, especially in the 1970s and 1980s. Since the 1950s, the Soviet leaders had insisted on having their sphere of influence over Eastern Europe recognized by an international convention of European states, the Commission on Security and Cooperation in Europe (CSCE), which gathered as of 1972 and led to a solemn declaration, the Helsinki Final Act of 1975. Western governments agreed to the Soviet demand after setting conditions. While Henry Kissinger, national security adviser and, later, secretary of state in the Nixon and Ford administrations, insisted on a linkage with a reduction in military forces on both sides of the Iron Curtain, the then nine members of the EC laid down their own condition: respect for political principles such as sovereignty and the inviolability of borders, and for "human rights, fundamental freedoms, including the freedom of thought, conscience, religion, and belief" (CSCE 1975). In a nutshell, the Soviet leaders entrapped themselves in the foolish belief that material borders alone mattered while ideas could be stopped. They agreed to the West's conditions, exposed their rule to scrutiny and blame at follow-up conferences, and provided dissidents with the legal instruments that doomed communism, and contributed to the leaders' own demise (Andréani 2005).

Suffice it here to say that political pressures and societal influences dovetailed remarkably with each other. Certainly, Western European governments sometimes connived with Eastern European regimes, and favored rapprochement over change—to hark back to the slogan of "change through rapprochement," which West German leaders had coined in the early 1960s. However, the Helsinki Final Act not only committed all signatories but also allowed citizens' surveillance committees to monitor Eastern European governments. This led to the creation of Helsinki Watch, in particular the Moscow Helsinki Group and other citizens' groups in Eastern Europe, Western Europe, and the United States. Numerous other nongovernmental organizations (NGOs) or networks, such as the Ost-West Netzwerk (East-West Network), or the Jan Hus Association, mushroomed to support dissidents and dissenters in Eastern Europe. Seminars took place in Warsaw or in Prague, sometimes organized by embassies. Radios broadcasted the voices of Europe and America. In short, the CSCE was not about conditions alone.

The whole CSCE process was a perfect example of coordinated foreign policies, transnational connections and influences, and trans-societal ties, a rare example indeed of a successful European policy, especially when looking at later attempts, for instance, the EC/EU's policy vis-à-vis the southern shore of the Mediterranean, which pales by comparison (see chapter 4). It was all the more remarkable because the incipient foreign policy of the nine EC/EUmembers, EPC, was too often dismissed as mere talking shop. The CSCE served as a matrix for a European order promoting rights and civil liberties, and eventually contributed to overcoming the division of the continent. At the time, though, enlargement to Central and Eastern Europe was not in the picture.

As the history of the CSCE epitomizes, the imposition of conditions was not linked to enlargement alone. It was embedded in a broader international framework. Conditions gradually became a diplomatic instrument in the context of human rights policy, in the United States, in international institutions such as the World Bank, and in Europe itself, in the 1970s and 1980s. One should not forget that successive American administrations, international NGOs, and European governments concurred to put human rights and civil liberties on the agenda. While shaken by horrendous human rights abuses in Uganda in the 1970s, the EC came to link development aid to Africa, Caribbean, and Pacific countries (ACP) with respect for human rights provisions. Yet conditions gradually became more stringent within the CSCE, and primarily within the framework of enlargement. In both cases, the EC held the keys to a future others aspired to, and this gave it the power to impose conditions.

The Birkelbach Report

From the very beginning, conditions were attached to enlargement. As mentioned earlier, Article 237 of the Rome Treaty set out one explicit condition—namely, that European states alone could apply. From that point on, the application of the UK, Ireland, and Denmark, and the desire of the Spanish government to enter an Association Agreement, led the EC to spell out conditions that had been implicit. In December 1961, the European Parliament produced and unanimously adopted a report bearing the name of its rapporteur, Willi Birkelbach, which laid down the conditions under which countries would become members or associate members.

The report underlined that the adjective "European" had a political component, and called for political conditions to be heeded.[11] In particular, it raised the question of the political structure of applicant countries, hoping that "it will not turn [the applicant] into a *body foreign to the Community*," adding that "the states the governments of which do not enjoy democratic legitimacy and the people of which do not partake in the decisions of the governments, either directly or indirectly through freely elected representatives, cannot pretend to be admitted in the assembly of peoples which constitute the European Communities" (European Parliament 1961, my emphasis).[12] To prevent democracy from being perfunctory, "illiberal" one would say today, and characterized only by formal elections, the report explicitly referred to Article 3 of the Statute of the

Council of Europe, which stresses the preeminence of law, human rights, and fundamental freedoms (European Parliament 1961: points 24, 25, and 26).[13]

The Birkelbach report further stressed the necessity for applicants to strengthen their economies to sustain the shock of competition inside the Common Market (European Parliament 1961, point 20), to comply with institutional rules, and to accept the body of laws, rules, and regulations known as the *acquis communautaire*. It also stressed the importance of the *finalité politique*, that is, further integration and the union that the Rome Treaty called for, one might say the ultimate purpose of the European construction (European Parliament 1961: points 73 and 78; Rome Treaty, preamble).[14] Heterogeneity would make it more difficult for a community or a union to make decisions and move forward smoothly together. It would create uncertainty. The report stressed the importance of a candidate taking on all obligations. Though foreign and security policy was very much in limbo at the time, the report stressed that "participating in foreign and defense policy cooperation would . . . require a disposition which would go beyond a general sympathy for the Western world and imply a clear commitment in this area" (European Parliament 1961: point 28).[15] Obviously, Willi Birkelbach and the European Parliament were insisting on a high degree of what I call "Euro-compatibility" between newcomers and the Community, that is, political, economic, and institutional compatibility between the applicants and the organization they wanted to join or be associated with. Potential members or associate members had to fit into the Community without disrupting it.

At the same time, however, the report entailed limitations. First, as detailed and encompassing as the report tried to be, it raised questions that could not be answered, which will be dealt with in the next chapter. For instance, while future members or associates were supposed to withstand economic shocks, what kind of shocks were foreseen, or unforeseen? The crisis that broke out in 2008 was beyond predictions. The report requested that future members and associates respect the *finalité politique* put forth in the Rome Treaty. Yet what did an ever closer union entail? Second, the report was not legally binding. In fact, heads of states and governments only briefly heeded it. The report was commissioned to judge the appropriateness of an associate partnership with authoritarian Spain, and warned against it. According to Marianne Kneuer, Willi Birkelbach went so far as to contend that the EEC would do Spain a greater service by shunning its regime, because association could not per se foster liberalization (European Parliament 1961: point 87; Kneuer 2007: 166). Nonetheless the member states insisted that negotiations were after all essentially commercial. Certainly negotiations started only in 1967 because of Franco's policy of repression, and because of difficult negotiations between the EC and the West and Northern European applicants. A preferential commercial agreement was concluded in 1970, but after the execution of Spanish Basque prisoners in 1975, the EC halted negotiations over its renewal, and member states withdrew their ambassadors (Kneuer 2007: 170–171).

With the benefit of hindsight, the report, though not legally binding, was trailblazing. It incorporated all the specifications that would be turned into conditions decades later, in the 1990s, through the so-called Copenhagen criteria. The Copenhagen criteria were not invented in 1993 in Copenhagen. From the very inception of the Community, it was clear that membership or association depended on democratic and economic institutions, and required strict commitments. *Only* full-fledged democracies and market economies could join or associate themselves with the EC. *Only* "similars" could apply, that is, states that were "Euro-compatible." Nondemocratic regimes could not apply, but in-between situations were not foreseen. The conditions were not put forth to transform or help transform states and societies that aspired to become democracies and market economies but had not yet reached that stage.

From Conditions to Conditionality: The Copenhagen Criteria

Hence, when states and societies shook off authoritarianism and communism, and looked to the EU for help, their accession should not have been taken into consideration according to the Birkelbach report. In particular, the states and societies of Central and Eastern Europe had suffered from over thirty years of communism, and had been altered to degrees unknown in Southern Europe. Yet the EC/EU had to rise to the challenge of securing and reunifying the continent, and invent tools to help the new democracies and conceive a European order. European decision makers gradually adapted conditions to support reforms in the newly liberated countries, while trying to ensure that these conditions would not be tampered with. They turned conditions into an instrument to promote reforms, and transform large swaths of the European continent. The conditions underpinning enlargement were transformed into an instrument of transformation. The EU endowed itself with "transformative power" (Youngs 2005; Grabbe 2006). This did not mean, however, that the EU was performing "regime change." It was helping countries to transform themselves.

Conditions were now supposed to remodel foreign bodies into "similars" that would fit into the Union, to Europeanize them, or EU-ize them. A huge body of literature has been devoted to the concept of Europeanization, "a process of construction, diffusion and institutionalization of formal and informal rules, procedures, policy paradigms, styles, 'ways of doing things' and shared beliefs and norms . . . first defined and consolidated in the making of EU decisions and then incorporated in the logic of domestic discourse, identities, political structures and public policies" (Radaelli 2000: 4). To prepare the new democracies for membership, information, advice, and practices regarding principles, rules and regulations were transferred from West to East. A whole strategy was devised piece by piece. The EC/EU was in a position to stipulate conditions and impose a negotiating structure. Its attraction and structural power, and the reluctance of some member states to accept new members, turned applicants into supplicants. Hence, it could lever its resources. And it found the will to do so. From a nonstrategy, enlargement surreptitiously became a strategy. On the basis of procedures, the EU invented a policy (Hillion 2011: 193). Incrementally, the EC/EU specified conditions, and expounded the steps to fulfill them and give them an increasingly binding character. Conditions thus evolved into a systematic body of requirements linked to a specific aim: conditionality. Conditionality entails the definition and implementation of a strategy to reach an aim, a road map that enunciates benchmarks, sets out intermediary stages, and provides monitoring. International organizations, in particular the world financial institutions, the United States, and the EU all gradually and incrementally devised and applied conditionality.

Over the years, a series of steps were indeed taken to systematize and operationalize the conditions that had gradually emerged. Signed in 1992, and coming into force a year later, the Treaty on the European Union, or

Maastricht Treaty (which turned the EC into the EU), marked an important watershed insofar as it made explicit, in Article 2, the values of the
EU, and, in Article F, pertaining to membership, referred to the necessity for all member states to be endowed with a democratic government.
Article 49 required that applicants respect the principles of the EU. It
further specified the procedures to be followed. All these provisions have
been incorporated into subsequent EU treaties.[16] In June 1993, the European Council meeting in Copenhagen adopted the so-called Copenhagen
criteria. The criteria closely followed the script that Birkelbach had written. Accordingly, they stated that "membership requires that a candidate
country has achieved stability of institutions guaranteeing democracy,
the rule of law, human rights, respect for and protection of minorities,
the existence of a functioning market economy as well as the capacity
to cope with competitive pressure and market forces within the Union.
Membership presupposes the candidate's ability to take on the obligations
of membership including adherence to the aims of political, economic and
monetary union" (Council of the European Union 1993). Applicants were
further required to heed the common foreign and security policy *acquis*,
join the economic and monetary union at a later date, and adopt all future
policies agreed upon (as detailed below); this would not prevent "older"
member states from securing opt-outs.

However, the Maastricht Treaty was binding only on the signatories,
and the declaration of the European Council meeting in Copenhagen
in 1993 was also a unilateral document. At the beginning of the 1990s,
conditions still had to be turned into prescriptions that both compelled
and prompted the candidates to abide by the rules of the EC/EU game.
First, membership had to become a concrete goal. In December 1997 in
Luxembourg, the six most advanced countries were given the signal that
negotiations would start, and, in December 1999, the Helsinki summit
invited six more countries, lagging behind more advanced applicants, to
the negotiating table. Second, a detailed road map had to be specified,
and benchmarks defined and monitored by the Commission. A preacces-
sion strategy, Agenda 2000, was adopted in 1997, and accession partnerships were struck the following year. During the 1990s, the EC/EU also
devised financial and technical instruments to help candidates overhaul
their economies, fulfill the prerequisites to membership, and bolster the
credentials of reformers: financial and technical help became a kind of

in-between reward before the ultimate prize of membership.[17] Technical help, in particular, was to provide information and the transfer of knowledge, know-how, and ways of thinking and doing things in various areas—administration, for instance. It was to "socialize" the newcomers, as the process came to be described, with a grain of condescendence, in the academic literature, to change habits and minds and "emulate" the West.

Conditions were never set in stone. They never ceased to develop, and were adjusted according to specific cases. In particular, increasing stress was laid on state capacities (Grabbe 2001, 2002, 2006; Schimmelfennig and Sedelmeier 2004; Pridham 2005; Vachudova 2005; Kutter and Trappmann 2006). Political conditionality, that is, respect for political criteria, became a *conditio sine qua non* to start the accession process: Slovakia was not invited to become a candidate before 1998, when a democratic government was elected. In the case of Croatia, the opening of negotiations was postponed by a few months in 2005 until the arrest of the presumed war criminal general Ante Gotovina. At the turn of the millennium, when it became obvious that some of the candidates had weak administrative and judicial capacities, and that corruption could be a major problem, further concrete conditions were added, such as the independence and strengthening of the judiciaries (see chapter 2). Child care and the social, economic, and cultural rights of minorities received particular attention in the case of Romania and of countries harboring a significant Roma minority. Further stipulations included the necessity to cultivate good relations with neighboring countries, added at the Helsinki summit in 1999, and subsequently the requirement for states born out of the ruins of the former Yugoslavia to cooperate with the International Criminal Court (ICC) and the need to allow the return of refugees (see chapter 2). The necessity to entertain good neighborly relations had already been alluded to in the late 1970s, when Greece's tense relations with Turkey had raised concern, but Prime Minister Konstantin Karamanlis had waved it aside. It nevertheless gained relevance in the 1990s in the wake of the Balkan wars, and with the situation of minorities in Central Europe.

The Community and the Union came to organize the continent "in a fit of absent-mindedness." Enlargement was not conceived first as a strategy going beyond the vision of some of the founding fathers who dreamed of a united Europe. Rather, it was driven from the outside, by neighboring countries that strived to join. To most in the EC/EU institutions and member states, it was a source of embarrassment. The newcomers were often greeted with reluctance, as the EC and the EU, engrossed in their own travails, pursued a never-ending construction, and tackled dissent and crises. Some member states looked upon newcomers as competitors or potential spoilers, disrupting the balance of power in the EC/EU, even though others understood the strategic necessity to embrace them. To ensure the sustainability of the European construction, the EC/EU sought at first to accept only similar states, with similar polities and economies—a concept vague at best. The European Parliament had attempted to circumscribe what it understood by similarity, that is, "Euro-compatibility." It stressed that newcomers or associate members had to respect democracy, the rule of law, and the rights of minorities, and withstand economic shocks. The vetoes that French President de Gaulle presented in opposition to the application of the UK, which he deemed unwilling to fit into the European project, underlined the loopholes of the Birkelbach report: "fitting into" the EC could take many forms.

The differences, supposed or real, between the applicants of the West, and later of northern and central Western Europe, and those of Southern, Central, and Eastern Europe, that is, between consolidated and rather prosperous democracies, and states, economies, and societies that had just come in from the cold, led the EC/EU to systematize conditions and dictate conditionality. Whereas the Birkelbach report barred "foreign bodies" from joining the EC, conditions and conditionality became a tool to transform the Southern and Eastern states and, thus, the continent. Conditions became increasingly detailed and specific in the face of new predicaments. Under the pressure of events, enlargement became a strategy, more or less surreptitiously. The process was incremental at best, and muddled at worst, as Council and Commission wavered between holding up enlargement and supporting it. In this shifting constellation, Germany played a crucial role.

This process, however, entailed limitations, which will be delved into in the next chapter. Paradoxically, the EU's "transformative power" is both considerable and limited. It is considerable, on the one hand, as it rests on a combination of soft and hard power: on attraction, which induces other governments and societies to seek membership, but also on the ability to impose conditions, that is, on a certain form of coercion, and on intrusive monitoring. To that extent, the EC/EU's power over applicants is not soft. It infringes upon the independence of countries that seek membership in the EU yet may resent intrusion. On the other hand, the EU's "transformative power" is limited in nature precisely because it relies on the applicants' willingness to comply with requirements, on their desire to join, on their attraction to the EU model, and on their understanding of the rules of the game. Hence, it is limited in time, as long as applicants seek membership. "Transformative power" cannot rule out backlashes, as members may not abide by the rules of the game, and transformations may become exceedingly demanding, threatening to overload the Union.

2

THE LIMITS OF ENLARGEMENT

The End of Certainties

> To extend the Monarchy to the peoples of the Balkans? To inflate it
> into an empire of a hundred million inhabitants? To corral together
> nations most diverse because of past and culture? To imagine that
> one would thus be stronger, and not even for one fleeting moment
> envisage that one might be weakened instead? Of course, it would
> then be possible to marshal very many soldiers, but what props
> up dynasties are not bayonets, but century-old traditions and a
> multiplicity of social links.
>
> —MIKLÓS BÁNFFY, *Vos jours sont comptés*

Hardly had the Union enlarged to ten, twelve, and thirteen new members than it threatened to unravel. Hubris was followed by crisis and dismay. Since the early years of the new millennium, the EU has been confronted with the quadruple task of helping to create new states and institutions on its southeastern border after failing to preserve the Yugoslav federation and peace in the Balkans; dealing with new member states that have either imitated democracy without adopting good governance or rolled back democracy; accommodating members that increasingly doubt the merits of membership, whether they want to withdraw from the Union, as the UK decided to do, or ask for specific exemptions and special treatment in a tailor-made EU; and handling the long, drawn-out process of enlargement to Turkey, even though the EU and Ankara have never been in step with each other in the past, and probably never will be in the foreseeable future.

Is the EU's enlargement policy running into limits? Limits refer both to restrictions and to boundaries or borders. Empires were always vulnerable at their boundaries. Insecure margins meant sedition, raids and incursions, wars and invasions. In order to survive, empires had to secure their peripheries by integration or intervention. This, however, often entailed overextension and overreach, drained and depleted resources, and overstretched capacities, and eventually led empires to withdraw. Empires also faced sedition from within, and provinces seceded. Today's EU faces similar challenges. As it wants to secure its surroundings by expanding its mode of governance, it encounters poor and often weak states, some of which emerged from the ashes of the Yugoslav federation, and it meets Turkey, the easternmost frontier of Europe, a former empire, a pole of civilization that never considered itself as Europe's periphery. And it must also deal with members that have grown rebellious, defy the very principles on which the EU is based, and undermine democracy, or members that question parts or the whole of the European project.

Overreach or Overload?

Has the EU been overextending and overcommitting itself? And if so, are the reasons to be found in the history of enlargement, in the lack of strategy and the belief that all members would share the same aims, the same principles, and the same institutions? The first part of this chapter will delve into the ambiguity of the so-called criteria for membership and their limited validity in time and space, the relevance of political culture or the resilience of bad governance, and the scramble for makeshift solutions to tighten the conditions of access to the EU. The rest of the chapter will be devoted to a difficult partner, the UK, and to an elusive candidate, Turkey, both of which in very different ways encapsulate some of the risks the EU is facing.

Conditions are very demanding and very intrusive, yet they fulfill a simple purpose, namely, to guarantee that a country that wants to join the EU does not remain "a foreign body in the Community," as the Birkelbach report put it. This is part of an implicit trade-off between the EU and newcomers. Enlargement has to entrench democracy in countries in transition, and help them reform. It offers them guarantees and support.

It extends stability beyond the EU's borders. In exchange, the EU verifies the applicants' credentials in order to hedge its bets, and ensure that it will not import instability by opening up to new members. In short, it has to receive assurances against future reversals of fortune. It seeks a "re-insurance" on the insurance policy that membership offers (Le Gloannec and Rupnik 2008).

Politics vs. Technicalities? Ambiguous Criteria

Yet candidate countries and EU members and institutions often have different time frames, or different "time-zones." The former want to join as soon as possible, and the latter to include new members as late as necessary. It is important, even vital, for a candidate country to join as soon as possible, and for reformers to deliver early on in order to entrench their positions against those who stand to lose out and try to hamper reforms or tamper with them. For the EU, however, it is advisable to let a candidate join as late as possible to make sure that democracy has taken root.

The argument, however, can be turned upside down. Even though a country may still be unprepared, early membership can entrench democracy, bolster reformers, and send a strong political signal. Poland, for instance, was admitted as a member in spite of shortcomings. The most important candidate country in Central Europe could not have been left aside for security and economic reasons, and Germany, its immediate neighbor, would not have allowed it. The same applied to Romania, for other reasons. Heads of state and government, first and foremost Tony Blair, the British prime minister, and Gerhard Schröder, the German chancellor, wanted to reward the country for having participated in the NATO campaign against Serbia over Kosovo in 1999, a "baptism by fire," as Romania had just joined the Atlantic alliance. The EU may also show its goodwill and reward a country in advance. When negotiations were about to start with Croatia in 2005, the chief prosecutor of the International Criminal Tribunal for the former Yugoslavia (ICTY), Carla del Ponte, gave a green light even though the country had not fulfilled a major requirement: the delivery of Ante Gotovina, a presumed war criminal.

Eventually, accepting a country's application and later membership is always a matter of judgment. The decisions that the Council and member states make are in essence very political, a bet on the future—even when enlargement has an aura of inevitability. It was indeed a bet when, based upon the Commission's opinion, the European Council decided to open negotiations with Portugal. Was it safe to do so? Would it invigorate democratic forces in the country? Was it too early to admit the country's candidacy? As for Greece, would membership provide a counterpoise to instability inside the country there and in the eastern Mediterranean as a whole? In this particular case, the European Council decided to overrule the negative opinion of the Commission. Bets may go wrong. Greece, Romania, and Hungary have all been difficult members (see below), as have Slovenia, once deemed the model citizen of the Balkans but now ranked as highly corrupt, and Croatia, which a few days before becoming a member, in 2013, indicated that it did not want to adopt the European arrest warrant (EAW), which is valid across the member states of the EU.

Hence, the criteria that emerged in 1993 at the European Council meeting in Copenhagen relating to the conditions for membership are deceptive and misleading. They convey the idea that boxes can simply be checked when benchmarks are reached. This is not the case—even when enlargement happens by default, the decisions are up to the member states, which might decide to procrastinate or go with the flow. Not only are these decisions essentially political, but the criteria inherently lack precision, for at least two reasons. First, the criteria were never set in stone. They are not valid at all times and in all circumstances. Each enlargement is embedded in specific constellations and obeys specific dynamics. The governments of certain candidate countries complained recurrently about the Copenhagen criteria being "a moving target," which indeed they are, and there is nothing wrong with this. From the very beginning, accession criteria never stopped evolving, according to the specific problems that each candidate poses, and according to lessons learned from the past.

Second, since institutional capacities in the new democracies were lacking in the beginning, Western experts had to give advice. However, their opinions sometimes contradicted one another, and incoherence prevailed—as the reform of the judiciary in Romania epitomized. Coming from different legal traditions, French and German experts offered different models (Coman 2006). Advisers were also often self-serving, as the European Court of Auditors uncovered (European Court of Auditors 2003a, 2003b). In the absence of a clear, unambiguous, and unequivocal template in the Union, the necessary requirements were sometimes vague (Grabbe 2006; Pridham

2005, 2007, 2008; Schimmelfennig and Sedelmeier 2004, 2005a, 2005b; Schimmelfennig 2008). In the absence of a template valid for all, and because democracy is embedded within national frameworks, the EU had to rely upon complex ad hoc alliances between member states and candidate countries, which were sometimes at odds with one another. Criteria were adapted rather than adopted. The EU could export the *acquis*. It could not export democracy itself.

Failings and Failures: A Tale of Two or Three Countries

As eager as the EU was to contract a reinsurance policy against future setbacks, it could not be certain of the results, for several reasons. Leaders with limited democratic credentials may profess a European identity and apply for membership to access resources. Ingrained institutions and habits sometimes thwart transformation and hamper reformers. Finally, reversals of fortune do happen once a country becomes a member, and duly elected governments may turn against the EU to follow a nondemocratic path. The policies of EU institutions reinforced all these failings and failures, either because the EU overlooked the persistence and relevance of cultures, or because it unwittingly stoked lingering resentments in the new members, as detailed below.

The call for Europe may hide murky motivations. After all, Franco himself stressed Spain's "European vocation" when he first sought to associate the country with the incipient Community (Franco, in 1975, quoted in Martin de la Guardia 2004: 99). President Tomislav Nikolić, head of the Serbian Democratic Party and close associate of former president Slobodan Milošević, turned out to support European integration after being elected president of Serbia in 2012, despite dubious credentials, as did Aleksandar Vučić, his prime minister as of 2014. The true motivations of candidates may elude those who screen potential candidates.

Beyond or behind motivations, political cultures imbue and skew the adaptation process in each candidate country. However, until the latter part of the first decade of the new millennium, the European institutions and member states, political scientists and sociologists alike, largely ignored the notion of political culture in the context of enlargement and "Europeanization." A concept first put forth by Gabriel Almond and Sidney Verba in the 1960s, political culture refers to a set of representations that are socially transmitted and shared over time, decades and sometimes centuries, and that shape views, behaviors, and actions, notably in the political, economic, and social spheres (Almond and Verba 1963). In the course of enlargement, differences in political cultures, that is, in values, behaviors, and institutional patterns, in the various candidate countries were brushed aside. Pondering the case of Greece, Kevin Featherstone and Dimitris Papadimitriou deplored in 2008 that analytical thinking on the influence of long-term patterns of culture on attitudes and agenda had gone out of fashion (2008: chapter 3). It seemed that the notion of political culture was tainted with cultural essentialism, and critiques of superficial forms of Europeanization were typecast as conservative.

Political cultures, however, must not be understood as immutable, as the product of an essentialist vision, but rather as ways of thinking and doing things that can be changed through education and social interactions, albeit slowly and sometimes painfully over years and decades. Conditionality may be insufficient to change mental patterns and behaviors. What has been patronizingly dubbed "socialization" was supposed to transform these ways of thinking and doing things, and "Europeanize" candidates and new members by showing and doing rather than by imposing. However, changes may happen only in the long run, within reformed institutions, in particular after the dismantling of ensconced networks and corrupt institutions.

In Greece, for instance, which Featherstone and Papadimitriou characterized as a member state with "a reputation for being the 'black sheep'— standing aside from common declarations on foreign policy, failing to meet agreed targets and . . . upholding EU legislation"—a culture of clientelism and political patronage grounded in group values, and the historical weakness of the bourgeoisie and of truly liberal modernizers, have left their imprint on Greek politics and society, "though how far is debatable" (2008: 5 and 40). As a result, "within government and between government and other domestic actors there is a political struggle over the adaptation to EU policies, especially where there are distributional issues involved," a diagnosis that sounds very relevant to understand the backdrop of the budgetary, financial, and economic crisis that broke out in 2008–2009 (9).

In Romania, as in Greece, institutional structures lived on, beyond the fall of the regime in 1989, and entry into the EC/EU in 2007. The implosion of 1989–1990 in Romania was not a revolution. It was a coup. State structures persisted, and networks lived on. And not only did ensconced institutions survive, but old habits also prevailed—a political culture inherited from decades of informal rules, "a culture of omitting laws" (Mungiu-Pippidi 2007a: 124). The judiciary was notably impervious to change. In December 2004, a government that tried to inflate its credentials appointed Monica Macovei minister of justice to reform the judiciary. In April 2007, a few months after the country had joined the EU, it dismissed her, rebuffing reformers. To prepare for Romania's entry, the European institutions had negotiated with a government led by a man, Adrian Năstase (2000–2004), who would be indicted in 2012 on grounds of corruption. The Commission failed to listen to the opinions of experts in Brussels, and to Romanian professionals, individuals, and associations that were looking for allies to compel their government to implement the rule of law and promote democracy (Gallagher 2009).[1]

The European institutions showed a lack of political acumen. Of course, they had to deal with elected governments, but they did not attempt to empower the democratic opposition. They took for granted a Europeanization process that was in fact a "pseudo-Europeanization," as Tom Gallagher dubbed it, whereby post-Soviet elites in Romania and elsewhere claimed to emulate EU rules and ways of doing things without actually reforming (Gallagher 2009: 11 and 89). Furthermore, the European institutions structurally promoted those very elites that were undemocratic at heart, insofar as they advocated privatization, while the communist and postcommunist networks lingered on and reconfigured themselves to grab assets. Only once before the country's accession did the European Commission attempt to exert pressure on the Romanian government, but that pressure had a bizarre twist. Insisting that Bucharest tackle corruption, Brussels threatened to delay Romania's entry by a year, which meant that whatever happened, membership was on the map.

On the other hand, Hungary is "the first post-communist country west of Minsk—and the first member state of the European Union," before Poland, "to slide back into authoritarianism." The leaders of a "nationalist conservative revolution" are "busy dismantling constitutionalism and the rule of law," and rolling back the Constitutional Court and independent media (Müller 2011: 5). The current authoritarian government of the prime minister, Viktor Orbán, firmly established its grip on Hungary thanks to the carefully built control of important sectors of political and public life, and to the masterful manipulation of resentment. For the past two decades at least, during which he held various public offices, Orbán has systematically pursued a policy of placing key allies not only in political offices but also in various sectors of public life, including the media—though his predecessors had previously attempted to do so, albeit less systematically and less successfully (Lendvai 2010). With the help of a two-thirds majority in Parliament in the national elections in April 2010—lost, however, at a by-election five years later—the prime minister was able to introduce a new constitution, which limits the rights of the Constitutional Court, curtails the independence of the judiciary and the media, weakens checks and balances, and creates what János Kornai calls an "overreaching state" (Tavares 2013; Kornai 2015). He inspired followers in neighboring Poland. After its election in October 2015, the Law and Justice government (Prawo i Sprawiedliwość, PiS, Law and Justice) promptly emulated its Hungarian counterpart, and, much more rapidly than Orbán's government, incapacitated the Constitutional Court, muzzled the media, and appointed followers to ministries and independent institutions, capitalizing on widespread resentment.

Viktor Orbán also carefully cultivated resentment, a resentment with two faces. World War I and the Treaty of Trianon of 1920—whose anniversary is now celebrated as the "day of national cohesion"—marked the end of greater Hungary and the loss of territories to neighboring countries, and fueled rancor against the victors.[2] The economic and monetary crisis, and the rapid impoverishment of parts of the middle class, lured by Western European banks into accepting cheap credit, often denominated in Swiss francs, further stoked resentment against the West. As in Romania, the EU bears some responsibility for having advocated a policy of liberalization in the absence of strong institutions, which led to privatizations that benefited former communists and Western companies.

The two forms of resentment, past and present, resonate with each other and feed a narrative of victimization, where former communists, liberals, and the EU play the role of villain, or worse, of the foreign villain, conflated with a heavy dose of anti-Semitism and xenophobia. In the eyes of many, liberalism has lost its virtue. The post-1989 experiment is being discredited, while its main proponent and supporter, the EU, is entangled in a vital crisis. The myth has faded, and the model has lost its attraction. Even though the EU contributes more than 3 percent of the Hungarian budget, over €32 billion between 2007 and 2013, dwarfing Hungary's commitments to the EU, the prime minister lambasts the imperial interference of the EU.[3] In April 2012, for instance, Orbán branded as blackmail a loan that the EU, together with the IMF, wanted to grant Hungary, conditional upon reform of the judicial system (Orbán 2012). In 2014, in a speech delivered at Băile Tuşnad (Tusnádfürdő), a Romanian locality inhabited by the Hungarian minority, the prime minister praised "illiberal democracy" (Orbán 2014). Left, however, with few options, public opinion expects little. Forty percent of the electorate abstained from voting in the parliamentary elections of 2014, 8 percent more than in 2010. Actually, only one in four voters cast a ballot in favor of FiDeSz (Fiatal Demokraták Szövetsége, the Alliance of Young Democrats), the main party in power. Almost 70 percent believe that Hungary is on the wrong track (Stolz 2013; Capelle-Pogàcean 2011: 9). The extreme right party, Jobbik, garnered 16 percent of the vote in the 2010 elections, and 20 percent in 2014. Nihilism begins to capture people's minds.[4]

Expiry Date

After accession, when candidates become decision makers, conditionality tends to lose its efficacy. It comes with an expiry date attached. To counter backlashes and relapses, the European institutions have invented new postaccession instruments. The former Romanian justice minister Monica Macovei, Romanian associations, intellectuals such as Alina Mungiu-Pippidi, who heads the European Research Centre for Anti-Corruption and State-Building in Berlin, and supporters in Brussels, in particular in the European Parliament, which Macovei entered in 2009, struck a powerful alliance that was instrumental in prompting the Commission to create mechanisms to monitor and pressure new members. A Mechanism for Co-operation and Verification for Bulgaria and Romania (CVM) was set up at the time of the two countries' accession, to support and monitor the establishment of an "impartial, independent and effective" judicial and administrative system (European Commission 2010b; Pridham 2007; Spendzharova and Vachudova 2012). Citizens in both countries, who are very critical of their corrupt political class, appreciate the role of the CVM (European Commission 2012c). The European Commission and Romanian reformers also successfully pushed for a change in the criminal code, in 2009–2010, which gave the DNA (Direcţia Naţională Anticorupţie,

National Directorate against Corruption) sweeping powers of investigation and arrest. Further measures involved the suspension of funding, and the postponement of Romania's—and Bulgaria's—accession to the Schengen Area, which the citizens of these countries highly value.[5]

Pressures have been applied. When, in total defiance of the EU's aims and policies, the Romanian prime minister, Victor Ponta, engineered a coup by stealth, in 2012, dismissed the presidents of the Chamber of Deputies and the Senate, and judges of the Constitutional Court, and tried to sideline the president of the Republic, and tamper with the impeachment procedure that targeted him, the presidents of both the European Commission and the European Council scolded him. In 2015, he was indicted on corruption charges and resigned. However, peer pressure may be to little avail. In Romania, the fight against corruption has had limited success (Mungiu-Pippidi 2015).[6] Victor Ponta remains a prominent figure in political life. The European Commission, the European Council, the European Parliament, the Council of Europe, the US administration, and numerous civilian associations have failed to sway the Hungarian government (e.g., European Parliament 2012; Council of Europe 2011; Tavares 2013). Nor, so far, have they influenced the Polish government.

As for sanctions, they are either too limited, though not entirely without effect, or too drastic. Delays in bailout agreements, and prosecution by the Court of Justice of the European Union, fall into the first category. In 2012, the Commission took the Hungarian government to court over the early retirement of judges, prosecutors, and notaries, and the independence of data protection. In 2013, it threatened to do so again over further contested measures, regarding political campaigning in particular, and this led Budapest to backtrack and amend decisions. However, limited sanctions that are supposed to bring about changes depend on the goodwill of the government in power. More often than not, modifications are cosmetic or nonexistent. The Hungarian legislative assembly has passed amendments that hardly modify original laws, or when they do, the new laws are not implemented (Kornai 2015: 39–40; Human Rights Watch 2013).

Potential sanctions are too drastic. In 2001 and in 2008, the member states incorporated Article 7 into the Nice and the Lisbon Treaties, which allows them to determine whether there is a "serious breach by a Member State of the values referred to in Article 2" (paras. 1 and 2), and, if so, address recommendations (para. 1) or decide to suspend the violator's voting rights (para. 3). Unanimity of all member states, minus the offender, is required for the European Council to determine that there is a breach (para. 2). The changes were introduced a year after the member states scrambled to impose puny and controversial sanctions on the Austrian coalition, which the FPÖ (Freiheitliche Partei Österreichs, Freedom Party of Austria) had joined, and froze diplomatic relations, without much effect. In a report published in 2013, the European Parliament advocated the creation of a new mechanism to effectively enforce Article 2 and operationalize the sanctions referred to in Article 7, and asked the Commission, in June 2015, to propose opening a procedure against Hungary (Tavares 2013).[7] The Commission and the Council chose to merely establish a "rule of law dialogue" with Hungary and Poland, a relatively weak procedure indeed.

The Commission, however, treats the two countries differently. In January 2016, in the case of Poland, it initiated a three-step process, and launched an inquiry to assess whether the government violates EU rules. The third step would involve sanctions (European Commission 2014c). Fearing contagion, and also because Poland is a middle-sized country that has played an active and constructive role in the EU, the Commission is upping the ante. Sanctions, however, are unlikely since Hungary—and other EU member states—will certainly oppose their adoption. Moreover, Article 7 has the quality of "an atomic bomb," and the implementation of sanctions would be tantamount to burning bridges. Were sanctions— drastic or not—to be adopted, citizens might close ranks behind the government. Finally, it is doubtful that the EU institutions have the capacity to overrule a democratically elected government. The 2000 episode when the member states tried to influence Vienna by imposing limited sanctions proved all these points. This is the reason why the Commission has abstained so far from resorting to Article 7 against Hungary and Poland.

On the whole, it has been relatively easy to exert pressure on Romania, a rather marginal country on Europe's periphery, which harbors a lively civil society that has come to see the European institutions, Commission, and Parliament as allies in the fight against corruption. However, disenchantment due to low standards of living and lingering corruption has led to setbacks, and since the elections of 2016 the powers of the judiciary are being curtailed, following a pattern familiar now in Hungary and in Poland. In the latter two countries, governments have established overall control over many institutions limiting the liberals' capacity to make themselves heard.[8] Similar methods and the antiliberal ideology that both governments extol bring Warsaw and Budapest closer to each another. Hence, EU institutions now face the quandary of having to confront two countries that present a more or less united front. Each can veto the Commission's proceedings against the other. All this casts a shadow on the EU's so-called transformative power (Rupnik 2007; Mungiu-Pippidi 2007b, 2015).

Mission Creep

The European institutions and the member states never did regime change. Revolutions and changes had to come from within. In very dire circumstances, though, the EU and its members have nonetheless taken on very different, various, and, on the whole, daunting tasks, such as postconflict stabilization, reconciliation and regional cooperation, border drawing, state building, economic development, and political and social engineering in the Western Balkans. For the EU, this amounts to doing what it never did before, namely, engineering states and democracies where there were none, while conflating enlargement with state and institution building. It amounts to doing what Soeren Keil and Zeynep Arkan (2014) aptly dubbed "member-state building." This task is all the more difficult as the geopolitical situation is far from stable in a number of post-Yugoslav states.

In the 1990s, the EU had failed to contain or solve the conflicts that tore down the Yugoslav federation (see chapter 3). Yet it was drawn into the wars that broke out in its neighborhood. Since then, the EU has built a very strong and multifaceted presence there. It has directly contributed and continues to contribute to security missions, with the first and largest ever military and police missions set up under its European Security and Defence Policy (ESDP), later the Common Security and Defence Policy (CSDP), in Macedonia, Bosnia-Herzegovina, and Kosovo. It has been administering and continues to directly administer two states born from wars, Bosnia-Herzegovina and Kosovo, creating de facto international European protectorates. Even though both countries are independent, and international supervision officially ended in Kosovo in 2012, both are still under some kind of supervision, of the High Representative in Bosnia-Herzegovina, and UN and EU missions, UNMIK and EULEX, in Kosovo.

Financially, the EU's considerable support amounted to more than €5 billion for the period 2000–2006, including macrofinancial assistance and Community Assistance for Reconstruction, Development, and Stabilisation (CARDS), the Community assistance program created in 2001.[9]

Last but not least, the EU has gradually devised a complex scheme to stabilize and draw the Western Balkans into its orbit, and embed them within a multilateral framework involving more than forty international, governmental, and nongovernmental organizations to rebuild the region and create new states. It uses a three-pronged approach to the region. A regional program encompasses the actors in the Balkan region to foster cooperation between them. Concurrently, the EU has devised association and stabilization agreements to consolidate state and institution building. Lastly, it has sketched a European perspective for the region (Council of the European Union 2000, 2003; Amato 2005; see also chapter 1).

On paper, all three facets of the EU's approach to the region dovetail with one another. State and institution building, and regional stabilization, logically precede membership. In reality, the rationales of postconflict state and institution building on the one hand, and the accession process on the other, contradict one another. Though enlargement implies a degree of imposition, it rests primarily on the will of reformers to overhaul institutions. Yet the international community helped to create new states and state institutions where there were none. It condoned the emergence of new borders and states, pushed for the independence of the former Serbian province of Kosovo, drew administrative borders in Bosnia-Herzegovina, and laid down reforms.[10] The EU foisted upon the Montenegrins a short-lived federation comprising Serbia and Montenegro, which only an unheard-of majority of 55 percent of Montenegrins could legally dissolve. According to the so-called Bonn powers adopted in 1997 to implement the Dayton agreement of 1995 that put an end to the war in Bosnia-Herzegovina, the international representative could impose legislation and dismiss politicians.

Certainly, the EU both displayed flexibility and flexed its muscles. Diplomats and civil servants inventively coined the formula "standards before status" to promote and implement democratic principles, delaying the question of Kosovo's status till 2008. Though five member states of the EU abstained from recognizing Kosovo, EULEX, the rule of law mission in Kosovo, is supported by all member states, and it is accepted that the country's future lies ultimately in the EU (Ker-Lindsay and Economides 2012: 78). Likewise, the EU granted Serbia the status of candidate, and started negotiations after having settled a number of practical questions with Kosovo despite Serbia's disagreement over the latter's independence.[11]

However, this method has run into limits. Relations between Serbia and its former province have not been normalized. In Bosnia-Herzegovina, it is extremely difficult to break the political and administrative stalemate that the Dayton Peace Agreement created when it anchored the constitutive power of all three nationalities of the Republic: Serbs, Croats, and Muslims. This model entrenches nationalist claims, as it entices the leaders of each entity to overemphasize national characteristics. In spite of the joint efforts of the American administration and the EU, no agreement on constitutional reform has been reached. In other words, the policies of the international community and of the EU entail perverse consequences. In Bosnia-Herzegovina, too, instead of promoting independence, the international community and the EU have unwittingly nurtured a history of dependency, first on the former Austro-Hungarian Empire, and later on the defunct Yugoslav federation (Knaus and Martin 2003). The efficiency of EULEX in establishing the rule of law in Kosovo is contested by European institutions (European Court of Auditors 2012). A system of high wages for those working for the international administration raised rents and prices, and distorted expectations.

As a result, a lack of political legitimacy and democracy fuels, and is fueled by, a manipulation of historical and ethnic claims, clientelism, inefficiency, an extraordinary level of unemployment, bouts of violence, and apathy accompanied by a brain drain and the disaffection of young people in most of the former Yugoslavia. Corruption is endemic "at every level," and the region is rife with smuggling and trafficking of all kinds (Ashdown, in House of Lords 2006: 52; Rupnik 2011; Institute for Regional and International Studies 2012; Prifti 2013). In some countries, almost half of the young people want to leave, mostly for Germany, and have swelled the ranks of refugees in 2015, even though public support for membership in the EU has dwindled in most states but Serbia (Hurrelmann and Weichert 2015: 41–42).

Eventually, time is suspended in a despairing fracture between postconflict traumas and construction, and a future within the EU. The reward of membership remains distant. Not only is time fractured, so is space. In spite of its efforts, the EU has not succeeded in creating a unified region, a *Yugosphere*, and dissonances arise between the more advanced Slovenia and Croatia, both of which are EU member states, and even Serbia, and the central and southern part of the former federation, as well as between minorities (Rupnik 2011: 24). The EU is mired in tasks for which it was never conceived (Chandler 2006, 2007; Knaus and Martin 2003).

The Return of Politics?

For a few decades, enlargement was a default drive, and opposition to enlargement was too marginal to be taken into account. In member states, peoples' representatives ratified enlargement treaties, while citizens did not have to vote. Referenda on membership took place only in those countries that were about to join—or, in the case of the UK, two years *after* joining the EC. Only in the late 1990s and the early years of the new millennium, when enlargement by twelve new members was looming, did the issue gain in salience. Two years after the inclusion of ten new states, European citizens showed distrust about the benefit of enlargement. Forty-five percent favored EU enlargement while 42 percent opposed it, and an overall majority of 68 percent felt uninformed (European Commission 2006a). Three years later, only a minority of EU citizens, 46 percent, supported enlargement (European Commission 2009b).

Concurrently, Euroskepticism, defined as either qualified or absolute opposition to European integration, grew (Mudde 2011). In 2005, the Constitutional Treaty that was supposed to endow the Union with a constitution was rejected by referenda in France and the Netherlands. The economic and monetary crisis further brought the European construction to the fore in political and public debate. It does not fall within the remit of this book to analyze correlations between opposition to enlargement and Euroskepticism, and their respective natures. Suffice it to underline that increased politicization and discontent in most countries mesmerized governments and institutions that grew wary of accepting new members into the EU. Enlargement, which had gradually become an EU policy instead of being a mere default drive, lost its aura of inevitability, and came to a standstill, at least temporarily, in the mid-2010s. More than that: enlargement became reversible, either because a candidate country might never join the EU or because a member state might leave the Union—a provision that the Lisbon Treaty introduced.

Firebreaks

To answer the rising distrust of elites and public opinion alike, vis-à-vis further enlargements, the EU compartmentalized the enlargement process and introduced firebreaks to stop the *engrenage* ultimately leading to membership. At a meeting in Brussels in December 2004, the European Council decided that the closure of each chapter of negotiations would depend on the implementation of benchmarks, and call for constant and strict monitoring. It further introduced the possibility of "long transition periods, derogations, specific arrangements or permanent safeguard clauses"—the very safeguards that the EU toyed with to delay the accession of Bulgaria and Romania—and warned that financial support would not be as generous as before (Council of the European Union 2004: point 23; Phinnemore 2006, 2009).

It is now easier to interrupt negotiations. A qualified majority in the Council may suspend negotiations, while a unanimous vote is necessary to restart them (Council of the European Union 2004: point 23). Suspension for violation of political conditions was raised, though not exercised, in the case of Romania over child protection, a topic that the European Parliament took up. Furthermore, the Council and the Commission are now keen to tackle the most difficult issues at the very beginning of the negotiating process, such as the fight against corruption that is at the core of the negotiations that began with Montenegro in 2012.

Compartmentalization of the accession procedure is reflected in the various stages that a country seeking membership has to go through. After being given a "European perspective," a potential candidate becomes eligible for candidacy if it meets the requirements set out by the EU. Once negotiations start, membership is not guaranteed, as the European Council meeting in Brussels in December 2004 stressed (Council of the European Union 2004). Germany, which had often driven enlargements in the past, strongly pleaded in favor of open-ended negotiations. This may be interpreted in two ways: the door is either gradually being closed or being left open.

Certain countries have introduced their own special provisions to prevent "inevitability" and unwanted outcomes. A German ratification law, amended in 2009, increases the powers of the Bundestag (Hillion 2011: 210). The French government modified the country's constitution to allow referenda in case of enlargement. According to the French Constitution revised in 2008, Article 88–5 stipulates that a referendum may be called to ratify a treaty concerning a state's accession to the EU, unless the National Assembly and the Senate decide by a two-thirds majority that parliamentary approval will suffice. The National Assembly ratified Croatia's accession. Yet it is widely understood that a referendum would be needed to approve Turkey's accession, were the latter to conclude an accession treaty with the EU. In the past, the member states, gathered in the European Council, played a role in pushing or blocking a candidacy or simply going with the flow. Now additional national constitutional provisions may hamper the enlargement process. Yet even in the absence of constitutional requirements, governments remain the gatekeepers of enlargement, since every step toward membership is subjected to the member states' unanimous approval within the European Council. Any member state can interrupt the enlargement process.

The state of the Union is increasingly taken into account. In the 1960s, the Birkelbach report and the first enlargements had stressed that the candidates had to respect the *acquis* and the *finalité* of the EC to prevent a "foreign body" from joining the EC. The Copenhagen criteria tried to encapsulate this into the rather hapless expression of "absorption capacity," later "integration capacity," which the Lisbon Treaty enshrined as a precondition. It is defined as the capacity to admit new members "without jeopardizing the political and policy objectives established by the Treaties" (European Commission 2006b: 5). The definition remains vague because it is highly political, as the EU is confronting a series of challenges, from the economic and monetary crisis and the rollback of democracy in Central Europe to the so-called refugee crisis and the rise of nationalist and xenophobic parties Europe-wide. Addressing the European Parliament upon his election on 15 July 2014, Jean-Claude Juncker, the new president of the Commission, announced: "As things now stand, it is inconceivable that any of the candidate countries with whom we are now negotiating will be able to meet all the membership criteria down to every detail by 2019" (Juncker 2014b). In other words, Juncker was careful not to close the door on the "tragic region" of the Western Balkans, as he called it, but also very skeptical and wary of further enlargement. Before his election he had emphasized that the Union had to "digest the addition of 13 new states in the past 10 years" (Juncker 2014a).

Last but not least, the Lisbon Treaty, which was adopted in 2007 and went into force in 2009, introduced a clause that recognized the member states' right to pull out of the EU. According to Article 50, "Any Member State may decide to withdraw from the Union in accordance with its own constitutional requirements." Up to that date, no government had shown any willingness to withdraw, except Greenland, an autonomous territory that is part of Denmark, and up to 2016 no country had held a referendum on continued membership or exit.

Uncertainty

All this signals that the return of politics means the return of uncertainty, that is, uncertainty over outcomes, be it enlargement at the end of a negotiating process, the makeup of the EU, or continued membership. Much will depend on the member states, governmental majorities, and public opinions. Public demand for increased participation in EU affairs, in particular through referenda that give citizens the possibility of vetoing further transfer of sovereignty, membership, or association, such as the—nonbinding—referendum by which Dutch citizens rejected an Association Agreement with Ukraine, in 2016 (see chapter 6), or the British referendum on the UK's continued membership in the EU, that same year, will affect future enlargements. Whereas over decades, enlargement had gained an aura of inevitability after the French vetoes over the UK's application had been withdrawn, it can now be interrupted by the will of the people and the assertiveness of governments. Permissiveness belongs to a bygone era. Furthermore, while uncertainty was always present, because societies are imbued with different experiences, institutions, and political cultures, and nourish different interests, and different views and visions, it has increased with heterogeneity, as the EU has come to encompass an ever-increasing number of states and societies and as it has had to accommodate various demands on the part of governments.

Two countries encapsulate the quandaries of uncertainty: the UK and Turkey. The former is a decades-old member, a long-established democracy, and a prosperous country. The latter, a decade-old candidate, is poor in spite of booming growth in the first years of the new millennium, and has undergone an authoritarian turn under the rule of Recep Tayyip Erdoğan. A comparison of the two would be irrelevant. As far as Turkey is concerned, the major challenge for the EU is—or has been—to anchor the country in the West, both in terms of democracy and in terms of geopolitical orientation. One of the major uncertainties it is now facing is whether Turkey relinquishes democracy and further distances itself from the EU. Meanwhile, the main issue regarding the EU's relations with the UK was and is the complexity of accommodating the UK as a member—or as a nonmember, after the June 2016 referendum that led to the first ever exit of a member state. Nonetheless, the history of both countries' relations with the EC/EU epitomizes the uncertainties that, for different reasons, plague the European geo-political construct and create risks. The referendum held in the UK on 23 June 2016 saw a member pulling out of the European construction, halting the UK's journey in the Union, shattering the EU's image, and threatening to engulf the EU and the UK in long, drawn-out negotiations that might distract them from fully addressing other major challenges, and even weaken the security fabric of the transatlantic world. Turkey's lack of democratic credentials, Erdoğan's authoritarian turn, and his grab for sweeping powers run counter to the Union's principles and criteria. For decades, Turkey has been looked upon as a major issue in the eastern Mediterranean, and both advocates and opponents of the country's membership based their arguments on security concerns that the authoritarian turn further stokes, while the UK's vote to leave the EU can be looked upon as a security issue that impairs the cohesion of the EU and of the West. To what extent then can the EC/EU address and tolerate diversity—and what type of diversity can it accommodate without exposing itself to fragmentation? To what extent does the UK's withdrawal and Turkey's reversal reveal and reinforce the EU's weaknesses?

The "Awkward Partner"

On 23 June 2016, a majority of British citizens voted in favor of leaving the EU. With the benefit of hindsight, one might argue that Brexit, as the UK's exit from the Union came to be known, was the logical outcome of decades of lukewarm engagement, special regime, and conspicuous rancor toward the European construction, which manifested itself through intense domestic strife over membership. To put it bluntly, Brexit was a "disaster decades in the making" (Younge 2016). In any case, the UK had always been an "awkward partner," as Stephen George aptly said in the 1990s (George 1998). Not only did the UK join late—as mentioned earlier, it did not partake in the initial negotiations that led to the creation of the Communities; it applied in 1961, one year after having launched EFTA to compete with the burgeoning common market, encountered a veto, and was admitted only in 1972. It also joined the EC on the basis of a misunderstanding. While the founding fathers of the Communities/Union had devised a political project that called for an "ever closer union," enshrined in the preamble to the Rome Treaty, the British ignored the commitment. In practice, the UK's hesitancy and reluctance translated into special arrangements that various governments wrenched from their partners in Brussels, and, domestically, they inspired deep strife that poisoned British political life.

In Britain's relations with the EC/EU, successive prime ministers secured special arrangements that mostly met Britain's requirements but deprived it of decisive influence, as the UK did not participate in a number of schemes. These arrangements included the following: a rebate on the British contribution to the EU budget, which Conservative prime minister Margaret Thatcher (1979–1990) extracted from her counterparts at the Fontainebleau European Council in June 1984; opt-outs on a number of policies, especially social policies, such as the Social Chapter and the Charter on Fundamental Rights, which spelled out and guaranteed basic social and economic rights, and which the UK eventually adhered to in 1997, under Labour prime minister Tony Blair's leadership (1997–2007); nonparticipation in the Economic and Monetary Union (EMU), as the UK never adopted the euro despite Tony Blair's timid pledges; and a guarantee of nondiscrimination in case EMU members achieved further progress in the banking and financial sectors, as well as exceptions to some provisions regarding the treatment of EU migrants, and the recognition that the UK is not tied by the vow to pursue an "ever closer union." The latter three concessions—which were eventually fairly limited—were obtained by Conservative prime minister David Cameron (2010–2016) from his counterparts in the run-up to the 2016 referendum.

This helped to consolidate a system of differentiation, defined "as the process that allows some EU member states to go further in the integration process, while allowing others to opt not to do so" (Chopin and

Lequesne 2016: 531). Though differentiation may entail the risk of fragmentation if the member state that seeks opt-outs deems accommodation to be insufficient, it was invented to allow the expansion of the Union and an increased heterogeneity while permitting further integration. Other states have secured opt-outs, too: Denmark first and foremost, while Sweden and a few Eastern European countries have not yet adopted the Euro, although they were or are supposed to. However, no state other than the UK has so insistently and repeatedly sought accommodation.

While these arrangements were devised to protect British interests, some of them actually prevented the country from decisively shaping the EC/EU. As David Cameron renegotiated some key points with his EU partners before the 2016 referendum, he did not obtain the right to veto the development of financial regulation, nor did he secure exemptions to EU rules in this respect, even though he obtained guarantees that countries outside the euro could voice their concern over decisions pertaining to the euro and that they would not have to contribute to bailout funds. Four years earlier, David Cameron had claimed exemptions from EU financial markets regulation. Unable to wrench concessions from his partners, the prime minister had vetoed the so-called Fiscal Compact, that is, the Treaty on Stability, Coordination and Governance in the Economic and Monetary Union, which aimed at tightening budgetary and deficit guidelines that member states are to follow. However, Britain's partners chose to agree on an intergovernmental format that allowed bypassing Britain's veto. To that extent, 2012 marked a watershed and demonstrated the vanity of British blocking tactics. Yet, in a way, the defeat of 2012 was avenged by the 2016 referendum.

Domestically, the question of membership in the EC/EU had been haunting British political life. Of all EU member states, including those that managed to secure opt-outs, such as Denmark, the UK put membership at the heart of British political life and turned it into a quasi-existential issue—ironically enough for a country that consistently sought to secure a semidetached status. More than anywhere else in Europe, skepticism tore apart the main political parties, and pitted them against one another. As early as 1974, one year after the UK joined the EC, Harold Wilson, then leader of the Labour Party, promised in the election manifesto to hold a referendum on Britain's membership. The Conservative prime minister Edward Heath (1970–1974), who had led the UK into the

EC, eventually held such a referendum in 1975 after having renegotiated the financial terms of membership. However, Labour's opposition to the EC did not relent, on the ground that economic sovereignty and, in particular, the ability to devise socialist economic policies were lost. Eventually, the Labour Party split over the EU: the Social Democratic Party, a splinter party, the only truly European party, was created and later merged with the Liberal Party to create the Liberal Democrats, who were practically swept away in the 2015 general elections. The Conservative Party was also ridden with internal strife over membership. David Cameron organized the 2016 referendum both to placate his Euroskeptic backbenchers and to rein them in. The campaign, however, turned out to be a bitter battle fought between two sides of the Conservative Party, with Labour standing on the sidelines.

Actually not only were the two main parties torn apart. Three prime ministers, all of them Conservative, fell on the "European question" as they proved unable to stop the advance of an "ever closer union." Having wrested a rebate from her European partners, Margaret Thatcher railed against the advances of federalism, which an increased resort to majority voting (qualified majority voting, QMV) linked to the Single European Act (SEA) and the looming Maastricht negotiations seemed to entail. Yet the prime minister could not translate into deeds her clear, articulate, and forceful opposition to federalism, aired at the Collège of Europe in Bruges in 1988 and in the House of Commons in 1990, where she emphatically dismissed Jacques Delors's plan to launch a political union (Thatcher 1988; Crines, Heppell, and Dorey 2016). Her powerlessness partly contributed to her demise in 1990, and weakened her party. Her successors from the Conservative Party did not fare well either. John Major (1990–1997), who had convinced Thatcher to bring the UK into the European Exchange Mechanism (ERM) in 1990, eleven years after it had been set up to tie a number of European currencies to one another, had to withdraw the pound from the exchange system after massive and detrimental speculation. David Cameron (2010–2016) chose to put a referendum on the table in order to "settle this European question in British politics." As a leader of the opposition, he had criticized the transfers of sovereignty that the Lisbon Treaty of 2007 wrought, and promised to consult British citizens on any further transfer. He reiterated his promise in 2013 during his reelection campaign. He insisted on keeping the UK in the EU, albeit in a reformed EU, and lost (Cameron 2013). Meanwhile, none of the British prime ministers actually strengthened the UK's European commitment. Edward Heath was the exception. John Major wanted to bring the EU back and failed. In the opposition, Tony Blair supported more QMV, and signed the Social Charter and the Charter for Fundamental Rights, but he quietly dropped the promise to introduce the euro in the UK. David Cameron failed both to block EU advances on the Fiscal Compact and to keep the UK in the EU.

For a long time British citizens did not have much influence on the debate, or if they exercised some influence, it was mainly through their representatives and through the recurring invocation of a referendum, which kept creeping into political debate. After the 1975 referendum, which the leader of the opposition had called for and a Conservative prime minister initiated, Labour toyed again with the idea of a referendum when the establishment of a common European currency came into focus in the 1990s. In the first decade of the new millennium, the idea was repeatedly aired by Tony Blair, by Nick Clegg, the leader of the Liberal Democratic Party (2007–2015), and by David Cameron, both as a leader of the opposition and as a prime minister. In 2016, British citizens were given a voice.

A Marriage of Convenience

"Awkwardness" had many causes. In contrast to those countries that had just discarded authoritarianism and communism, the UK did not look for new models, nor did the Scandinavian countries. Their own national model shaped their identity and was a source of pride. They all joined the EC/EU for economic reasons, at a time of domestic downturn. They looked at membership through the prism of economic rationality. This was one of the reasons why General de Gaulle opposed the UK's application. The UK's economic model, and in particular its relation with the Commonwealth, seemed alien to the European construction, an opinion that the Commission and other member states, the Federal Republic of Germany in particular, shared. This did not mean that de Gaulle's motivations were essentially, let alone solely, economic, since the European construction had an economic makeup but a political intent, and the economic rationality that London followed could not be divorced from its own domestic constitution and identity (Ludlow 1997, 2012; Gloriant 2014).[12]

Accession negotiations were also difficult. Not only did General de Gaulle veto Britain's application. Not only did the UK misunderstand that it had to abide by the rules of a game devised by the EC (Ludlow 1997). It also negotiated from a position of weakness, since it had refused to participate in the negotiations that led to the creation of the European Communities, and chose instead to promote EFTA, the free trade area it deemed best suited to its preferences. EFTA, however, did not turn out to be the economic success it expected, while the EC underwent a period of growth. Yet when the UK—and Denmark—joined the latter, the EC was entering a recession following the first and second oil shocks. This may have nurtured the impression that the dice were loaded—though the referendum held in 1975, two years after accession, produced a strong majority in favor of membership.

While an economic rationale brought the UK closer to the EC/EU, the history of a kingdom that, though embroiled in intra-European wars, was less at risk than continental powers, the careful balance of powers the UK sought to maintain between the latter, the imperial legacy, a global strategic culture, ties to the USA and to the Commonwealth, an open economy and society that in a way embraced the whole world, all this weighed on British membership in the EC/EU—as de Gaulle had feared. As Tim Oliver put it, "Underlying all this has been a feeling that the relationship is a transactional one, a marriage of convenience with membership as a means to an end. That end has never been the EU's ideal of 'ever closer union,' but more of enhancing British wealth and power in the world" (Oliver 2015: 413).

The rejection of an "ever closer union," first implicitly, and later as an explicit demand that David Cameron put forth and obtained when renegotiating with the EU in view of the 2016 referendum, seemed to encapsulate the misunderstandings and differences between the UK and the EC/EU—or at least some of its bigger members—over the European project, and to summarize the UK's degree of commitment toward the EC/EU. At the same time, though, it was much ado about nothing, for various reasons. While increasingly binding, the notion of ever closer union always remained vague. In the preamble of the Rome Treaty, the heads of state and government declared that they were "determined to lay the foundations of an ever closer union among the peoples of Europe." Preambles establish guidelines, and are therefore nonbinding, but the subsequent treaties regarding the European Union included the notion of an ever closer union in the main provisions.

As to the substance, what was to be understood as ever closer union remained unspecified. What kind of union was it supposed to be? What kind of union would withstand the vagaries of unforeseeable events? These are questions that many legal scholars have pondered. The constitution of an "ever closer union" primarily reflects a process: "The journey is its own reward" (Everling, quoted in Blanke and Mangiameli 2013: 58). The Maastricht Treaty, for instance, stated that it marked "a new stage in the process of creating an ever closer union among the peoples of Europe" (Maastricht Treaty 1993). The journey being its own reward, it is open-ended. Hence, different states could—and do—offer different interpretations varying with time. Furthermore, since the adoption of the Lisbon Treaty, a state can now interrupt the journey. Finally, the vast majority of governments and citizens in the Union have abandoned the dream of an "ever closer union," if they ever cherished it.

A Comedy of Errors

While the result of the 2016 referendum was logical, it was not inevitable. Forty-eight (48.1) percent of British voters cast their ballots in favor of continued membership in the EU. More important, even if some Brexiters voted to give the UK, freed from EU constraints, a broader economic and political role in the world, others voted primarily to protest against evolutions that have little to do with the EU. Noting that Labour's historic heartland, in coal-mining and shipbuilding areas in northeastern and southwestern England, disproportionately voted in favor of Brexit, the British political economist Will Davies attributed a part of the anti-EU vote to austerity policies of Conservative governments but also to the makeshift policies of Labour governments, which offered " 'redistribution' but no 'recognition.' " Not only did the mainly white industrial working class experience a deterioration in its socioeconomic situation, but it also suffered from cultural marginalization and uprooting insofar as it lost attachment and status when Labour, a political party and a cultural home, transformed itself into New Labour (Davies 2016). As Davies underlines, redistribution could not buy gratitude and political votes; it rather nourished resentment. A disaffected segment of British voters longed for a return to old certainties. Though national policies and globalization, that is, delocalization of employment and migration flows, were to be blamed for the socioeconomic and cultural implosion of the working class, immigration and "Europe" provided simple explanations for alienation and dramatic changes in life circumstances; in short they served as code words that accounted for the loss of control over one's country and one's life. Brexiters turned their backs on mainstream elites, left and right—though, paradoxically enough, the new elites the Brexiters turned to, from the United Kingdom Independence Party (UKIP) to Conservative leaders, were as cosseted and as aloof as traditional elites.

All these themes resonated deeply with long, drawn-out debates in other countries, such as the rift over the EC/EU, which tears up political parties; the rise of anti-European parties or movements, and of a Euroskepticism that feeds on the estrangement of citizens from established political parties; the latter's lack of clear vision; an increasing divide between haves and have-nots; the weakening of the middle class and the impoverishment of the working class; and last but not least the many crises that the EU has been facing since the outbreak of the euro crisis in 2009: all these issues have been transforming the public political debate over the past years in Europe. In the UK and on the continent—or in the United States with Donald Trump's bid for power—resentment and anger displaced facts and expertise, identity politics won over economic arguments. Debates that hovered over the referendum campaign in the UK pitted simplicity against ambiguity. The advocates of a British exit from the EU had an edge because referenda require a yes/no answer, and because the political proponents of a Brexit articulated a simple, passionate answer, easily conveyed by tabloids. On the contrary, the prime minister did not have a forceful message, unable as he was to juggle two levels, both European and national. A fierce critic of the EU, David Cameron fought in favor of the UK's continued membership while having to concede that his demands were not met during the negotiations preceding the referendum.

The consequences of the UK's exit from the EU are mostly a matter of guesswork. Astonishingly enough, both sides, namely, proponents of continued membership and those who wanted to throw off the shackles of the EU, were utterly unprepared. If the former's lack of preparation was understandable, the latter's was not, as if those who led the UK to Brexit had not thought through what the future ties of the UK with the EU and with third countries might be. During the campaign, the proponents of a Brexit were at a loss to present a blueprint for a UK untethered from the EU, wavering between a Norwegian model, a so-called Bosnian one, or a WTO as a one-size-fits-all solution (Michael Gove, Lord Chancellor and Secretary of State for Justice [2015–2016], quoted in Cadman and Mance 2016). After the referendum, they proved to have no plan. As a result, the UK is a country in disarray, a country in parenthesis, which faces formidable tasks in the months and years to come, and pulls a weakened EU in its wake. The challenges that the UK confronts are multiple.

The UK will have to redefine its relations with the EU and with each EU member state, as well as with every country in the world, and hammer out new agreements. This will consume government and civil servants, and feed uncertainty, which business dreads. This will discourage investments and put decisions on hold. Engrossed in negotiations and entrapped in a time warp, the UK will be isolating itself instead of opening up to the broader world, all the more so as the United States is drawing in upon itself economically and politically, and will be more inward-looking. It will also be weakened, not only economically but also politically. The referendum revealed cleavages more than it created them. And it certainly accentuated them. The significance of the UK might dwindle, especially if Scotland and Northern Ireland redefine their position within the kingdom. In view of these far-reaching consequences, the absence of preparation betrays absent-mindedness on the part of those who triggered the crisis. In other words, the UK has been sleep walking into a crisis that threatens its reputation, riches, and role in the world.

Concurrently and consequently, the EU has not been left unscathed. As Brussels negotiates the modes and costs of divorce and sets up new arrangements with London, as well as between its members, resources and goodwill will be drained at a time when the EU is facing many other crises. Rancor poisons relations between London and a number of other capital cities on the continent. More generally, the economic difficulties or straits that might poison the British economy, in particular a weakening of the City's role, temporary or not, will reverberate on the continent. Politically, Brexit spells disaster in the EU as it offers a mirror to other populist parties, from Italy's Cinque Stelle and Denmark's Dansk Folkeparti to Hungary's FIDESZ, which see in it an opportunity to lure citizens by offering their own versions of exit. Other countries might be tempted to follow suit. In 2016, 45 percent of Europeans interviewed in eight countries—Belgium, France, Germany, Hungary, Italy, Poland, Spain, and Sweden—thought that their country should hold a referendum on EU membership (IPSOS Mori 2016). Paradoxically, the rank and file of pro-Europeans seem to swell as citizens realize what they might lose. In the months following the UK referendum, opinion polls in the EU underscored both evolutions (IFOP; Reuters, 20 July 2016). Brexit also casts a shadow on the EU's legitimacy and authority. For the first time in its history, the EU is confronted not with enlargement but with shrinkage. Not only is it possible to criticize the EU; it is also possible to leave it. The EU is undermined and falls prey to fragmentation, its standing in the world is weakened, and the West is in disarray. Brexit reveals and enhances the existential crisis in which the EU is mired.

An Unlikely Candidate

Turkey's first encounter with the Community dates back to 1959, when, at the same time as Greece, Ankara asked to be associated with the Community through agreements that uniquely raised the possibility of membership. It applied for membership in 1987. The Customs Union, also foreseen in the Association Agreement, was established in 1995. Yet Turkey was not considered a candidate before 1999, and the European Council did not specify a date for the beginning of the negotiations, which started only in 2005. Negotiations have proceeded haltingly for more than a decade. At the time of this writing, only one chapter, on science and research, has been closed. Some chapters have been blocked by the European Council over the question of Cyprus, others by Cyprus itself; others were temporarily blocked by the French president at the time, Nicolas Sarkozy, and finally, Turkish laws regarding some chapters, such as public procurement, are incompatible with the *acquis*. Turkey's predicament is similar to none. Since its first application in 1987, many other candidate countries have overtaken Turkey. Denmark, Ireland, and the UK joined in January 1973 after a brief three-year period of negotiations. It took Greece five and a half years, and Portugal and Spain nine years, from the moment they submitted their application to the time they actually joined the EC, and most Central and Eastern European states waited about ten years.

This fuels doubt that the EU has any inclination to open its doors to Turkey, all the more so as criteria for membership have increased. For instance, the European Council, which bestowed candidate status on Turkey in 1999 did not set a date for accession negotiations, since new candidates first have to comply with political criteria, and respect democracy, the rule of law, and the rights of minorities. It was only after the AKP (Adalet ve Kalkınma Partisi, Justice and Development Party) came to power in 2002 and adopted reforms—some of which were not implemented (as seen below)—that the European Council delivered in turn, and gave a green light to Turkey.

For its part, Turkey is an unlikely candidate, for reasons that pertain to its geopolitical role in the eastern Mediterranean, and, since its prime minister and later president Recep Tayyip Erdoğan took an authoritarian turn, to the evolution of democracy in the country. To ascribe Turkey's predicament solely to the EU's reluctance, to its rejection of Islam and fear of a country, large and poor, that would alter the balance of power within the EU institutions, and weigh upon the common budget, disregards the internal and external dynamics of Turkish policy as well as the dynamics of EU-Turkey relations. The latter are a story of missteps, where Ankara sought membership too late and too unconvincingly, of mutual distrust over the Cypriot deadlock, and of mutual defiance over the dire state of democracy in Turkey and the travails of the EU.

Geopolitical Quandary

After the signing of the Association Agreement, fifteen years went by before Ankara applied for membership. Successive Turkish governments failed to properly assess the EU's security concerns in the eastern Mediterranean and understand that Greece would gain a veto power upon joining the EC in 1981. Greek-Turkish relations bore the mark of enmity. Each had fought its blood-drenched war of independence against the other (Onar 2009). In 1974, the invasion of Northern Cyprus by Turkish troops, following a Greek attempt to annex Cyprus, rekindled tensions. When Greece submitted its application for membership in 1975, the secretary-general of the Commission, Emile Noël, discreetly suggested to Ankara that it should follow suit (Bossuat 2011: 304). Whatever Noël's motivations may have been, the Commission was wary that Turkish-Greek enmity would embroil the EC in security crises. When it delivered its opinion on Greece's application, it called for Greece and Turkey to "find 'a just and lasting solution' to their differences," though it did not want to give Ankara a say on the rapprochement between Athens and the EC (Verney 2007: 311).

Mired in domestic problems ranging from political instability to economic crisis, Ankara failed to respond. Turkey did not apply for membership until 1987, after a brief military parenthesis (1980–1983). Yet it was too early and too late (Yılmaz 2008: 4; Öniş 2001). It was too early because the latest military episode had just ended, and a policy of economic and political liberalization had hardly started. In its opinion published in 1989, the Commission recommended postponement because of economic imbalances and the weakness of democracy. The EC was also engrossed with the completion of the Single Market, and enlargement to Turkey might have "weaken[ed] the Community's capacity to pursue the internal and external policies required for the very success of the Single Act" (Commission of the European Communities 1989).

It was also too late, since Greece could exploit to the full its position in the Council. It was the only member to oppose Turkey's application, even though some European governments certainly appreciated hiding behind the new member's veto. As of 1981, Greece was able to dictate the pace of Turkish–EC/EU relations, and repeatedly block them. It derailed Ankara's candidacy at the end of the 1980s. In 1986, it opposed the resumption of the Association Agreement between Turkey and the EC, frozen after the 1980 military coup, and the release of financial aid because of disagreements over Cyprus and military tensions with Turkey. In 1994, it countered the finalization of the Customs Union Agreement, and only agreed to it in March 1995 when the EU decided to open accession negotiations with Cyprus.

Greek-Turkish tensions were running high at the time. Many issues that arose from a common, contentious past were poisoning relations between the two countries: the delimitation of the continental shelf, the extension of territorial waters, sovereignty over contested islands and air space, the status of the Greek Orthodox minority in Turkey, and above all the Cypriot quandary. The contest between Ankara and Athens over Cyprus, the aborted coup that the Greek colonels engineered in 1974 to take over the island, and the subsequent invasion of Northern Cyprus by Turkish troops brought about the demise of the junta in Greece but consolidated the military's grip in Turkey. Though direct negotiations between the two parties on the divided island looked more promising in the 2010s—that is, between the internationally recognized Greek government of the Republic of Cyprus (RoC), which legally represents Cyprus, and the Turkish Republic of Northern Cyprus (TNRC), recognized by Ankara only—the question of the status of the island is still unresolved, troops of a country that desires to join the EU actually occupy part of an EU member, and the deadlock over Cyprus poisons the EU's relations with Turkey as well as with NATO, of which Turkey is a member.

All the parties involved in the conflict contributed to the stalemate. After joining the EC, the Greek government lobbied in favor of its Cypriot protégé to strengthen the links between the island and the continent, and build up Greece's clout within the EU. The European Council accepted Cyprus's candidacy in 1994, and accession negotiations opened the following year—in return for which Athens stopped vetoing the Customs Union. The Greek Cypriots and the Greek government further insisted that Cyprus join the EU regardless of its status. The Commission had underlined that negotiations would start once the prospect of a "peaceful, balanced and lasting settlement" became certain, but the European Council had to shelve conditionality at its December 1999 meeting in return for Turkey's candidacy, which the German chancellor and the French president were then promoting (European Council 1999b). In spite of a warming of relations with Turkey, the Greek government had threatened to block the EU's enlargement to the CEECs, were Cyprus left aside. Consequently, Cyprus joined the EU in 2004 in the absence of any settlement. The Greek Cypriots rejected by referendum a reunification plan that UN Secretary-General Kofi Annan had brokered. Certain of joining the EU, they had no incentives whatsoever to espouse a plan that did not heed their preferences for a centralized federation. Conversely, the Turkish Cypriots voted in favor of reunification to access the EU (Tocci 2004). Contrary to what the enlargement commissioner contended, then, the outcome of the referendum was entirely predictable.[13]

As conditionality ceased to bear on Cyprus, that is, on the Greek Cypriots who represented the whole island, it increasingly weighed on the Turkish Cypriots and their Turkish patron. This was predictable and yet paradoxical, since the Turkish Cypriots had overwhelmingly favored the Annan plan, and Turkey professed then to follow a European path. The

December 1999 summit stressed the importance of good-neighborly relations. Henceforth, Turkey's membership in the EU depended on the resolution of the Cypriot conflict. The EU also put the onus on the TRNC. Contrary to earlier promises of the Commission to foster trade with the nonrecognized entity to alleviate its isolation and reward it for having voted in favor of reunification, trade was suspended because the latest member of the Union, the RoC, exercised its veto. The Commission has nonetheless been able to mitigate the TRNC's isolation at the microeconomic, legal, and social levels, and promote connections and reconciliation. Since 2006, the EU has provided assistance to Turkish Cypriots, who legally are EU citizens.

For its part, the Turkish government has not in the least contributed to a settlement. Not only does it station troops on EU territory. It has also refused to apply to the RoC the 2005 Ankara Protocol, which extends the EU-Turkey free trade provisions to all new EU members, and balks at opening its ports and airports to Greek Cypriot sea and air ships. Time and again, it has threatened to annex the TRNC. It is Ankara that will eventually define, approve, or reject the terms of the negotiation between Greek and Turkish Cypriots. This, in turn, bears on the negotiations between the EU and Turkey, and on the relations between the EU and NATO, metastasizing at all levels. Citing Turkey's refusal to fulfill its commitment, the EU decided, in December 2006, to freeze eight chapters of the accession negotiations, Cyprus blocked some chapters, and Ankara retaliated by ignoring the rotating presidency of the Council, which Nicosia held in the second half of 2012. It also bears on the relations between the EU and NATO. A member of NATO, Turkey prevents Cyprus's participation in all kinds of NATO and NATO-EU activities, including the exchange of information, joint operations, and operations where the EU would borrow NATO infrastructures and capabilities. US pressure and the inventiveness of EU and NATO diplomats alone can partly bypass the interdiction.[14]

Alla Turca, Alla Franca?

Geopolitics alone does not account for the impasse in the accession negotiations. Turkey's path to democracy has been difficult. Since it first applied for association with the EC, three military coups took place in as many decades, in 1960, 1971, and 1980. For more than fifty years during which Turkey has been associated with the EU and sought membership, one question has repeatedly come to the fore in Brussels and in the member states, that of Ankara's democratic credentials. Only in October 2004 did the Progress Report of the Commission judge that Turkey was meeting the political conditions required, even though Turkey was not a full-fledged democracy meeting all political criteria. As often in similar circumstances, the decision to open up negotiations with Turkey was political, to bolster the credentials of reformers after Ankara started undertaking major economic and political reforms in the late 1990s, under Bülent Ecevit (1999–2002) and, as of 2002, with Recep Tayyip Erdoğan (prime minister 2003–2014 and president since 2014).

Certainly public and political debates in the EU echoed many concerns, such as the possible repercussions of Turkey's membership on the EU's makeup, a climate of suspicion vis-à-vis Muslims after 9/11, support for the Armenian cause and criticism of Ankara's denial of the genocide committed at the end of World War I, and the denunciation of the lack of religious freedom and the murder of proselytizers (Le Gloannec 2008). Within the context of growing opposition to enlargement, wariness toward immigrants, and mistrust of Islam, public opinion in France and Germany has, over the years, become increasingly hostile to Turkey's membership, and governments in Paris and Berlin withdrew their backing. It was Nicolas Sarkozy's government that initiated the freeze of ten negotiation chapters, in particular all those that dealt with matters that would lead to membership only, to the exclusion of other forms of association.[15]

The illiberal turn that has taken place under the leadership of Recep Tayyip Erdoğan has strengthened opposition to Turkey's membership. On assuming power in November 2002, the AKP government pursued the liberalization process that its predecessors had initiated. In a context of amazing economic growth and societal awakening, the new government represented a break with the past and promised a democratic renewal. It empowered an electorate that in the past had been shunned and literally disenfranchised by a secular, liberal, and Western-oriented elite, but had nonetheless built a powerful economic and financial basis in the years of economic opening (ESI 2005). In a seminal book published in 1972, the sociologist Şerif Mardin pointed at the duality between center and periphery to understand the mechanisms of Ottoman domination, and later a modernization imposed by the Kemalist regime against a "suspect" periphery (Mardin 1972, 2006). The election of the AKP in 2002 and its hold on power since then could be interpreted not only as the inclusion of the periphery in the center, but also as the revenge of the periphery.

The AKP professed to democratize politics and policies, overhaul the judiciary, roll back the army, and recognize the rights of minorities. Many reforms were adopted in the first years of the AKP government, between 2002 and 2006, including the abolition of the death penalty in 2004. However, some of the reforms were mostly cosmetic, even before the swift and massive power grab that Erdoğan engineered after the military coup that failed in July 2016. The reform of the judiciary was sluggish. The new version of Article 301 of the penal code, that bars insulting Turkishness, was the old one in disguise. Imprisonment without charges or trial was the rule. In 2014, governmental control over the judiciary was legally tightened. The government forcibly removed prosecutors and police officers in charge of corruption investigations targeting the prime minister, and allowed a wave of prosecutions against members of the military on the basis of tenuous or dubious evidence, but the rollback of the military has not been matched by greater democratic accountability. Only small steps were taken concerning the recognition of religions other than Islam, and the use of Kurdish. Press freedom was curtailed, and journalists and academics fired, sued, jailed, and even murdered. This paved the way for the massive curtailment of liberties and fundamental rights that followed the coup in July 2016. An ill-prepared coup by a military that had been partly brought under the control of the executive was followed by the imposition of a state of emergency and by the dismissal and/or arrest of more than 100,000 lawyers, academics, teachers, journalists, and members of the Kurdish Peoples' Democratic Party (Halkların Demokratik Partisi, HDP), who were supposed to have connived with Erdoğan's former longtime ally, Fetullah Gülen. In a sense, this was the real coup that brought Turkey under Erdoğan's control, in open violation of the EU's fundamental rights and requirements.[16]

Erdoğan's ambition to strengthen, constitutionally or de facto, the powers of the presidency to which he was elected in 2014, and the triumph of his party in the November 2015 elections, coming after a narrow defeat a few months earlier and the resumption of war in the eastern, Kurdish part of the country, demonstrated that his popularity, rooted in the revenge of the disenfranchised, and his grip on power remain firmly anchored despite his authoritarian streak, suspected embezzlements, and huge demonstrations in 2007 and 2013. Yet it came at the cost of the country's unity, rekindling tensions and strife after the failure of long, drawn-out talks with the imprisoned leader of the Kurdish Workers' Party (Partiya Karkerên Kurdistan, PKK), the split with Fetullah Gülen and his followers, and the battle against liberals, secularist or Muslim, which was akin to a *Kulturkampf* and reflected a deep-seated cleavage that had lingered through decades and centuries.[17]

Cleavages between center and periphery, between liberals and conservatives, between the old Kemalist guard and the formerly disenfranchised newcomers, do not necessarily overlap, yet resonate with an entrenched tension between a Western type of identity and a more Turkish one, between *sivilizasyon* and spirituality, which, since the first part of the nineteenth century, those in power have been juggling (Hanioğlu 2008; Gökalp [1915] 2008; Keyman and Öniş 2007: 9–11). The adoption, adaptation, or rejection of Western, that is, European, values set Turkey's—as well as Russia's and Prussia's—quest for identity against the backdrop of lingering distrust of the West, which the long involvement of European states in Ottoman affairs, and the dismemberment of the empire at the end of World War I, nurtured (Zarakol 2011; Türkmen 2014).[18] Hence, accession negotiations and other negotiations, for instance, over the refugee question, were viewed through the prism of sovereignty. It is doubtful that a Turkish regime will ever cast itself in the role of an applicant, let alone a supplicant, agree to play by EU rules, and compromise. The accession process is not about bargaining, however. There is a disconnection between Brussels's conditions and rules, and Ankara's insistence on trying to negotiate from a position of strength and resorting to a tit-for-tat policy—besides the Cyprus quandary (Öniş 2007: 248).

Compounding diverging views over the tactics and purpose of membership negotiations, Turkey's application had lost steam as both sides lost interest. The liberal elites in Istanbul and Ankara felt betrayed by an EU that empowered the so-called AKP reformers, who are not of a mind with Western democrats (Pamuk 2006). Abandonment was even more painful as the EU struck a deal with Ankara in March 2016 over immigration (see below and chapter 5), at a time when the regime strengthened its grip on the liberal opposition. The EU was viewed as giving up on its very values.

Concurrently, the EU's reluctance to embrace Turkey, the reversal of France and Germany in particular, and the crises the EU faces undermined its attraction and legitimacy—which Erdoğan did not hesitate to ridicule. Public opinion in Turkey showed new support for membership, while coveting the visa liberalization that the March 2016 agreement with the EU promised. Intellectuals too doubted the validity of the European project. In "The Fading Dream of Europe" (2010), Orhan Pamuk, the recipient of the 2006 Nobel Prize for Literature, lambasted a confused, anxious, and even panicked Europe that shuns outsiders and is oblivious to "liberté, égalité, fraternité."

Within the context of a weakening Europe and a withdrawing West, Turkish decision makers, business leaders, and politicians alike looked away from Europe. In the first decade of the new millennium, Turkish enterprises strengthened their stakes in neighboring countries, in Iraq and Syria, and in Africa. Up to the so-called Arab Spring, the government, with Ahmet Davutoğlu as foreign minister, tried to invent a future outside the EU, and independent of the success or failure of an elusive accession process.[19] In contrast to the government's grand strategy, however, Turkey ended up embedded in a hostile and inflammable environment, especially after the start of the war in Syria in 2011, the military coup in Egypt in 2013, and the nightmare of a Kurdish alliance across borders, while dangerously trying to manipulate the so-called Islamic State (IS) for its own purposes, and to reestablish a military and political sphere of influence over parts of Syria and Iraq.

All this left Turkey isolated in the Middle East. Before the establishment of sweeping controls over Turkey's civil society, Ahmet Davutoğlu, who thereafter served as prime minister between 2014 and 2016, sketched a rapprochement with the EU, especially in the context of the refugee crisis, partly to counterbalance the regime's illiberal turn and partly to carve out a niche for himself in a system that Erdoğan was seeking to presidentialize. Twice in the latter years, the EU hesitatingly opened up new chapters: a chapter on regional policy after the repression of demonstrations in 2013, when liberals insisted that they not be left out in the cold, and a chapter on financial and budgetary provisions in 2016. The March 2016 agreement between the EU and Turkey, pertaining to the refugee crisis, went further and mentioned the reinvigoration of the negotiation process—before unraveling. After July 2016, Ankara's bid for membership came to a standstill, and the European Parliament recommended, in a nonbinding vote, to suspend talks. Turkey's candidacy is anything but alive.

The European construction always had to accommodate heterogeneity. The original member states and those that joined later did not have the same motivations to partake in the European construction, nor did they cast the latter in the same light, all the more so since the treaties were conspicuously vague regarding the nature of an ever closer union. The EC/EU had to accommodate heterogeneity for the sake of survival, and eventually for the sake of democracy. The necessity to embrace diversity in order to sustain the viability of the union led the EC/EU to invent so-called opt-outs that allowed certain countries, such as the UK and Denmark, not to participate in specific EC/EU policies. The irruption of public demands for democratic participation, especially in the new millennium, also called for increased flexibility. Yet this entailed a fateful twist—the risk of fostering fragmentation and even breakup instead of allowing for diversity in unity. This was the main lesson of the 2016 referendum in the UK and of other referenda that might follow.

Concurrently, the EU institutions sought to introduce homogeneity within diversity through criteria for membership, which were, however, so ambiguous that they had to be specified over time. Yet this did not prevent countries that had joined after being vetted from turning their backs on the very principles on which the EU rests. Such is the case of Hungary, a member of the EU, and that of Turkey, a candidate member. In other countries, norms and habits inherited from the past put a brake on reforms. For many years, EU institutions, experts, and decision makers too easily glossed over national characteristics and idiosyncrasies. Political cultures can be changed over time, through education and reforms of institutions. Yet such changes take generations and must come from within. The EU alone cannot be blamed for failing to transform a specific country, nor can the onus be put on the latter only. Success or failure lies in the interaction between the EU's influence and power, and the will of governments and/ or citizens to bring about changes in countries that may apply. To that extent, enlargement has always been a political bet about the future, a bet that entailed uncertainty and risks. For decades uncertainty was covered up by technicalities, criteria, commitments, or opt-outs. With the rise of Euroskepticism, and the illiberal turn of a few member states or candidate countries, uncertainty has come to the fore.

PEACE, WAR, AND CONFETTI

An Elusive Security Policy

> Yet, there was no army in sight, marching on. Throughout the desert
> of the Tartars, the road alone unwound like a ribbon, a singular
> sign of human order in this most ancient solitude. No army came to
> launch an attack. Everything was left, suspended for who knows how
> many years.
>
> —DINO BUZZATI, *Il deserto dei Tartari*

The Communities were to create a new pattern of intra-European relations that banned war from the continent, through democracy and prosperity,
shared sovereignty and shared policies. Foreign policy did not belong to
the remit of the new organization that came into being, and, aside from
the ill-fated attempt to constitute, in the early 1950s, a European Defense
Community (EDC), the Europeans relied on the American protector to prevent or thwart a Soviet attack. Yet conflicts always simmered or flared up
at the ever expanding borders of the EC/EU. Some were rooted in decades
or centuries of strife, from Ireland to the Middle East, from Cyprus to the
Caucasus.

Toward the end of the 1960s and into the 1970s, wars (the Vietnam
War, the Arab-Israeli wars in 1967), the 1973 oil embargo imposed by
Arab states on Western countries that did not share their views, and the
accession to the EC of the UK, which, like France, had an imperial past
and an understanding of world affairs, demonstrated the vacuity of foreign ministers' meetings addressing all kinds of issues but foreign policy.

A fledgling European foreign policy (European Political Cooperation, EPC) emerged in the early 1970s, replaced in the 1990s by the Common Foreign and Security Policy (CFSP), deemed to be more robust, and beefed up by the Lisbon Treaty, which came into force in 2009. Meanwhile the Europeans' impotence in the former Yugoslavia led to the European Security and Defence Policy (ESDP) in 1999, which the Lisbon Treaty revamped into a Common Security and Defence Policy (CSDP) as of 2009. Did this help the EU deal with conflicts in the neighborhood? Much has been written on the civilian nature of the EU since François Duchêne pithily observed that the EC was "long on economic power and relatively short on armed force," a civilian power that relied on American military power (Duchêne 1972: 12–20; Maull 1990; Bull 1982). A lengthy academic debate ensued as to whether the EU was a normative power thanks to its civilian touch (Manners 2002, 2006).

What instruments are at the EU's disposal? Can the Union mediate, cajole, and coerce? Does it do peace? Can it do wars? How successfully? A decade after the EC/EU failed to prevent the violent breakup of Yugoslavia and the return of wars and genocide to the continent in the 1990s, a European defense vanished in the sand dunes of Libya, and the Europeans stood by helplessly as internecine wars gripped Libya, and Syria descended into chaos. Mediation efforts have also been puny in the Middle East and the Caucasus. In Ukraine, where Russia holds the commanding heights, the Europeans have been cautious at best. The difficulties the EU and its member states have encountered in trying to pacify the surroundings by diplomatic or military means are the focus of this chapter, while the Europeans' role in Ukraine will be analyzed in chapter 6. The difficulties faced by the EU depend on the parties to the conflicts, their relations with the EU, and their value to EU member states according to past experiences and present interests. They also depend on the orientation of the governments in power.

The Delusions of Mediation, Support, and Conflict Transformation

In 2002, a dozen Moroccan constables occupied tiny Parsley Island, thirty-eight acres of emptiness under Spanish rule off the coast of Morocco. The EU member states diverged and dithered. The president of the Commission offered to mediate, but mediation between one of the member states and a third party was deemed awkward, and rejected. Eventually, the US secretary of state, Colin Powell, arranged a settlement with the unobtrusive support of the High Representative for Foreign Affairs and Security Policy (Monar 2002).[1] A few years earlier, in January 1996, in relatively similar circumstances, Greece and Turkey had almost gone to war over ten acres of uninhabited rock off the Turkish coast. That winter, the Europeans were just as helpless as they would be in the summer of 2002, and it was thanks to the United States that the matter was settled. In both cases, the organizer of the continent, the EU, which appeared to be at the height of its might, transforming Europe through enlargement and extending its area of peace and prosperity to Central and Eastern Europe, was incapable of solving two relatively minor quarrels over tiny, forlorn islands on its fringe, hindered by some of its own members. It had to call in its American ally.

The truth is that the EU cannot mediate when both parties to the conflict are members, and rarely can it do so when one state is a member and the other is not—as with Greece and Turkey. However, what about mediating between parties that are not EU members, yet part of its neighborhood? The prospect of membership may induce the conflicting parties to resolve their disputes, and give the EU some leverage. True to the requirements it spelled out in the 1990s, the EU has insisted, more often than not, on the establishment of good-neighborly relations before admitting new members. In 1992, Hungary and Slovakia, which both eyed membership, turned to the Commission over their dispute regarding the construction of a dam on the Danube at the border between Gabčíkovo and Nagymaros, which the postcommunist government in Budapest wanted to halt on ecological grounds. The Commission convinced both parties to bring the case to the International Court of Justice (K. Smith 2004: 151–155). In 1994, the EU convened a Stability Pact for Hungary and its neighbors to guarantee the rights of minorities. At the beginning of the new millennium, the Commission intervened in the Slovenian-Croatian maritime and land border dispute, whereby Slovenia, already a member of the EU, threatened to derail Croatia's EU and NATO accession and relented when pressed by the enlargement commissioner and the EU president. In 2011, a dialogue started between Kosovo and Serbia under the High Representative's auspices, leading to an agreement in 2013. Certainly, not only does the prospect of membership play a role; domestic considerations do as well. In Slovenia, public opinion, consulted by referendum, proved to be less obdurate than the government, while a change in prime ministers in Croatia opened the door to an understanding.

Window Dressing: The EU and the Georgian-Russian War

What about mediating between parties that are not candidates for membership, yet lie in the EU's neighborhood? EU representatives have been mediating between parties, to no avail in Egypt, successfully in Tunisia, thanks to a process in which the local actors played a primary role, recognized by the Nobel Peace Prize in 2015, and in Libya, where mediation led to a unified government, which transnational terrorist movements nonetheless challenge. Many variables interfere in a mediation process that is supposed to end an international conflict, such as the regional balance of power, the presence of the EU on the ground, and each party's respective importance for the EU or some of its members. All these elements devise constellations that affect mediation.

The EU's mediation between Russia and Georgia to halt the war in the late summer of 2008 was certainly not the success that the French government, then in charge of the EU's rotating presidency, claimed. Of the two conflicting parties, Russia was dominant, present on the ground in Georgia and the Caucasus. The EC/EU, and the United States as well, had long shunned the area and had only started to meekly venture into it in the first decade of the new millennium. In the early 1990s and at the beginning of the new millennium, the role of the EU, or of the West for that matter, had been extremely modest, though the conflict between Russia and Georgia had been simmering since the implosion of the USSR. The Caucasus seemed far away, and, engrossed as they were in the reunification of the continent, Europeans and Americans left to the Russians the task of supposedly pacifying their neighborhood. Russia, however, played contradictory roles, as self-proclaimed peacekeeper and upholder of public order, and as patron of two minorities in Georgia, Abkhaz and Ossetian. This pitted Moscow against Tbilisi and, in an extraordinarily personalized and embittered contest, Vladimir Putin against Mikheil Saakashvili, after the latter's accession to power in 2004. Nor did the EU take part in the negotiations that were supposed to solve the inner-Georgian conflicts (Popescu

2011).[2] For more than a decade, the role of the EU was confined to that of purveyor of economic, financial, and technical aid and help.

In the early years of the new millennium, as the wars in Afghanistan and Iraq, the alleged presence of terrorists in the mountainous gorges of the region, the EU's expansion to the Black Sea, and the development of energy corridors in that area gave the Caucasus new geopolitical significance, the Europeans stepped up their presence, albeit modestly and inconsistently.[3] What later turned out to be Europe's weakness was partly of its own making. When Russia refused to renew the Organization for Security and Co-operation in Europe (OSCE) mission in Georgia in 2005, some of the EU governments most critical of Russia, the Baltic states and the UK, for instance, advocated sending a border mission. France, Germany, Italy, Spain, Belgium, and Greece rejected the proposal, lest they be dragged into a conflict with Russia (Socor 2005; Popescu 2007: 10–12). The support team that the EU eventually dispatched was merely designed to reassure the Georgian government (Popescu 2007: 12). An opportunity was missed.

In August 2008, however, the EU found a new role, that of a mediator. Or, rather, the French president, acting in his capacity as president of the European Council, did. On 8 August, the Georgian government had ordered its troops to attack Russian troops massed on the border, and suffered a crushing defeat. The interest of the EU, considered as a whole, was to restore peace between a major country, Russia, with which a number of European capitals, Berlin, Paris, and Rome, above all, seek to cultivate good and profitable relations, and a small country in the European neighborhood, which had been trying to elude Russia's grip, follows a somewhat democratic path, and serves as an essential conduit of energy to Western Europe. Before the war, as tensions mounted, the American administration, the EU, and individual EU member states had multiplied high-level visits and initiatives. Yet it had been "too little, too late" (Asmus 2010: 145).

The eventual cease-fire agreement signed under France's auspices was underwritten by the Russians first, and handed over to the Georgians, who in disarray could only subscribe to it. The French government hailed the agreement as a success, and boasted about convincing the Russian government not to invade Tbilisi. Yet did reality match rhetoric? First, the agreement was vague. It did not specify the territories from which the Russian troops were supposed to withdraw, nor differentiate between Russian peacekeepers and Russian troops, nor spell out the "additional security measures pending international mechanisms" that the Russians were allowed to seek. It did not even refer to Georgia's territorial integrity (Asmus 2010: chap. 6).[4] In the fuzzy spaces left by unspecific wording, a window was left open that Moscow exploited. Though the Russian authorities ultimately withdrew their troops behind the administrative borders of South Ossetia and Abkhazia, except from a small area, they built up their military forces, officially recognized the two entities, and since then have kept increasing their presence there, and pushed the so-called border farther into Georgian territory.

Second, and most important, whether or not the Kremlin meant to invade Tbilisi, it was dictating the rules of the game.[5] Controlling the capital city and the Baku-Tbilisi-Ceyhan oil pipeline from the commanding heights of South Ossetia, some fifty kilometers north of Tbilisi, was—and is—probably enough for any Russian government to remind its Georgian counterpart and Western allies of its permanent superiority in the region. The Kremlin's main purpose may have been to teach the Georgian government and the West a lesson, and destroy any hope for Georgia of joining NATO, after the Bucharest Summit of the Atlantic Alliance, in April 2008, promised Tbilisi a Membership Action Plan (MAP), a first step toward membership, though it did not grant Georgia immediate accession, because of Germany's and France's opposition. It is unlikely that NATO will accept as member a state on whose territory Russian troops are stationed. The Kremlin was drawing a red line to stop the expansion of Western influence, a rehearsal before the war it launched in Ukraine six years later. Led by an active French presidency, the EU displayed a fair degree of cohesion during the negotiating process. Yet years of division over how to deal with Russia had left an imprint. While five presidents from Estonia, Latvia, Lithuania, Poland, and Ukraine showed up in Tbilisi on 12 August 2008 to support Mikheil Saakashvili, the French presidency ruled out sanctions against Russia: "If there are still problems, we will not talk about sanctions" (Kouchner 2008). Negotiations on a renewed Partnership and Cooperation Agreement (PCA) with Russia were merely frozen. Limited to "confetti," to borrow the description by an astute observer, the EU lacked the paraphernalia to impress and impose.[6] It could not play the role of a mediator who entices, cajoles, and warns. It was not the United

States. Yet in the absence of the latter, which chose not to act, it was the only party available (Asmus 2010). It essentially served as a conduit, a go-between, which one party used to dictate its will to the other.

The EC/EU and the Arab-Israeli Conflict: A Doctrine without a Policy

The Arab-Israeli conflict is one of Europe's oldest foreign policy concerns. No sooner had the EC sketched an incipient foreign policy in the early 1970s, than the Arab-Israeli conflict became a priority. Never has the EC/EU invested so much for so long in an area torn by such a deep-seated conflict, punctuated for decades by wars, simmering tensions, and bouts of violence, which the claims and clashes around the Temple Mount/Haram esh-Sharif in Jerusalem encapsulate. This is easy to understand. The Middle East is on Europe's doorstep. Geostrategically, historically, economically, and demographically, a combination of European commitments, interests, interconnections and enmeshments, responsibility, and lingering guilt ties Europe to the Middle East, and conflicts in the Middle East resonate on the Old Continent. Nonetheless the EC/EU has played a very limited role, not commensurate with its ambitions and input. Reasons are to be sought in the domineering role of the United States, in the Europeans' lack of influence and cohesion, and in the evolution on the ground.

Certainly, the EC/EU's repertoire of actions in this conflict has been most versatile: diplomacy, trade, research cooperation, election monitoring, institution building, humanitarian aid, deployment of civilian missions, participation of member states in peacekeeping operations, attempts at reconciling political factions, and promotion of people-to-people contacts. Above all, the EC and, later, the EU came to devise the broad parameters for a future settlement of the Arab-Israeli conflict. To that extent, the EC/EU has been more innovative and daring than when dealing with other conflicts.

With the inception of EPC, the members of the EC narrowed the gap that opposed members, like France, which supported the Arab cause, and those, like Germany, which had turned "Israel's security" into their *Staatsräson* (Sonne 2013). The members of the EC gradually pared down their differences, and prepared the ground for the Venice Declaration of

13 June 1980, later complemented by the Berlin Declaration of 24–25 March 1999 (Dosenrode and Stubkjaers 2002: 87). Trying to accommodate both parties, not only did the Venice Declaration of 1980 call on Israel to withdraw from territories occupied in the 1967 war, condemn attempts to modify the status of Jerusalem, denounce settlements in the occupied territories, and underline the necessity of a peace agreement following the resolutions of the United Nations Security Council (UNSC). It also asked for the recognition of the Palestinian Liberation Organization (PLO) as the Palestinians' representatives, and proclaimed the Palestinians' right to self-determination (European Council 1980).[7] Gradually, the EC inched toward the idea of a Palestinian state (Dosenrode and Stubkjaers 2002: 87). The Berlin Declaration enunciated the Palestinians' permanent and unrestricted right to have their own state, at a time when the Oslo Agreement, struck by Israel and the PLO to outline a negotiating process, was unraveling, and the Arab parties were asking for increased involvement of the EU (European Council 1999b).

All these declarations and statements go beyond what has too often been dismissed as a declaratory policy (Musu 2010: 123). They add up to a doctrine, the basis of the EU's foreign policy on the Middle East, that performs twin functions. The first function is internal to the EC/EU. It is in a way an *internal foreign policy* of the EU, incorporated in the *acquis* that new members of the EU are supposed to adopt. The second, external function defines the building blocks of an international settlement, relying upon resolutions of the UNSC. Though denounced by Israel and the United States, the Venice Declaration foresaw the Oslo Agreement. A decade later, in June 2002, George W. Bush adopted the two-state solution advocated by the Union in Berlin. The shuttle negotiations that the Germans and also the French pursued, at the beginning of the new millennium, led to the definition of a peace plan adopted by the ministers for foreign affairs of the EU, in 2002, and offered, a year later, the blueprint for a road map endorsed by the Quartet, an international framework set up in 2002 by the United States, the UN, the EU, and Russia.

To that extent, the EU helped to formulate the main prerequisites to any solution to the Middle East conflict. Yet this came too early, and it was too vague. The Venice Declaration never came to be known as the "EU parameters," as one speaks of the Clinton Parameters, accepted by both Israelis and Palestinians, and specifying the guidelines for a permanent agreement, covering issues that the Oslo Agreement had left open, such as the status of Jerusalem, the question of refugees, and the security of all.

In parallel, while under American auspices, bilateral peace treaties were signed by Israel and Egypt in 1979 and by Israel and Jordan in 1994, and international negotiations were launched, the EU carved out a minor political role for itself. Sidelined at international negotiations on the Arab-Israeli conflict, in Madrid in 1991, it merely presided over one of the working groups set up by the Oslo Peace Process, the Regional Economic Development Working Group (REDWG). It devised the Barcelona Process, which should have served as a complement of and a counterpoint to the diplomatic track (see chapter 4). In the first years of the new millennium, the EU became increasingly involved politically, either as a union or through its individual member states. It contributed to the Taba negotiations in 2001, which took place after the failed Camp David Summit in 2000, and became one of the four members of the Quartet, set up in 2002 to revive the moribund peace process.[8] Yet it never played a defining role like the United States and/or Israel.

As long as the United States ultimately underwrites Israel's security, does it matter that France, the UK, and Germany have declared they would uphold it, even though the first two countries have always insisted on Israel's right to security, and the latter emphatically declares Israel part and parcel of its *Staatsräson?* On many questions, substantial or formal, Israel strongly, and the United States often, disagree with the EU. In spite of international condemnations of expanding settlements on the West Bank, Israeli governments have repeatedly insisted on securing defendable borders beyond those that predated the 1967 Six-Day War. Though disapproving sometimes of Jewish settlements, various American administrations have vetoed UNSC resolutions that condemn them. Eventually, Israel's policy on borders and settlements, tacitly condoned by various American administrations, chips away at the substance and existence of the Palestinian state, which the EU supports, and which a number of EU member states have recognized.[9]

Nor has there been any agreement in the past between the EU, the United States, and Israel on the tactics to follow, or the partner to engage. Both Israel and the United States objected to negotiating with Yasser Arafat, when he was leader of the PLO, and later president of the Palestinian National Authority (PNA), which the Oslo Agreement had helped bring to life. Americans, followed by Europeans, refused to recognize the electoral victory of Hamas in 2006, the Islamist party that now administers the Gaza Strip, though some European governments entertain contacts with it. As regards format, the EU advocates a multilateral format of negotiations, while the United States and Israel favor a bilateral or trilateral format or even, as far as Israel is concerned, unilateral policies. Bi- or trilateral formats, with the United States, Israel's main ally and protector, as an intermediary, empower Israel. In parallel, the United States has little interest in a multilateral format, partly for the same reasons as Israel, and partly because it looks upon the EU as an adjunct that has to support American initiatives and bolster their legitimacy.

Resources without Leverage

The EU's lack of clout seems all the more surprising as EU resources flow to the region. Both Israel and the PNA have signed Association Agreements with the EU and are part of its Neighbourhood Policy (see chapter 4). Indeed, one of the Europeans' main achievements has been to bolster the PNA's political and economic substance, symbolically, institutionally, and materially, in order to redress the asymmetry between both sides, and turn the Palestinians into a viable, democratic, and trustworthy negotiating partner.[10] This effort entails an enormous amount of assistance, financial, economic, and humanitarian support, and the transfer of knowledge and know-how to build and reform institutions. The EU provides the PNA with approximately €500 million a year, directly or indirectly via the European Commission Humanitarian Office (ECHO) and the United Nations Relief and Works Agency (UNRWA), to which another €500 million must be added from individual member states (Bertrand-Sanz 2010; Musu 2010). However, as is the case with other countries of the neighborhood, the EU has often failed to specify conditions, and so has curtailed its leverage (Tocci 2005; Yacobi and Newman 2008). It was with Salam Fayyad as Yasser Arafat's finance minister (2002–2007), and later in his capacity as prime minister (2007–2013), that a decisive fight against corruption was launched—that is, when the decision was taken in Ramallah to push for decisive reforms in order to create a state.

The EU's relations with Israel are also dense, because of geographical proximity—"Europe is Israel's hinterland," as one Israeli personality put it—and because of the extraordinary technological development of Israel in the last ten to fifteen years. The EU is the primary market for Israel's exports, and its second source of imports after the United States. The Association Agreement encompasses free trade for industrial goods and a number of agricultural products, freedom of establishment, free movement of capital, the harmonization of regulation, as well as social and cultural cooperation, and a political dialogue. EU-Israeli cooperation further involves technical, scientific, and research cooperation, such as agreements on procurement, civil aviation, and participation in the European Global Navigation Satellite System, Galileo. No other third country has such close relations with the EU. Israel is a member by stealth, a "member of the European Union without being a member of the institution," as Javier Solana stated in 2009 (quoted in Ahren 2009). And it is due to become an even closer partner. At a July 2012 meeting of the Association Council set up by the Association Agreement, the EU and Israel agreed to upgrade their relations.[11] After the war on Gaza, in December 2008 and January 2009, the EU had, for the first time, shelved closer political ties, without mentioning sanctions. Later on, prudence translated into ambiguity. Officially, the upgrade in relations was merely called an "intensification of relations."

In spite of close ties with Israel and Palestine, the EU does not enjoy the trust of either country. Indeed, Israeli public opinion and elites view the EU and some of its member states as biased toward the Palestinian cause. The political credit that France had enjoyed in the 1950s and early 1960s was badly damaged by General de Gaulle's political swerve in 1967, which changed France from a major supporter of Israel into an abrupt critic. The Euro-Arab rapprochement in the 1970s, and the ties forged with the PLO, took place at inauspicious times, after the massacre of Israeli athletes by a Palestinian group at the Munich Olympics in 1972, and the Yom Kippur War, in 1973, when a coalition of Arab states attacked Israel. Since the turn of the millennium, rising numbers of attacks against Jews, in France in particular, have led to an increase in emigration to Israel. Compounded by a "thousand years of pogroms and anti-Semitism" culminating in the Holocaust, deep suspicions about Europe coalesce into resentment (Pardo and Peters 2010: 74–75).[12]

Vis-à-vis the PNA, the EU is also relatively powerless. The PNA is too dependent on the EU for the latter to impose sanctions. The Palestinians wield the power of the powerless, and constrain the EU's margin of maneuver. The EU also suffers from a lack of credit derived from its own contradictions and double standards, for not having recognized Hamas in spite of helping to organize the 2006 elections, and for not enforcing the regulations concerning goods produced in the occupied Palestinian territories.

As in many other instances, a lack of coherence also afflicts the EU. In particular, enlargement has weakened unity. New member states, such as the Czech Republic or Romania, reluctant to criticize Israel and wary of antagonizing the United States, have settled on the position of some older member states, such as the Netherlands and Germany. They oppose any linkage between progress in EU-Israeli relations and the Israeli government's commitment to the peace process. Some member states have recognized the Palestinian state. Others have not. A similar cleavage opposes an alliance of old and new member states to another group keen on engaging Hamas and integrating it into the political game, though all EU members underline that Hamas and any Fatah-Hamas government have to fulfill the requirements set by the Quartet.[13] Thus, agreements have become more difficult to reach. According to one observer, "Every single word, every sentence is poised in the hand for hours and hours, these texts are the most difficult to negotiate, even more so than in the case of Russia."[14]

Worse still, the relevance of EU policies to the Israeli-Palestinian conflict paradoxically dwindled in the first decade of the new millennium. Because of wars and violence, the EU's economic, financial, and technical aid to the PNA has changed in nature. Once a supporter of a future Palestinian state, the EU has become a provider of assistance to Gaza in particular (Le More 2008; Bertrand-Sanz 2010: 44). Lately, the West Bank has undergone an entrepreneurial boom, partly funded by the EU. Yet between recurring destruction and wars, and booming pockets on the West Bank, it is the very existence of a Palestinian state that is at stake. The deterioration of the situation on the ground, the shrinking of the Palestinian territories, divided into two so far irreconcilable entities, and eaten up by Israeli checkpoints and settlements, the rampant fragmentation of the Israeli political scene, which skews governmental policies toward the right wing, an awkward combination of inward-lookingness and globalization that has taken hold in Israel in recent years, and the lethal interaction between states and transnational terrorist movements in a region at war, all this annihilates efforts to solve the Arab-Israeli conflict in the coming years. In other words, the EU lost relevance at the very moment it was joining an array of international negotiators in the so-called Quartet to promote a settlement that ultimately never happened.

The Remains of the Day: The EU and Conflict Transformation

Within a context where the EU is unable to help settle conflicts through mediation, it has often pursued another track: conflict transformation. Conflict transformation, however, has to run in parallel with a political process, even if the latter is not in European hands. While it is instrumental to the success and viability of a political settlement, the latter is essential if conflict transformation is to succeed.

Conflict transformation aims at redressing socioeconomic grievances to allay the causes of dissent and conflict. It borrows the very ideas that presided over the creation of the EC, which was to foster peace by pooling resources and bringing people together to work on concrete projects. This approach was reinvented in the Northern Irish context. While a political solution was being negotiated at the Northern Irish and British-Irish levels under the auspices of international actors, the EU sought to use the means at its disposal. Just after the military arm of Sinn Féin, the party standing for Irish sovereignty, announced a unilateral truce on 31 August 1994, the president of the European Commission, Jacques Delors, swiftly grasped an opportunity (Grardel 2009: 57–66).[15] He met with members of the European Parliament (MEPs) representing Northern Ireland, some of whom, moderate nationalists, offered to involve radical nationalists in a program specifically designed for that area, and increased regional aid. The EU Special Support Programme for Peace and Reconciliation in Northern Ireland and the Border Region of Ireland (PEACE) was born, at a European Council meeting in Essen in December 1994.

Still in operation, PEACE funds a number of very concrete projects, such as the protection of the environment, water supplies, the development of communications and transportation, training and education, and the reintegration of former political offenders. It encourages cooperation between all parties, Catholics and Protestants, in Northern Ireland and in the northern counties of the Republic of Ireland.[16] Though earlier programs had already been activated for Northern Ireland, the PEACE program offers a major comparative advantage, that of involving societal actors. It aims primarily at improving living conditions of the poor communities in Northern Ireland, and at easing if not erasing socioeconomic differences between Catholics and Protestants. It further aims at blurring the border between north and south by promoting cross-border interactions. It is about bringing all the various parties together to alter perceptions and understanding of the conflict, and turn a "zero-sum game" into "win-win solutions."

Last but not least, the EU offered a model for the parties to emulate, and a framework in which they could socialize. As a 2008 report of the European Economic and Social Committee on the role of the EU in the Northern Ireland peace process underlined, "[The program] provided for UK and Irish decision makers to experience the consensus-building style of EU law-making. In Council negotiations, Member States used a new style of multilateral dialogue, trade off and compromise which was a valuable tool in local political talks" (European Economic and Social Committee 2008; also Diez, Albert, and Stetter 2008; Hayward 2006, 2007; Hayward and Wiener 2008). Though the EC/EU could not mediate between the parties, the political intent of the program was unmistakable.

The Good Friday Agreement was signed in 1998, whereby London devolved political power to Northern Ireland, and institutions were created to encompass both parts of the island. Yet it took a decade before it started to bear fruit. The conflict abated. However, the resumption of violence in the winter of 2012–2013, and the brief detainment in 2014 of Sinn Féin's president, Gerry Adams, for a murder committed during the Troubles stirred deeply ingrained resentment. Hence it is reasonable to ask whether the EU transforms identities, and redirects loyalties toward Brussels. Looking at both political and societal levels, answers have to be cautious for four reasons.

First, distrust still separates communities. In 2008, a mere 6 percent of all children attended school integrating Catholics and Protestants (European Economic and Social Committee 2008; Coakley 2008: 105). Curbs painted with the Irish tricolor or conversely with the colors of the Union Jack define territories and identities. Certainly, walls do not disappear in the wink of an eye. Indeed, full integration is not yet in sight. Second, some of the actors involved in the political process appear to be more willing to instrumentalize EU institutions and procedures than to genuinely adopt them, something that one finds in other cases (on Cyprus, see chapter 2). Of course, it is difficult to scrutinize hearts and minds. One of the most prominent pro-EU politicians of the moderate Social Democratic and Labour Party, Nobel Prize winner John Hume, certainly was a genuine Europhile. Others may have simply learned to play the European game.

Third, one should distinguish between elites and the broader public. According to analysts, public awareness of the EU's actions is very limited (Hayward 2007). Last but not least, reconciliation is not about erasing national identities. It is about shedding hostilities and prejudices (Hayward 2007: 263–264). In any case, peace is still fragile. Scottish demands for independence might reverberate on the island and exacerbate divides, just as a British exit from the EU may unsettle the balance between the Republic of Ireland and the UK (see chapter 2).

On the whole, the success of the EU in transforming conflict is difficult to gauge. Since it is more about changing the broader context and reconfiguring perceptions of the conflict rather than manipulating the terms of negotiation, the EU's contribution is less visible, and less translatable into words, op-eds, or photos than is an American intermediation. It is more elusive, but still palpable. In the Northern Irish conflict, the EU contributed to the nitty-gritty work on the ground, necessary to underpin a political settlement; it offered a framework where officials and civil servants from both countries could interact, created a congenial environment, and provided a method to reach an understanding. This is the Union at its best, in spite of uncertainties as to long-term bets.

Indeed, the EU has tried to transfer the Irish "tool kit" to other terrains from Cyprus to Moldova, from the Middle East to the Caucasus. However, while this template has been dovetailing with political negotiations in Northern Ireland, its efficiency in the absence of a political settlement is worth questioning in Georgia or in Palestine. In all the years preceding the Russian-Georgian war of 2008, the EU provided help and brought together people from different communities.[17] Prior to the Russian-Georgian war, the results were extremely mixed. Some "grey zones," "a space for cooperation," had been created, yet they were always threatened by political authorities seeking to reassert their control. The August 2008 war eliminated them. Since then, the work of the EU has been hampered by the almost complete closure of South Ossetia, and Abkhazia's partial closure. Furthermore, assisting Abkhazia may contradict the official EU policy of nonrecognition, though it is also a way to try to lure the secessionist entity back to the Georgian fold.

Assistance may also simply paper over a lack of political will on the part of the EU, or a lack of political agreement between member states for that matter. Moldova is a case in point (Popescu 2011: 38–65). While the EU has hardly played a role in the fledgling negotiations, it sent a civilian mission to help build, control, and monitor the border between Moldovan Transnistria and Ukraine after the presidents of both republics requested EU support in a letter addressed to the president of the European Commission and to the High Representative in June 2005. Still in operation, the EUBAM border mission to Moldova and Ukraine advises border services, provides infrastructure, trains customs officers, and helps with inquiries. Corruption, including among border agents, has been reduced, the number of illegal migrants has dwindled, and the volume of illicit traffic has declined. Companies based in Transnistria have to register according to Moldovan laws, helping Moldova to reassert its sovereignty over Transnistria, at least in this particular sector. EUBAM, however, is not an ESDP mission. It is in the hands of the Commission, which makes it an "advisory technical body . . . more palatable to Russia" (Kurowska and Tallis 2009). It thus appears less risky to some of the member states of the EU.

In the Arab-Israeli conflict, the same pattern is recognizable. At a time when Arab-Israeli negotiations have been put on hold, and the conflict is not abating, let alone resolved, the EU's contribution to people-to-people contacts is limited. In 2004, it set up a Partnership for Peace, with an annual budget of €5–10 million, the Middle East Peace Project, to support local and international civil society initiatives to rebuild trust within and between societies, promoting, for instance, the Palestinian-Israeli NGO Forum and the Israel-Jordan Integrated Emergency Medical System Concept.[18] In the absence of negotiations, such programs partly fill a political void. Yet they also suffer from the asymmetry between Palestine and Israel, and seem to condone the occupation. In the absence of any agreement between member states, the EU runs the risk of dispersion and dilution. As multifaceted as its presence on the ground may be, from Ireland to the Caucasus and the Middle East, EU policy may amount to mere trickles, to "confetti," without clear strategy.

Baptism by Fire?

As the northern republics of the Yugoslav federation declared their independence, and the central government in Belgrade sought to reassert control over them by military means in 1991, the EC resorted to diplomacy. However, it did not have the power to impress, let alone the paraphernalia to impose a lasting solution. It did not have the military means that it might have threatened to use to back a settlement at a time when the United States was withdrawing, and James Baker, US secretary of state, famously claimed that "we have no dog in this fight" (Danner 1997). Worse, the Europeans, mainly Bonn, London, and Paris, disagreed on the means to solve the looming crisis: to send troops or stay away, to recognize the republics that claimed independence or keep the federation, to maintain a semblance of unity or display divergences. Divergences were difficult to grasp, though, since all in the EC shared the same interest, that is, the need to circumscribe the conflict. In fact, London, Paris, and Bonn interpreted the conflict differently according to their past experiences and their political culture. As the federation unraveled, they learned to narrow their differences, and eventually, at the turn of the decade, together with the United States they drove Serbia out of Kosovo and prevented the outbreak of a conflict in Macedonia. However, lessons learned in one area cannot be transferred to another. The unity the Europeans forged in the course of the 1990s in Yugoslavia, and the will they mustered to build a military force, remained a relatively isolated episode. In Libya, a limited number of Europeans intervened, while the EU stood on the side. And they mostly stayed away from Syria.

Yugoslavia's Fragmentation and Europe's Divisions

Initially, the Europeans misjudged the causes of the wars. In the 1980s, the EC and its member states had overlooked the undercurrents that were sapping the foundations of the Yugoslav federation (Rupnik 1992; Woodward 1995; Glaurdic 2011). Engrossed as they were in Germany's and Europe's reunification, the EC/EU and the United States were turning a blind eye to a country that had shed geopolitical significance, once the Soviet Union ceased to pose a threat to Western Europe. Instead, the West was fixated on the financial and economic crisis unfurling in Yugoslavia, and thought reforms had to be introduced by the central authorities. For a while, it seemed that the Yugoslav prime minister, Ante Marković, was delivering. Yet even though the West praised him in words, it lent him hardly any financial support (Glaurdic 2011: 60). The Europeans, and the West in general, also misunderstood the impact of economic reforms on the federation.[19] The northern republics of Yugoslavia, the only ones to enjoy full employment at the time, resented budgetary redistribution from the richer to the poorer republics, and the centralization impact of the reforms. Marković's program was also undermined by the nationalist policies of Slobodan Milošević as head of the Communist League of Serbia and, as of 1989, president of Serbia, who aimed at tightening his grip on the federation and, as the republics were breaking loose, at gathering together the Serbs scattered across Yugoslavia (Garde 1991; Rupnik 1992). Last, the EC ignored the structural impact and the force of attraction it exerted on its surroundings. Slovenia and Croatia, in particular, toyed with the idea of joining the EC quickly, even though no promise had been made (Woodward 1995: 154–156).[20]

Certainly, once fragmentation loomed large and wars began in 1991, the EC, and primarily some of its member states, resorted to diplomatic means to prop up the federation. The Europeans thought that they could swiftly bring peace to the country. Jacques Poos, foreign minister of Luxembourg, in charge of the rotating presidency of the Council of the European Union, famously claimed that "the hour of Europe" had dawned (Riding 1991). He jumped in to mediate between the federal center and those republics that were the first to seek independence, Slovenia and Croatia, and, a few months later Bosnia-Herzegovina, which was caught in the maelstrom of internecine dissolution. After Belgrade attacked Slovenia and Croatia to reassert control, EC foreign ministers brokered a short-lived cease-fire and agreement between Belgrade, Ljubljana, and Zagreb, concluded on 7 July 1991 on the island of Brioni, to keep the Yugoslav federation alive. An international peace conference, chaired by Lord Carrington, former British foreign minister and EC mediator, was set up in 1992 in London, and later Geneva, while war was raging.

The agreement was a mere trompe l'oeil, based on a twin misunderstanding. Having misunderstood the causes of the Yugoslav Wars, and the determination of Slobodan Milošević to recreate a small federation of all Serbs—leaving aside Slovenia where there were none—the EC, its member states, and the international community at large miscalculated their responses. Actually, there was no peace to maintain, and no federation to preserve (Gnesotto 1994). The peace plans the Europeans devised afterward were not backed by rewards or sanctions. Those years were littered with vain promises of rewards, unimplemented sanctions, and empty threats of force.[21] Eventually, a small team of EC observers, civilian and military, was dispatched to Slovenia only.

The EC and its member states persisted, nonetheless, in a mediation that misunderstood the underlying aims of each party. They kept on advocating a loose federation. Yet at the same time, they set up, rightly so, an arbitration commission—the Arbitration Commission of the Conference on Yugoslavia, under the auspices of former French justice minister Robert Badinter—to devise the principles under which the breakaway republics would be recognized, in an attempt to reconcile two contradictory principles of international law, namely, sovereignty and self-determination (Arbitration Commission 1992). At best, the EC hedged its bets, in case the Yugoslav federation failed. At worst, it was incoherent. Nor did the member states agree on the purpose of the Arbitration Commission. The German government preempted its recommendation, though it delayed the formal recognition of both Slovenia and Croatia (Crawford 1995, 1996; Woodward 1995; Lucarelli 2000). Indeed, the Commission did not consider that Zagreb was meeting the requirements. This mix of incoherence and inconsistency was to become the very trademark of Europe's—and the international community's—management of the crisis. Each government interpreted the conflict through its own template.

From Discord to Unity in Irrelevance?

Whereas the EC had jumped into action in 1991, it soon shared responsibilities with the UN in trying to solve the conflict. In September 1991, the UNSC was brought in and imposed an embargo—after the EC had imposed its own. At the end of 1991 and early in 1992, the EC became one actor among many and certainly not the most decisive one. On the diplomatic front, Cyrus Vance, the special envoy of the secretary-general of the UN, was commissioned to devise a peace plan together with the

EC's representative. Further international peace plans followed that were all but unsuccessful and obsolete as soon as they had been put on the table, overtaken by events on the ground. Contrary to international law and to international and European covenants, Europeans and Americans accepted new borders carved out by force, trampling on the very principles they were supposed to uphold. Concurrently, the UN decided, in February 1992, to deploy a United Nations Protection Force (UNPROFOR) to Croatia, and later to Bosnia-Herzegovina, to facilitate the distribution of humanitarian aid to the local populations who bore the brunt of the war. Its mandate was very weak, and NATO was brought in for more robust protection. In March 1993, a UNSC resolution allowed NATO to shoot down planes that violated the newly created no-fly zones over Bosnia-Herzegovina.

In any case, the actor that really mattered, the American administration, was drawn in. After years of procrastination, 1994 and 1995 signaled a turning point. In 1994, the United States took the diplomatic lead, and created the Contact Group to streamline the decision-making process. The Contact Group (the United States, Russia, France, Germany, Italy, and the UK) breathed some coherence into European foreign policies. It brought the foreign ministries and governments of the four European countries closer together (Schwegmann 2000; Boidevaix 2005). In particular, the political directors of the British, French, and German foreign ministries developed a very close relationship, while, in parallel, high civil servants in the ministries of foreign affairs and defense were constantly in touch with one another. A kind of European spirit developed, an identity by default against the backdrop of American leadership and Russian isolation. Well into the Serbo-Croatian war and the deadly conflict that wrecked Bosnia-Herzegovina, decision makers and civil servants in the three capital cities eventually learned to narrow down their differences.

The same identity by default prevailed when in 1995, after dragging the Serbian president, Slobodan Milošević, to the negotiating table, the US assistant secretary for European and Canadian affairs, Richard Holbrooke, crafted a peace agreement in Dayton, Ohio, that put an end to that phase of the Yugoslav Wars, and designed the institutional makeup of the new state of Bosnia-Herzegovina. Though the French president, Jacques Chirac, the British prime minister, John Major, and the Dutch prime minister, Wim Kok, had mustered forces, and deployed a Rapid

Reaction Force to Bosnia-Herzegovina, finally convincing the Clinton administration of their will to intervene, the representatives of the EU member states, and the EU special envoy to the former Yugoslavia, Carl Bildt, were nonetheless bypassed at Dayton (Bildt 1998; Holbrooke 1998).[22] Though the procrastination of the Europeans and of European institutions merely reflected the impotence of the whole international community, it was nevertheless particularly embarrassing for the very Community that had claimed to come of age with a new CFSP, but could not stabilize its own backyard.

Hard Lessons Learned

As most Europeans sought to avoid military involvement, peacekeeping was preferred to peace enforcement, and humanitarian aid became a makeshift for political action, even though the necessity to protect humanitarian workers gradually drew the allies deeper into the conflict. This "containment with charity," as Susan Woodward put it, prolonged the wars and dragged in a reluctant community of states (Woodward 1995: 320). This deeply flawed plan had two major consequences, both for the peoples in the former Yugoslavia and for the EC/EU itself. The decisions taken by the Europeans, and by the international community, often led to perverse consequences. The arms embargo, for instance, benefited the Yugoslav army, under Serbian control. The deployment of peacekeepers on the ground, comprising Europeans mainly, prevented the use of force. Thus the Europeans, and the West at large, fueled the wars.

Meanwhile, the deployment of peacekeepers and humanitarian aid dragged the Europeans further into the conflict, in what Henry Wynaendts has called an *engrenage*, an unstoppable chain of events (Wynaendts 1993). The Europeans paid due tribute to the conflict. They footed most of the troops, sent their most brilliant generals, and provided the bulk of humanitarian aid. They oversaw the embargo. They took over the administration of the Herzegovinian city of Mostar, divided between Croats and Muslims. Having initiated the negotiations, they were present all along. Yet the EC and the Europeans failed dramatically. Eventually it was the United States that was credited for the actions undertaken. After the beautiful medieval bridge over the Drina in Mostar was destroyed in the fighting and then rebuilt with EU money, it was the American delegation at the bridge's inauguration in 2004 that was applauded, while EU representatives were relegated to the background. As a community, the EC was hardly present. National governments too often disagreed, and botched their way into the war.

Certainly, Europeans learned from their mistakes. The last war in the former Yugoslavia, which Belgrade unleashed in 1999 to drive out the overwhelming Albanian majority from Kosovo, the so-called cradle of Serbian identity, witnessed a European and American awakening. A NATO operation was launched against the Serbian leader to put an end to the repression and exodus of Albanian Kosovars, and the Europeans substantially participated in both the air campaign and the negotiations.[23] The Europeans also contributed to the stabilization of Macedonia. While tensions between Albanian and Slav Macedonians had been simmering for over a decade, the combined action of Europeans and Americans, resorting to the whole repertoire of show of force, arm twisting, threats, rewards, help, and the promise of a Stabilization and Association Agreement with the EU led, after a brief bout of violence, to the Ohrid Agreement in 2001, backed by a NATO mission and the EU's first ever Common Security and Defence Policy (CSDP) military mission, Operation Concordia, in 2003 (Eldridge 2007; Ilievski and Taleski 2009).

The CSDP seemed to take off.[24] The humiliation of not being able to bring Slobodan Milošević to the negotiating table underlined the necessity for the Europeans to resort to coercion and, hence, to acquire the means to coerce. The reluctance of the United States to intervene before the French and the British showed resolve led the Europeans to understand that they had to acquire the means to bear on their American allies. The Europeans had to demonstrate their will and capacity to intervene. After a 1998 Franco-British agreement in Saint-Malo, designed to endow Europe with an autonomous military capacity, decisions were swiftly taken to set up a CSDP (Howorth 2007). Remarkably enough, almost all member states of the EU followed suit and rallied the nascent CSDP, except for Denmark, which, however, makes a point in participating in military interventions.

Yet the EU has never waged a war (Howorth 2007; Youngs 2010; Toje 2010: 95–111). Will more than capability is lacking. Certainly, forces, civilian and military, have been deployed under the banner of the EU as postconflict stabilization instruments on European soil (Koutrakos 2013).

Some operations, many of them small, have taken place, in Africa primarily, to perform tasks, sometimes robust but mostly limited in time and space. Yet it seems very likely that in dire circumstances, when military interventions may look necessary but prove costly and counterproductive, nothing will happen at EU level.

Eventually, there were powerful reasons for the Europeans to intervene in the former Yugoslavia, albeit reluctantly and without much strategic thinking. Not only did the former federation abut the EC, but it was also surrounded by it, at the heart of Europe, a reason why the EU later signaled that it would give the new states membership once they meet the criteria. Moreover, the international environment was, in a way, conducive to a European outburst of mobilization. Certainly, the US administration procrastinated as much as the Europeans. Yet it provided support, though it bickered and mostly bypassed the Europeans, nonetheless driving them to define a European position. The UN and a considerable number of international organizations and NGOs worked together with the Europeans. Last but not least, Moscow was convinced to condone a settlement with Serbia at the end of the 1990s. Such a constellation will not necessarily form again. In other circumstances, the weight of political cultures, and of past and present experiences, hampers the definition of common positions and policies within the EU framework. When a war was launched against Colonel Gaddafi's rule in 2011, a decade after the inception of CSDP, the EU eschewed military responsibilities. A "coalition of the willing" took action.

We Don't Do Wars: Libya as an Epitome

The Desert of the Tartars

On 15 February 2011, soon after Tunisia had shaken off the grip of Zine al-Abidine Ben Ali, heralding what was for a while called the Arab Spring, riots started in Libya and soon spread out of control, igniting an all-out insurgency against Colonel Gaddafi's iron fist. Backed by the air force and propped up by the political support of Western and Arab countries, the insurgency led to the infamous death of Gaddafi and the demise of his regime. In the military intervention that lasted from March to October 2011, the EU as such played a very limited role, characteristic of the constraints it faces because of the disagreements between member states and their incapacity to act jointly.

Certainly, the EU took action. The least it could do was to suspend the Framework Agreement it was negotiating. After Muammar Gaddafi claimed, in the first decade of the new millennium, to have given up sponsoring terrorist activities, and to have forsaken weapons of mass destruction, Western governments had embraced him, all the more so as he was engaging in the control of illegal migration to Europe. From being a pariah, the government of this oil- and gas-rich country was suddenly regarded as a welcome partner. The Framework Agreement was supposed to "reintegrate" Libya into the international community of states (European Commission 2009a). The rebellion in Libya, followed by governmental repression, called the bluff of a man who had pretended to court respectability, and demonstrated the vanity of Western governments, which had allowed themselves to be deceived.

Furthermore, after the adoption by the UNSC of Resolution 1970, on 26 February 2011, and of Resolution 1973, on 17 March 2011, which condemned violence and imposed an arms embargo on Libya, bolstered by robust sanctions, not only did the EU and its member states implement these measures, but the Council also went beyond them (Council of the European Union 2011a). It extended, for instance, the asset freeze to a wider circle of Muammar Gaddafi's entourage, to financial and energy companies suspected of supporting the regime, and later to port authorities. This amounted to a de facto oil and gas embargo. The EU also resorted to a well-known repertoire, when it helped to evacuate from Libya EU member states' nationals, a total of 5,800 EU citizens, and third-country nationals, mostly immigrant workers from poor countries. More than 30,000 third-country nationals were repatriated with the help of the Monitoring and Information Centre (MIC), the operational heart of the EU Civil Protection Mechanism, based at the European Commission to facilitate assistance. The European Commission Humanitarian Aid and Civil Protection department (ECHO) provided humanitarian aid, and dispatched to Libya and its neighbors, Tunisia, Egypt, Algeria, and Chad, experts trained to aid and protect civilians.[25] In 2011, the EU set up a joint maritime operation to tackle illegal migration through its border management agency, FRONTEX, to patrol the seas, as the Italian government became overwhelmed by a rising wave of migrants from North African countries and requested help. On 22 May 2011, twelve days after the European Parliament passed a resolution that called on the Union to establish direct relations with the Interim Transitional National Council (ITNC), the transitional Libyan government set up during the rebellion, the High Representative opened a liaison office in Benghazi, the stronghold of liberated Libya.

Meanwhile, in April 2011 in a bold and yet mostly irrelevant move, the EU set up EUFOR Libya, a military operation supposed to support humanitarian and civilian assistance to Libya by securing sea and land corridors (Council of the European Union 2011b). Based in Rome, the mission was to involve about 1,000 troops. Yet, like Dino Buzzati's script in *Il deserto dei Tartari*, it was an operation that never took place.[26] Only a formal demand of the UN Secretariat's Office for the Coordination of Humanitarian Affairs (OCHA), the body responsible for bringing together humanitarian actors in a crisis, would have triggered it. Wary of using military assets for civilian operations, OCHA never made the request. The operation was stillborn. This eerie paradox of an operation ready to be launched though not likely to happen encapsulates the fate of EU's military power: too often virtual in dire circumstances.

Indeed, the EU was conspicuously absent from the military intervention. Individual European governments, the United States, Arab nations, and Turkey intervened militarily to protect civilians against Colonel Gaddafi's fierce repression. The UNSC was the center of authorization and legitimation. The Arab League and the Organisation of Islamic Cooperation (OIC) pushed for military intervention. An International Contact Group on Libya, made up of the countries that took part in the intervention, provided political guidance and legitimacy by involving Arab countries, and NATO coordinated NATO and non-NATO combatants. The International Criminal Court (ICC) was also involved in investigating alleged crimes in Libya. Only the EU did not participate.

Meeting on 11 March 2011, almost a month after the first riots, the Extraordinary European Council issued a "Declaration on the European Union's Southern Neighbourhood and Libya," calling for Colonel Gaddafi's resignation, but without mentioning an intervention. Though the latter was intensely debated at the time in London, Paris, and Washington—Resolution 1973, authorizing the use of force would be adopted six days later by the UNSC—the twenty-seven member states of the EU could not reach an agreement (European Council 2011). Germany, in particular, opposed a military intervention. The European Council became irrelevant. In any case, the UNSC was the locus of decisions, since its authorization was necessary, and both the UK and France were permanent members. When Resolution 1973 was put to vote and adopted, on 17 March 2011, Germany, a temporary member, abstained, as did Russia, China, India, and Brazil. To justify his position, Germany's ambassador to the UNSC, Peter Wittig, warned of the risk of a protracted conflict, possibly igniting the whole region, and the lack of an exit strategy (UNSC 2011).

Both Paris and London took the lead, behind the scene and up front. They aired the idea of establishing a no-fly zone over Libya to prevent Gaddafi's air force from attacking civilians, and Washington discussed it too. They took American and Arab allies on board, connected with the Gulf Cooperation Council (GCC), the OIC, and later the Arab League, which had called for a no-fly zone in early March, and drew them into the International Contact Group. In other words, the French and the British governments put the question of Libya on the agenda, framed the political answer, and couched it in military terms. Yet they differed over the framework for action.

The French president repeatedly acted single-handedly. He recognized the Libyan transitional council on 10 March 2011, ahead of his international allies whom he caught unawares—he even bypassed his own foreign minister. On Saturday 19 March, as the allies were in Paris attending a hastily convened conference, the French air force struck Colonel Gaddafi's troops marching on Benghazi. Again, the French president had taken his allies off guard, incurring the wrath of the British and the American governments, and "play(ed) directly to world opinion" (Rusi 2011: 4). He pushed for a military coalition of the willing, while his British allies favored a NATO-led intervention. Eventually, the French followed the British and the Americans. NATO could provide know-how, and constituted the necessary link between the United States and its allies after Washington withdrew its active participation although lending logistical support, or "leading from behind," as President Obama's policy came to be known. After a week of squabbles and negotiations, the NATO-led operation took over from what had been for a few days an unruly coalition of national operations.[27] The particular role of President Sarkozy is not to be underestimated. As Alastair

Cameron put it, "In several ways, the Libya military campaign would have been very different had France not led in the way it did. Interpreting the mission through the lens of France's own motivations throughout the Libya campaign helps to underscore the important role that France played in setting the early dynamics that affected the operational tempo, and ultimately, the political outcome" (Cameron 2012: 16)

On the whole, each of the three main EU countries, Germany, France, and the UK contributed, in its own way and for its own reasons, to kill the EU option: the German government by showing its opposition to the use of force, the French president by acting single-handedly and preferably outside existing institutional frameworks, and Britain by pushing for a NATO solution. Eventually, the French reluctantly and pragmatically rallied to the latter's position while the German government stayed on the sidelines.

One may wonder why the European countries espoused different and even diverging preferences. Differences in political cultures offer a convenient explanation (Meyer 2006; Biehl, Giegerich, and Jonas 2013; France and Witney 2013). Germany's abstention highlighted how much German political culture is risk averse and alien to military interventions. Though harshly criticized by German publicists and intellectuals, the decision to stay on the sidelines was backed by the wider public. Support for an intervention in Libya was limited to a mere 37 percent of the German population. Public support reached 53 percent in the UK, 58 percent in France, and 59 percent in the United States (Nyiri and Raisher 2012). The British and the French do not shun robust interventions, and the character of Nicolas Sarkozy, prompt to act and with a liking for grandstanding, certainly reinforced this feature. It would, however, be too simplistic to refer to differences in political cultures alone as the explanation for diverging approaches.

Interests do matter. An intervention in Libya conferred upon the British prime minister and the French president a certain prestige, particularly helpful in the case of France to make up for previous, unpalatable mistakes before the Libyan—and Tunisian—uprisings.[28] Germany's arguments also made sense.

Half Full or Half Empty?

The ambiguity of the resolution, and the political context in which it was taken, allowed different interpretations. This accounted for the reticence of the German government—and the fierce criticisms that Russia and China later voiced. Together with Lebanon, France and the UK put forth a "toughly worded UN resolution" (Rusi 2011: 3). Resolution 1973, which called for the reinforcement of the arms embargo and the establishment of a no-fly zone, authorized "all necessary means" to protect the civilian population, barring the deployment of troops on the ground (UNSC 2011). During the preceding weeks, it had become obvious on both sides of the Atlantic that a no-fly zone would require a military intervention, and the Western allies, the French in particular, dictated the means to be employed, namely, military force. In any case, the resolution meant to protect civilians, not to overthrow a regime. However, a number of governments called for Colonel Gaddafi's departure, especially the very governments that would lead the military intervention. On 11 March, the Extraordinary European Council demanded that Colonel Gaddafi "relinquish power immediately" (European Council 2011: item 7). A month later, US president Obama, British prime minister Cameron, and French president Sarkozy underlined in a joint letter that "our duty and our mandate . . . is to protect civilians. . . . It is not to remove Gaddafi by force. But it is impossible to imagine a future for Libya with Gaddafi in power" (Obama, Cameron, Sarkozy 2011). In other words, the desirable and desired political outcome, and the aims of the military mission, contradicted or at best interfered with one another. As Germany's ambassador to the UNSC, Wittig, underlined, the mission was "open-ended" (UNSC 2011).

Compounding this contradiction, the conduct of war involves offensive episodes. The enforcement of the no-fly zone and even more the protection of civilian populations entailed a number of tactical attacks, and eventually a genuine interference in the conflict opposing rebels and loyalists. As Gaddafi's forces and their opponents seemed at times embroiled in a stalemate, the French and the British tried their best to tip the balance, air-dropping weapons to the insurgents in spite of the arms embargo, and stepping up the attacks from July on. In short, they gave a very specific twist to Resolution 1973, which put them at odds with other governments that stuck to a narrow interpretation of the resolution.

In other words, the regime's brutality, the rebels' lack of experience and equipment, the allies' air power, and the sheer impossibility of neatly drawing a line between the protection of civilians and attacks that might destroy the capacities and threaten the survival of a regime at war against its own population, all skewed the war aims (Kometer and Wright 2013: 21, 8). This led to an *engrenage*, a mission creep, which was foreseeable—and this profoundly worried the German government. Later on, the Russian and the Chinese governments would use the Libyan precedent to block what they deemed as interference in the Syrian conflict.

Last but not least, most operations entail perverse consequences. The intervention in Libya had political consequences in the country itself and in the neighborhood, in Mali in particular.[29] Because of porous borders and chaos in Libya, men and weapons infiltrated neighboring countries, and fell into the hands of rebels and terrorist groups. Terrorist groupings that a dictator had previously crushed and perversely fostered connected with other networks in the region or in the Middle East, reaching the shores of Europe. It was not until 2013 that an EUBAM border mission was set up on the Libyan government's request to secure the country's borders, even though the country that Colonel Gaddafi had held together in a straitjacket was falling prey to warlords and squabbling factions between which the EU and the UN attempted to mediate. For all these reasons, be it the ambiguity of the mandate, the lack of clarity of purpose, the contradiction between aims and means, the dynamics of military involvement, the lack of exit strategy and political perspectives, and possible unforeseen consequences, some governments chose to abstain from intervening in Libya while others ignored such concerns.

The consequences are clear: if this analysis is correct, future European military interventions of this kind will falter on the same difficulties. Robust EU operations may well remain a mirage. In Syria, neither the EU nor the Europeans have intervened in the conflict that started in 2011. Only a few European governments did. In 2013, the French president, François Hollande, fleetingly referred to "safe areas" that should have been established to protect Syrian civilians, and a few months later, in August 2013, he called for a military intervention after Bashar al-Assad's government was accused of using chemical weapons. The French president, however, stood alone after the British House of Commons voted against such an intervention, and the American president refrained from acting despite the breach of what he had earlier declared a "red line." Together with the United States, France and the UK have nonetheless helped some of the opposition forces, deployed special forces, and engaged in military strikes, while Germany has sent reconnaissance aircraft and military personnel. A combination of American prudence (if not dithering), the presence of numerous state and nonstate actors on the ground, and the massive expansion of aerial, maritime, and ground presence by a Russian power bent on preventing a repetition of the military intervention in Libya that led to regime change, and on dwarfing Western presence in the Middle East, constrained those European governments that intervened. Paradoxically, as circumscribed as the role of a few European countries is, the EU turns out to be—apart from the Middle East—the region most exposed to the dramatic fallout of the war in Syria, the expansion of ISIS from the Mashrek to the Maghreb, and the arrival of thousands of refugees driven out of their countries by Assad's and ISIS tyranny, and by the massive Russian bombardments from September 2015 to March 2016.

Certainly, the responsibility for failings and failures does not fall on the Europeans alone. In Syria, the French and the British could not act by themselves. Some of the conflicts are intractable. Dictators have chosen and still choose to crush their own people rather than bow out. Nonetheless, the EU's and the Europeans' capacity to intervene and appetite for intervention, right or wrong, are limited. On paper, the EU has a wide repertoire at its disposal, ranging from diplomacy to military intervention. It has considerable resources, economic and financial, including the lure of its own market, which can be used for rewards or sanctions. Yet its ability to leverage its resources and influence its neighbors through foreign policy initiatives or responses has too often been paltry. A misperception of the conflicting parties' motivations and of the structural forces at work, a misunderstanding of unwanted consequences, failing credibility and trust, and a lack of strategic acumen, compounded by the Europeans' divergences because of different political cultures, interests, and interpretations of events, pull governments apart when the time of reckoning comes, and account for the EC/EU's failings and failures (Toje 2010; Youngs 2010). Even where the EU might seem to be in a position to make a difference on the continent, it is unable and unwilling to bully aggressors or would-be aggressors to the negotiating table. It is also unable to offer credible security guarantees to conflicting parties engaged in negotiations. For this reason, it is hardly a credible mediator—except in very specific circumstances, when two parties, as in Tunisia or Libya in the mid-2010s, seek professional mediation to reach an agreement. Eventually, the EU has instruments. It does not have a strategy.

4

BOUNDARIES AND BORDERLANDS

From Inside Out?

Borders uphold the centre, they give it a sense of gravity, keep it
alive. A centre without borders collapses and becomes a contested
space. In other words, it turns into frontier. . . . Yet the centre-
periphery relationship is never just about the power of the centre and
the subjugation of the periphery. The margins bleed into the centre,
thereby constantly undermining its influence by bringing their own
uncertainties and insecurities into play.

—LAIMONAS BRIEDIS, *Vilnius: City of Strangers*

Since their inception, the European Communities and the European
Union have enjoyed peace. The pattern of intra-European relations that
the EC/EU had invented in the 1950s kept war at bay. However, this did
not mean that civil strife was absent, in Northern Ireland for instance, or
that war did not return to the continent, beyond the EC/EU's borders, to
wreck the former Yugoslavia. As seen in the preceding chapter, there was
little that the Communities and the Union could do. Endowed with limited military instruments and a fledgling "foreign policy," they steered
clear of intervening militarily in Yugoslavia or later in Libya, let alone in
Syria, and did not manage to solve conflicts pitting communities against
one other, from Ireland to Cyprus to Georgia—though the EU is trying to
cobble together a makeshift agreement in Ukraine.

Yet didn't they have other means at their disposal? Could they not
transfer to their surroundings the very recipe that had turned them into an
area of peace, and "domesticate" their neighborhood, a notion that British

author François Duchêne had coined in 1972 to describe the effort of the EC "to bring to international problems the sense of common responsibility and structures of contractual politics which have been in the past associated exclusively with 'home' and not 'foreign,' that is alien, affairs" (Duchêne 1972: 12–20)? The Stabilization and Association Agreements that the EU signed with the countries that had emerged from the ruins of the former Yugoslavia aimed to establish peace by promising membership. What about those countries that the EU could not embrace quickly, if at all? At the turn of the millennium, as the enlargement to twelve new countries was looming, the EU conceived a neighborhood policy to project peace and prosperity beyond its borders, and surround itself with a "ring of friends," well-governed states that would prevent mayhem from spilling into the continent and the Union.

Of all policies that the EU ever devised, the European Neighbourhood Policy (ENP) has been one of its most proactive, one of the most brilliantly thought through, on paper at least. Unlike enlargement, the neighbors did not drive the EU. The EU devised—or meant to devise—borders and neighbors. Neighbors were addressees. This policy failed, however. The Arab Spring that started rather auspiciously in Tunisia and Egypt, in the winter of 2010–2011, was soon perverted. Upheavals, repression, and massacres, followed by a broad-based international military intervention in Libya, the suppression of civilian power and of civil society in Egypt, and the war in Syria, have created around Europe a chain of failed states or, conversely, have reinforced authoritarian ones. Eastern European states and societies are gangrenous with corruption, and democracy is a façade where it is not entirely obliterated.

Why did this policy fail? There was a contradiction between open and closed borders, embracing neighbors and keeping them at bay, offering concessions, withdrawing them, and then later ratcheting them up again to recoup some credit among the neighbors. There were also differences between policies vis-à-vis the East and policies vis-à-vis the South. The EU pretended to treat Eastern European neighbors and neighbors beyond the Mediterranean in the same way. Yet this was not the case. After pondering the notion of borders and boundaries, this chapter will stress how the EU, or rather some member states, turned a blind eye to nondemocratic practices, more in the Arab world than in Eastern Europe, and will set the stage for the following chapter, which will scrutinize how the EU turned to neighbors, democratic or not, to police its borders and keep migrants at bay.

Borders and Boundaries: Quest and Quandary

Borders and boundaries are not synonymous. They both distinguish an outside, a neighborhood or "outer world," from an inside, states, empires, or Union. Yet they differ in nature, and relate differently to the outside. A border is the outer edge of a state or of a union of states, while the notion of boundary refers to confines, margins, or frontiers. A border is a limit. Boundaries encompass swaths of territories.

The ultimate borders of Europe are unknown, and so are those of the EC/EU, since theoretically all European states might apply to the EU. Where does Europe end? To the East in particular, Europe is a mere "promontory on the Asian continent," as the French poet Paul Valéry put it. Where "natural borders" exist, delineated by rivers, straits, or mountains, they do not coincide with political borders. The Bosporus divides a city and a state, and the Urals became, by order of Peter the Great, an administrative border to emphasize the Europeanness of the imperial core as opposed to its Asian periphery, and to underline Russia's twin identities, European and imperial.[1] The French president Nicolas Sarkozy meant to convene a committee to discuss Europe's borders, to little avail. Eventually, a group of wise men, gathering under the leadership of Felipe González, left the topic untouched. The question of Europe's borders remains a mystery that geography and history cannot answer. Culturally and socially, borders have existed for a long time within Europe. Invisible, they furrow the continent, separating, for instance, different types of social structures, organizations, and practices. They may still influence political cultures in very subtle ways, though not all researchers agree with this statement (Bibó 1986; Szűcs 1985; Todorova 1997). Yet, intangible as they are, these borders that delineate different cultural and social Europes do not always draw clear lines, and Europe gradually merges into further cultures. Europe is borderless geographically, historically, and politically, as well as culturally.

Nonetheless, the EC/EU has definite borders, no matter how frequently they were and are altered, and no matter how far they are and will be pushed out—indeed, no matter whether they will be pushed out or rolled back. These borders, which can be called definite, separate members from nonmembers, they include and exclude. Changing with time, they nonetheless delimit an area proper to the Communities, and later the Union, endowed with a de facto constitution, common treaties, laws and rules and ways of doing things, joint policies, a specific type of governance, certain common aspirations, some elements of solidarity and internal cohesion, albeit shaky, contested, and battered by multiple crises, and Euroskepticism or populism, which nonetheless create or nurture streaks of a common identity.[2] They are political in essence (Foucher 1991). By virtue of its very existence the EC/EU delineates borders between members and nonmembers. Yet just as enlargement has been largely driven from the outside, the Union's neighbors also play a part in drawing these borders. They question them or transform them by the very act of yearning for membership, applying, and joining the EU, or by staying out.

Because the—changing—borders of the EC/EU and the—unknown— borders of Europe do not coincide, there are territories that do not belong to the EU yet consider themselves or may be considered European, though the characterization of a territory and its inhabitants as European may be contested both inside that country and within the EU. Outside of the EU, they lie in an in-between, in confines or boundaries. The countries on the southern shore of the Mediterranean Sea may also be considered part of the Union's boundaries. Even though they are not deemed European and cannot aspire to membership, they are neighbors in spite of, or because of, the Mediterranean Sea. In Roman times, the Mediterranean Sea, *Mare Nostrum*, did not separate two shores. North Africa belonged to the empire and produced some of its finest thinkers and rulers.

As long as a wall divided Europe, from the end of World War II till 1989, the question whether the Community should and could encompass the whole of Europe—as unknown as Europe's borders were—remained theoretical, since the EC was ensconced in its Western entrenchments. The question of eastern boundaries was theoretical, too. Beyond the Wall was off-limits. There were no boundaries per se. There were countries ruled from Moscow, lumped together under a single label: Eastern Europe. In the west, the sea delineated the borders of Europe, and there were, of course, no boundaries. To the south, after the 1950s when Algeria was still French, the southern shore of the Mediterranean was a source of concern, the addressee of policies, but it was not yet considered a boundary or an in-between between the EC and territories farther away.

After the demise of communism, in 1989, the question of borders and boundaries became pressing, for two reasons. The fall of the Wall opened up a new space. If Europe was to become whole, and wholly democratic, the question of Europe's boundaries loomed large. While some of the countries closer to the EU and better prepared to embrace democracy and the market economy joined the Union, others became new neighbors, on the EU's outskirts, both on the continent and on the other side of the Mediterranean, as southern members of the EU increasingly demanded that attention be devoted not only to Eastern Europe but also to the countries beyond the Mediterranean. Furthermore, what came to be known as the Schengen Area, called into life by the Schengen Agreement of 1985 and the Schengen Convention of 1990, abolished borders between a growing number of European states, mostly, though not all, EU members. At the outer limits of the Schengen Area, borders were erected. Policies had to be defined regarding neighbors, and regarding borders.

The EU and Its Neighbors: Power, Attraction, and Rejection

Neighbors, European or non-European, do not escape the structural power of the EU or its attraction—though to varying degrees. Indeed, countries left outside can be affected by negative externalities that ensue from the constitution of the Internal Market and the creation of the Schengen Area, such as the diversion of investments toward the Market, or the closure of EU borders.[3] Some countries depend more than others on the EU for trade. This is the case for Tunisia and Morocco. In 2014, almost 72.5 percent of the former's exports went to the EU, and 64.7 percent of its imports came from the EU. The figures for the latter were respectively 63.4 percent and 51 percent. Other countries are much less dependent, in particular those that draw their main revenue from oil. The EU represents Algeria's main source of imports, almost 51 percent in 2014, but does not belong in its top ten clients. The EU provides almost half of Moldova's imports, and absorbs a little over half of its exports (respectively 48.4 and 54.1 percent in 2014), while Ukraine and Belarus fall primarily within Russia's orbit. Though the EU was Ukraine's top trading partner, with 35.2 percent of all imports and exports in 2014, Russia was Belarus's major one, with almost 49 percent that same year (EU Commission, Directorate General for Trade 2015). In other words, the EU holds considerable structural power over parts of its neighborhood, though some countries escape its grip, willingly or not, either because they can rely on a wide base of customers for their plentiful energy supply or because they depend on a single client and provider, having failed to diversify and modernize their economy.

Asymmetry obviously skews the relationship between a small country and the EU-28, but structural power does not necessarily translate into influence. While the EU remains off-limits for the countries on Europe's southern and southeastern rim, Eastern European countries can pretend to join the EU, albeit in some hypothetical future. Nonetheless, just as Eastern European countries' trade dependence on the EU is split, their societies are cleaved, and rifts deepened by Russia. Certainly, since the beginning of the new millennium, some of the elites in power in Kiev, Chişinău, or Tbilisi proclaimed their desire to join the EU, but not all did so. Some of the Ukrainian oligarchs or diehards in Chişinău, let alone in Minsk, did not want to surrender their power. In 2013, Ukrainian president Viktor Yanukovych refused to sign an agreement with the EU that would have required reforms denting his power and privileges. A cost-benefit analysis too often pertains to the losses or gains authoritarian leaders may personally incur. Public opinion, however, may differ, as the Ukrainian revolt in the Independence Square—the Maidan—epitomized (see chapter 5).

In all these countries public opinion is divided. A broad majority of Moldovans and Georgians favored membership in the EU in 2008, 77 percent and 79 percent respectively.[4] A few years later, in 2013, a wider chasm seemed to separate Moldovans and Georgians—though all polls are subject to interpretation. As the Kremlin was pushing for its Eurasian Customs Unions (ECU) and Eurasian Economic Union (EEU) to counter the EU's further forays into former Soviet territories, 44 percent of Moldovans preferred joining the EU with over 40 percent rallying to the ECU (Serviciul Independent de Sociologie şi Informaţii, "Opinia" 2013: 10), while 83 percent of Georgians held it desirable to join the EU, even though they did not deem their country ready for membership (EPF 2013: 6; on ECU and EEU, see chapter 6). In other countries, opinions are even more deeply cleaved, sometimes showing wide, wild gyrations. Thus, between 40 percent and 65 percent of Ukrainians advocate membership in the EU, with a lower percentage in southern and eastern Ukraine more inclined toward Russia (Razumkov Centre 2010: 66; 2013a: 104). A poll taken in 2014, before the war in eastern Ukraine, indicated that slightly more than 50 percent of those interviewed would vote for joining the EU, while about 31 percent preferred the Moscow-led Customs Union of former Soviet states.[5] In Belarus, in 2010, 44.1 percent of the respondents were in favor of their country's accession to the Union, against a mere 26.7 percent a year earlier (NISEPI 2010–2011; Popescu and Wilson 2009: 28). According to a 2013 poll, the percentage of those advocating a union with Russia had plummeted from 56 percent to 32 percent between 2008 and 2013, while the proportion of those advocating a union with the EU increased in parallel, from 18 percent to 33 percent (Office for a Democratic Belarus 2013).

Despite variations according to countries and according to years, the EU recently scored better than the Kremlin in Eastern European perceptions. For Moldovans, for instance, the EU is associated with democracy (46.4 percent), peace and stability (30 percent), and lack of corruption (32.2 percent)—the ECU scoring 9.2, 6.1, and 18.2 percent on each of these three accounts (Serviciul Independent de Sociologie şi Informaţii, "Opinia" 2013: 3; see also Eurasia Partnership Foundation 2013: 7).[6] Kievan Ukrainians demonstrating in Independence Square called for a better life and for the dignity that the EU is supposed to embody. Georgians ask for European standards. Certainly, the relation a number of Eastern Europeans entertain with Western Europe may differ from Central Europeans' perceptions before the fall of the Wall. The Europe of Tbilisi's Georgians or Kievan Ukrainians may be less carnal, less vivid than the Europe Central Europeans yearned for in the 1980s. In many ways, the connections to Western Europe, understood now as covering the greater part of the continent, are probably more tenuous and fleeting than the web of ties that linked Central Europe to the West at the time of the Cold War. In the 1970s and 1980s, Polish émigrés lived in Paris. In the 1970s and 1980s, East-West societal networks consistently supported the dissidents in communist countries, and Western media, political or not, broadcasted from Budapest to Riga and Tallinn and farther away. For a long time, however, those connections were weaker the farther east one went, not only because of geographical and perhaps cultural distance, but also because the channels of influence, of socialization as some would say, were more limited. In the first decade of the new millennium, more Ukrainians visited Russia, Belarus, or Kazakhstan than countries of the EU, respectively 48 percent and 21 percent (Razumkov Centre 2013a: 106). Apart from these countries' immediate neighbors, Poland, Sweden, or even Germany or Slovakia, the West feels less concerned by the fate of East Europeans, though NGOs support their counterparts in Eastern Europe.

Never before had the EU encountered such poor, unstable, and even insecure confines on the continent, apart from the Western Balkans. Certainly, it had faced major challenges before, when it had to embrace former authoritarian regimes, polities, and societies in transition, when it opened up to poorer economies and eventually shared borders with Russia, and when it had to contain and put an end to the wars in Yugoslavia, which it could not do without the crucial intervention of the United States. Yet in the new neighborhood defined by the last wave of enlargement, the EU is in a quandary.

Moldova, for instance, is the poorest country on the continent, with a Gross Domestic Product (GDP) less than a third of that of its western neighbor Romania, and Ukraine's GDP, half that of its Polish neighbor a decade ago, was less than a fourth in 2014 (World Bank 2014). Even aside from Belarus, the "last dictatorship on the continent," democracy is not firmly anchored in either Moldova or Ukraine, or in the southern Caucasus—as the tugs-of-war in Chișinău, the upheavals, battles, and predicaments in Ukraine, and even past turmoil in Georgia epitomize.[7] State institutions are weak. Preparedness is lacking, and the ability of state institutions to carry out reforms may be questioned—as seen in chapter 6, Kiev is struggling to introduce some reforms. What is dubbed "convergence with the EU," and which is actually a unilateral effort demanded by the EU to meet its standards, will be much more difficult than in the case of the CEECs, though the EU helps financially, technically, and politically. Secessionist entities, supported by Moscow, challenge the sovereignty of some of these states: Transnistria in Moldova, Donbass and the Crimea in Ukraine, and Georgia's Abkhazia and South Ossetia—the latter three having been, de jure or de facto, incorporated by the Russian federation. Corruption networks, a shaky rule of law, and illicit trafficking from enclaves or exclaves often undermine Eastern European states.

However ambiguous the picture may look, the farther east, the less prepared are the newly independent countries to join the EU. Paradoxically, the countries that would benefit most from the EU's support and enticement to further democratization and liberalization are least able to do so because domestically they suffer from weak institutions and are often deeply divided over the path they want to follow. To the Union and its populations, the travail looks ever more daunting and less palatable than previous enlargements, especially at a time of dire economic straits and increasing challenges.

To the south and the southeast of the continent, countries beyond the Mediterranean Sea suffer partly from similar predicaments, but they also find themselves caught in totally different constellations, harbor very different perceptions of Europe, and nurture very different aspirations. The influence the EU exercises on North African and Middle Eastern governments and elites is more limited than on the European marches, because of past history and ties, recent policies, and the lack of a European future. The scars of colonization and wars of independence nourish accusations of European neocolonialism and interference, and imbue views of Europe that differ from those cherished in the eastern marches, except in Morocco, which mostly escaped colonization. Despite the EU's rhetorical endorsement of democracy and human rights, its inability to contribute to a solution to the Arab-Israeli conflict, its perceived indifference toward the plight of Palestinians or the civil war in Algeria, its connivance with authoritarian regimes in the Arab world, and the prioritization of its security concerns over the economic development and democratization processes, Arab countries, as seen below, nurtured negative views against what was deemed a policy of double standards.

The so-called Arab Spring hardly promised a meeting of minds between the two shores of the Mediterranean. When the Arab Spring shattered North Africa and the Middle East, starting in 2011, support came in the beginning from individuals, NGOs, and trade unions in Europe, not from officials. There was no embrace. Conversely, on the southern shore of the Mediterranean, there was no demand for models and recipes either before the Arab Spring or after. As an EU official put it, there was no Havel and no Wojtyła to call for them. While European ideas had infused this part of the world since the nineteenth century, in some countries more than in others, it was rather the words and work of Gene Sharp, an American professor and director of the Albert Einstein Institute for the promotion of change through nonviolence, that inspired many of those who fought against dictatorship, from Tunis to Cairo. After having shaped the minds of the Southern and Eastern European revolutionaries in the early years of the new millennium, from Serbia's Otpor to Ukraine's Pora, Sharp's book, *The Politics of Nonviolent Action*, was avidly downloaded by many of those who expressed their wrath in the Arab world. As an astute observer of the region puts it concisely, "The European Union has lost all its credibility," except in Morocco, "the only country where it has an audible voice."[8]

In the Middle East, limited structural power did not translate into influence, as it tapered off with geographic and historical distance, and as the EU and the Europeans encountered strong competition from other poles of influence in the Arab world, or other countries farther away, which exerted a powerful pull, and manipulated actors and actions. The United States constituted a pole of attraction for Israel, and for part of Lebanon and Jordan, for instance. Qatar, Saudi Arabia, or Iran offered money and appeal. Even China lured with its pattern of modernization without democratization. In Africa and in the Middle East, the ferocious repression that crushed rebellions, the descent into war of Syria, the fragmentation of Iraq, Syria, and Libya, the stasis that paralyzed Algeria and Saudi Arabia, had twin consequences affecting European societies and polities and the EU. These developments partly explained the rise of Islamist networks, of Daesh particularly (the Arab acronym of IS, the so-called Islamic State, also called ISIL, the Islamic State in the Levant, or ISIS, the Islamic State in Syria), and their expansion from the Middle East to Africa and farther away. Repression, war, paralysis, and deadly nihilism all contributed to drive local populations in droves to find refuge on the Old Continent.

Thus, Europe looks attractive to many individuals. A greater number of Moroccans and Algerians would rather join the EU than a regional framework (Martinez 2009: 14). Individually or in groups, migrants from the Middle East, from Syria and Iraq—which does not officially belong to the European Neighbourhood—and from Sub-Saharan Africa try to reach the northern shore of the Mediterranean in increasing numbers, often facing immense peril (see chapter 5). There is a striking paradox between individual strategies, whereby individuals see Europe as a safe haven that, right or wrong, respects human dignity, heeds the rule of law, and promises material well-being, and countries, North African and Middle Eastern, that will probably never join the EU and sometime look down on it or away from it—though Morocco applied to the European Communities in 1987, after the king had expressed his aspiration to join in a letter to François Mitterrand in 1985.

What kind of policies could the EU define toward its neighbors to the south and to the east while it enjoyed some economic leverage—at least in some countries more than in others—but limited political credit? Could and would the EU treat its neighbors, in the East and South, in the same way? Did it act coherently or did it implement different policies that did not necessarily dovetail with one another? In short, which neighbors, which policy, and what or whose purposes were, and are, at stake? Those very questions underline the confusion that imbued the European Neighbourhood Policy, or rather policies, toward the neighbors from the very beginning.

Embracing the Neighbors?

On paper, the neighborhood policy, or policies, understood as encompassing the Euro-Mediterranean Policy (EMP), dating from 1995, toward the Arab world, and the European Neighbourhood Policy (ENP), from 2004, directed at the whole neighborhood from Morocco to Ukraine, were beautifully coherent, designed to create a ring of well-governed states around Europe. They echoed past attempts, dating to the early 1970s, when the European Community, prodded by the French government, invented a "Global Mediterranean Approach," essentially commercial, that led to cooperation agreements granting most industrial goods and some agricultural products originating from these countries free access to the Community without reciprocity—and without prompting an economic takeoff either. The EC also halfheartedly opened a political front, again under French pressure, to pursue a Euro-Arab political dialogue at a time of economic and political turmoil and tensions, following the Yom Kippur War in 1973, and the subsequent imposition of an oil embargo by the Arab producers.[9] Eventually, against the backdrop of the Madrid Conference in 1991, and the Oslo Peace Process (for the Arab-Israeli conflict, see chapter 3), the European governments, in particular of France, Spain, and Italy, invented a policy that both fit into the conference and the peace process and offered a counterpoint to them, the Euro-Mediterranean Partnership (EMP, EUROMED, or so-called Barcelona Process).

Launched in 1995, the EMP was not meant to solve the Arab-Israeli conflict—this was the purpose of the Oslo Peace Process—but rather to address economic, social, and cultural root causes and to promote democracy, human rights, and the rule of law. It was to forge ties between the two shores of the Mediterranean, create a region despite wars, conflicts, and cleavages, overcome the deep socioeconomic chasm between both shores of the Mediterranean and the economic divide between Israel and the Arab countries, and foster democratic institutions and practices (Del Sarto and Schumacher 2005; Bicchi 2007). It was an answer to the Eastern enlargement, a complex interplay of EU policies, politics, and bargaining between institutions and states wrangling over programs and financial help, a kind of horse trading between the southern and the central and eastern EU member states (Maresceau and Lannon 2001). On the whole, it was far too ambitious for the recipients, ridden by conflicts and cleavages, and for the Europeans themselves, who could not live up to all the tasks they had set for themselves.

Elsewhere on the margins of the EU, the EU invented other cross-border programs, like the Northern Dimension, the Black Sea Synergy, and the Baltic Sea Strategy, which had to tackle specific national and regional concerns, and bridge the divide between the EU and its neighbors (Johansson 2001; Lannon and Elsuwege 2004; Behr 2010). Such programs eventually amounted to organizing the surroundings. Of all these endeavors, the European Neighbourhood Policy (ENP), adopted in 2004, was to be the crown jewel. Of all the policies that the European institutions crafted, haphazardly or not, the ENP is among the most proactive and figures prominently among the achievements of which the EU boasts. As the enlargement to eight and later ten Central and Eastern European countries loomed, the Spanish foreign minister Josep Piqué, whose country was holding the rotating presidency of the European Council, aired some of the problems that he thought might plague the Union after 2004. He referred to border crossings in particular, to illegal migration, organized crime, or illicit trafficking and urged the EU to craft a status for its neighbors (Foreign and Commonwealth Office 2002).[10] In 2003, the heads of states and governments approved the European Security Strategy (ESS), which called for the establishment of a "ring of well-governed states" surrounding Europe (European Council 2003). The following year, the European Council adopted the ENP, and charted a path to create the "ring of friends."

The ENP seemed essentially intended to stabilize the marches and prevent instabilities from spilling over into the EU, by tying in the new neighbors that would not soon join the EU, Ukraine, above all, the largest state in the East, and, thrown in for good measure, Moldova and Belarus were the latter to shake its despotic regime. After the Rose Revolution in Tbilisi, in 2004, which overthrew the post-Soviet regime, the neighborhood expanded to include Georgia, Azerbaijan, and Armenia. The countries of the South, from Morocco to Syria, were included to complete the "ring of friends," and underline that the status of neighbor did not imply candidacy, that, in short, the neighborhood policy was a makeshift for enlargement (Cottey 2009).[11]

Specifically, the Union claimed to expect far-reaching domestic, economic, and political reforms, agreed upon by the EU and its partner states and formalized in bilateral documents, the so-called Action Plans, in return for incentives. Its neighbors were to adopt part of the EU's governance, certain standards and norms, economic and political, and some of the *acquis*, to enforce policies, such as those designed to stem illegal migration and curb terrorism, to abide by the rule of law, and to respect human and civil rights, in particular minority rights (M. Smith 1996; Lavenex 2004). To support such reforms, the EU granted technical and financial aid, commercial concessions, involvement in European programs, projects and networks funded by the Commission, or participation in particular policies and agencies.[12] Benchmarking and monitoring also belonged to the panoply of instruments put in place and inspired by ENP and pre-enlargement mechanisms (Tulmets 2005; Kelley 2006).

Though proactive, the ENP was nonetheless incremental not only because it emulated previous policies but also because it was revised step-by-step, according to external pressures and internal dynamics. The Union indeed made one offer after another, scaling down or ratcheting up its proposals according to the fears or, conversely, ambitions of member states and the Commission. Some of the initial offers were grandiose. In a famous speech in December 2002 in Brussels, Romano Prodi, the president of the Commission, mooted the idea of sharing "everything but the institutions" (Prodi 2002; Commission of the European Communities 2003). If implemented, this would have amounted to another version of the EEA encompassing the rich Northern and Central European countries.

Prodi's vision of a single economic area, however, did not take into account the weakness of state institutions in the neighborhood, and the lack of infrastructure of all kinds, particularly in the legal field. In order to implement the four freedoms, namely, of persons, goods, services, and capital, all the partner states, governmental and economic actors, have to share similar institutions and norms, abide by similar laws and rules, and implement common standards. The four freedoms were abandoned for a more realistic approach, namely, a stake in the Internal Market and its regulatory structures. Offering now too little, the Union had to come up with new offers, round up incentives and upgrade rewards to regain credibility and clout, and encourage, for instance, the new government in Ukraine.

After the Orange Revolution in Ukraine, which brought down a government fraudulently elected in December 2004, European decision makers deemed it necessary to amend the proposals that had earlier been on the table. A ten-point plan, including EU support for Ukraine's membership in the World Trade Organization (WTO), the prospect of a free trade area (FTA), visa facilitation, and increased financial aid, was put forth in January 2005. Later, an "advanced" or "enhanced status" was invented as a reward for implementing the priorities set out in the Action Plans. Initially, the two potential powerhouses of the neighborhood, lying at the two ends of the ring, Morocco and Ukraine, were earmarked to receive this status. Morocco was granted an advanced status in 2008, and the EU started negotiating with Ukraine an Association Agreement and a so-called Deep and Comprehensive Free Trade Agreement (DCFTA), after the country joined the WTO in 2008, requiring the adoption of EU laws in many areas, and visa facilitation, including, for instance, the creation of common visa application centers.[13] That same year, the Eastern Partnership (EaP) was put forth, a component of ENP specifically tailored by Northern and Central European EU members for their East European neighbors, and a direct counterbalance to the Union for the Mediterranean (UfM), also launched in 2008.

The UfM was a loose collection of practical projects that never really took off, conceived as it was under adverse political auspices. The French president, its initiator, had first tried not to embed it in the EU, excluding some member states, and ignored political conditionality, embracing authoritarian leaders that the Arab revolutions soon swept away. On the contrary, the EaP is all encompassing, geographically and thematically, and based on conditionality. It sought to systematize the DCFTAs, and the political Association Agreements that embed them; and it devises regional and thematic programs. In 2011, another upgrade was conceived, ENP Plus, supposed to be yet another ambitious answer, to the Arab upheavals this time, and summarized by the motto "More for more": more money, more market access, and more mobility in return for more democracy and reforms. The Support to Partnership, Reform and Inclusive Growth (SPRING Programme) was to support democratic transition (European Commission 2011).

Democracy: Lost in Conditionality

Yet these projects revealed similar flaws, and upgrading fell short of expectations. The enhanced status conferred on some countries was initially looked upon as something specific, at least in the eyes of the recipients. Morocco, for instance, considers itself the "best pupil" or, at least, the most advanced of the southern Mediterranean countries (Jaidi and Martin 2010). Yet the "advanced status" it received was lagging behind the DCFTA extended to Ukraine. Rabat eventually opened negotiations with the EU on a DCFTA in 2013, and as other countries joined the waiting list, uniqueness was lost. Moreover, while the advanced status confers on Morocco recognition, if not weight, insofar as its representatives are consulted by the members of the Council within the precincts of the Political and Security Committee (PSC) in Brussels or in the General Assembly of the United Nations in New York, negotiations are not completed at the time of writing. Rabat has not obtained what it seeks regarding visa liberalization.[14]

In short, some of the rewards are more symbolic than substantial. Conversely, reforms that the EMP, the ENP, and the EaP demand can be costly for the countries concerned. Indeed, the cost of adjustment that the Union exacts from its neighbors may be higher, at least in the short term, than the advantages it is willing to grant. The price involves the political cost of reforms that elites will have to pay, and the economic cost of adjusting to the standards and rules of the Internal Market. Societies stand to lose: in most Mediterranean countries, small family enterprises with fewer than ten employees are the rule, so the burden of adaptation to the Internal Market is heavy. The incentives promised by Brussels have not been sufficient "to improve trade performance . . . or to reduce [the Mediterranean countries'] degree of vulnerability facing a more open economic environment" (Montalbano 2007: 61). In Eastern European societies as well, small and medium enterprises have to bear the brunt of adjustment (Shumylo-Tapiola 2012).[15] On the other hand, elites often obstruct those reforms that would put at risk their vested interests, and undermine or even overhaul established social and political structures, be it in the Arab world or in postcommunist states.

Whose Bargaining Power?

Nonetheless, neighbors do hold trump cards, specific assets that the Union values, and use them in an attempt to extract quid pro quos, even though the asymmetry between the Union and each individual country seems to favor the former and the bargaining structure it devises. Though Morocco has underwritten bilateral readmission agreements with EU member states that authorize the repatriation of Moroccan or foreign immigrants passing through Morocco to illegally enter these countries, it refuses to sign a readmission agreement with the EU as long as it does not obtain better travel conditions for its citizens (Coleman 2009: 150–157). Pressures from the Union may even backfire or at least peter out. When, in January 1992, the European Parliament froze the fourth financial protocol intended for Morocco, citing human rights abuses, the kingdom merely discarded European financial assistance, and reciprocated by cutting off negotiations on the renewal of a fishing agreement (Gillspie and Youngs 2002: 152–153). In 2016, it suspended contacts with the EU over an agreement on agricultural products because of a European court ruling that excluded Western Sahara from its remit.

More generally, the grip of European governments on the king's policy of small steps has been limited at best, though the country had been the largest recipient of European Neighbourhood Policy Instrument (ENPI) funds (European Commission 2013). Prior to the Arab uprisings, the king had undertaken a policy of "modernization without democratization," to borrow Kristina Kausch's tart formula (Kausch 2010). The "advanced status" was based on a promise to deliver rather than the result of strict conditionality. Instead of conditionality, Jacques Chirac and later Nicolas Sarkozy of France, and José Luis Zapatero of Spain, actually vied with one another to offer their patronage to the king in his quest for closer ties with the EU. The southern members of the EU and the EU itself turned a blind eye to the glitches and scratches that mar supposedly good-neighborly relations, such as the contest between Morocco and Spain over the Spanish Perjil islet and the Spanish enclaves of Ceuta and Melilla, and, aside from the aforementioned court ruling, the kingdom's claims over Western Sahara, and the plight of Sahraoui. The constitutional reforms that were adopted in Morocco in 2011 were not prompted by a European policy that was inconsistent and sometimes nonexistent. They were rather clever answers of a king who still enjoys religious and political legitimacy and understands so far how to co-opt political Islam to navigate between rebellion and repression, and to modernize and diversify the economy. They were also part of the king's grand design to put the country on a par with other European and American states, as close associate of the EU and the Atlantic community. Against the backdrop of mostly failed Arab revolutions, turmoil, and chaos, the king's strategy of incremental reforms, and of turning Morocco into an indispensable partner, accounts for what might be called privileged treatment.

In other words, there is little that the EU can impose upon its neighbors. Reforms and measures are jointly agreed upon in the Action Plans, and each government is free to subscribe to the reforms it chooses and the measures it wants to implement, and to follow the rhythm it sets, or does not set. In the Action Plan it signed with the Union in 2005, the Jordanian government, for instance, merely took over the national program of economic and social development it had earlier devised (Schmid and Braizat 2006). As a result, commitments all too often are vague, benchmarks imprecise, and the calendar hesitant. In its first years, the ENP was also criticized for both the complexity and the confusion of the conditions it enumerated. For instance, the Action Plan concluded with Georgia in 2006 listed the necessity to strengthen the rule of law, state institutions, and the independence of the judiciary, to improve the business and investment climate, to fight against corruption and illegal migration, to promote economic development and social cohesion, to manage borders, to solve conflicts, to increase regional cooperation, and to work on transport and energy, to name some of the plan's aims—a Christmas list in many respects. With time, requirements have become more specific. Yet no benchmark or time frame is set, an omission that also characterizes the EaP, and that NGOs on the ground bitterly criticize (Youngs 2008). It remains to be seen whether ENP Plus will be more specific and whether a step-by-step approach, a quid pro quo, can be implemented as announced, especially in a context that is not conducive to reforms.

As in the case of enlargement, reforms are essentially indigenous—though targeted pressures may bring limited returns. The EU adhered, or seemed to adhere, to this rationale when it subscribed to the concepts of partnership and "joint ownership." When reforms were and are indeed introduced and implemented, it is because of the will of the government—and its citizens. Certainly, the EU required some reforms from the Palestinian National Authority (PNA) in the early years of the new millennium, yet they really took off once Salam Fayyad, prime minister from 2007 to 2013, tackled them head-on. East of Europe, in Georgia or in Ukraine, reforms are primarily indigenous, in particular the fight against petty corruption under Mikheil Saakashvili's rule. After the Rose Revolution, which brought down the ex-communist regime in 2003, the EU increased somewhat its presence and support in Georgia. Yet it was under the leadership of President Saakashvili (2004–2007 and 2008–2013) that the country made headway on certain issues, but not on others: democratic institutions were consolidated, and elections became fairer (European Commission, High Representative of the European Union for Foreign Affairs and Security Policy 2013). The fight against corruption at the street level was ferocious, though not at higher levels. The recommendations of a European civilian mission, EUJUST, in 2005, which aimed at strengthening the rule of law, were not implemented.[16]

East vs. South: Look for the States

The EU had devised this beautifully logical and coherent category of "friends," logical and coherent at least on paper. Yet not only is each country a case in itself, but also Eastern neighbors and neighbors to the south of Europe end up being treated differently by the EU and its member states. Their treatment differs depending on whether they are Europeans, nurturing the hope to join the EU, or whether they face a different future. Hence, they differ in Europe's assessments and calculations. While some EU member states may place their hope in an Eastern Europe that would transform itself, the Arab world has long been neglected, except when it came down to short-term economic returns and cooperation in areas such as border controls. It has not found among EU members the supporters that some Eastern European states or societies have.

Between 1995 and 2006, the EU transferred €8.8 billion to the Mediterranean countries to support reforms, such as the introduction of new legal frameworks and new regulations. Compared with the amounts spent on helping the CEECs to adjust to enlargement, this sum was limited. Between 1 and 6 euros were disbursed per head per year for the Mediterranean countries, which by all accounts is much less than the 209 euros spent on the CEECs (Moisseron 2005: 109; Larabi and Martin 2010: 68–69). In 2014, a new instrument (ENI) was instituted to ratchet up the previous one, ENPI (2007–2014), whose budget of €11.2 billion had increased by €1.2 billion in May 2011 after the beginning of the Arab upheavals (European External Action Service 2014).[17] Half of ENI's €15.4 billion (2014–2020) goes to the southern neighbors, 32 percent to the East—and 15 percent to Russia. Again, a higher number of southern neighbors receive relatively less than the East does. In any case, structural help has hardly been able "to bring about changes in the institutional environment," and technical assistance programs fared badly. In the past, a number of projects were "either (being) delayed or simply cancelled," according to one expert familiar with the programs of the EU in the Mediterranean. Hence, it proved difficult to attach robust conditions, and even more so to interrupt disbursement in the absence of reforms as it risked "bring[ing] . . . about a political crisis" (Moisseron 2005: 78–79).

Though influencing autocratic or pseudodemocratic governments, be it in the Mediterranean basin, be it east of Europe, proves to be elusive, a comparison between the Union's and its member states' policies toward the East, and toward the South and Southeast further shows a marked difference in their dealings with the two regions. The EU and its member states have been investing less in the latter than in the former, not only financially but also politically—leaving aside the Palestinian-Israeli conflict discussed earlier.

In Belarus, even though the president, Alyaksandr Lukashenka, has been clinging to power for two decades, the EU has nonetheless attempted to bring pressure to bear on the regime, upon the insistence of some of its member states. Early on, sanctions were raised on the Belarusian government. The PCA, signed in 1995 with Minsk, never came into force because of the 1996 referendum that extended Lukashenka's powers. Technical assistance was rescinded, and a visa ban targeted four officials after the disappearance of opposition politicians and journalists. Following parliamentary elections and a referendum in 2004, which further extended Lukashenka's term in office, and the 2006 presidential elections, the EU broadened its list of sanctions, banned an increasing number of officials from entering the EU, froze assets, and removed Belarus from its Generalized System of [Commercial] Preferences (GSP). Pressures multiplied, through the mobilization of European embassies in Minsk, for instance.

However selective and targeted the sanctions are, they may end up playing into the hands of a government that turns self-isolation into a policy, and into those of a domineering Russia, which seeks to exploit the weaknesses of its neighbors and strengthen its political and economic grip on them. Hence, as early as 2001, the Union devised incentives, and offered a policy of gradual normalization in return for progress regarding the respect for human rights and democratic principles. After the last wave of enlargement, direct neighbors of Belarus—Poland, Lithuania, Slovakia, and the Czech Republic—questioned the rationale of sanctions and underlined the value of engagement. Polish elites knew how much they owed to an open-door policy, when the West embraced Polish dissidents in the 1970s and 1980s. Despite a lack of improvement in Belarus, the stranglehold that Moscow had on the country's economy and infrastructure, in particular on its gas transit system, and the burgeoning sovereignty that Minsk started to cultivate emboldened the advocates of engagement.

The efforts of the Union seemed to converge toward an opening between 2008 and 2010. After the liberation, in August 2008, of three political prisoners that Minsk claimed to be the last, and also owing to the fact that it had not recognized the secessionist entities of Abkhazia and South Ossetia after the Georgian-Russian war in 2008, the Union suspended sanctions and offered a political dialogue, economic cooperation, and financial assistance, contingent on free and fair elections. It invited Belarus to take part in the EaP and participate in multilateral projects, though not in the bilateral dimension of the ENP. All this, however, was to little avail. Even though, during the run-up to the presidential elections in Belarus, held in December 2010, the contest seemed more open, and outside observers were allowed in, the elections were rigged, and opposition candidates and campaigners were beaten and detained. As four European foreign ministers put it in an open letter, continued positive engagement was "a waste of time and money," though "engagement with the democrats of Belarus [remains] essential" (Bildt et al. 2010). Increased repression led to new sanctions in 2011, 2012, and 2013 that the Polish foreign minister, Radosław Sikorski, who had formerly been at the forefront of the policy of engagement, criticized for their weakness.[18] The German and French governments in particular were more reluctant to oppose the regime because of their commercial ties with Belarus (European Parliament 2012). Yet they did not block the policy agreed upon, and when Slovenia opposed a veto, the latter was quickly overturned.[19]

However, not only has the EU been unable to influence the Belarusian regime. It has also watered down its policy and principles since 2014. In 2015, the EU suspended most of its sanctions against Belarus. After mixed signals from Alyaksandr Lukashenka in 2015, his rigged reelection to a fifth term in office—that an OSCE report only mildly criticized—the liberation, yet again, of political prisoners, and tensions between Moscow and Minsk over the establishment of a Russian military base in Belarus, the EU suspended most sanctions, for a number of reasons. First, with Brussels and Moscow vying for influence, Lukashenka seeks profits where opportunities arise, and withstands pressures wherever they come from, under the motto "Take the money and stay." On the whole, the president has rather carefully—or should one say desperately?—managed so far to navigate between Russia—and even China, which granted Minsk loans in 2011 and 2013—and the West. Second, as part of this game, Lukashenka has consolidated to some extent its independence from Moscow (Ioffe 2008). He objected to the Kremlin's plans to impose countersanctions on the West after the latter sanctioned Russia, following the annexation of the Crimea and the invasion of Donbass, and to federalize Ukraine, which bode ill for the future of his own country. Third, the geopolitical turn of 2014, and the Russian war in Ukraine, dissuaded some or most members of the EU, Germany and France in particular, from berating the regime. The EU must have deemed it necessary not to throw Lukashenka into the arms of its bigger neighbor, especially after Brussels failed to convince the Ukrainian president, Viktor Yanukovych, to sign the Association Agreement and the DCFTA in 2013 (see chapter 6). Some of Belarus's western neighbors wanted to avoid opening a new eastern front, while they were doing their utmost to hammer out agreements with Russia on Ukraine and Syria.

Though the EU could not influence Minsk, and wavered between isolating Lukashenka and engaging him, eventually surrendering to a policy of quasi accommodation, one may contend that it did, at very least, search for a policy. Debates frequently took place in European institutions, launched by some of the Eastern and Northern European member states that sought to nurture the seeds of democracy. The fact that the same EU actors advocated different policies over time reflected intense soul-searching and the desire to look for the most appropriate answers. The geopolitical upheavals in Eastern Europe, however, have skewed principled policies. Now that some of the EU member states have taken the measure of the threat that the Russian regime represents, its policy regarding Belarus might come to emulate the timid one it has pursued in the Arab world. There, not only did the capacity of authoritarian regimes to resist change thwart EU policies, but some of the member states also stood in the way of a unified front. Those EU governments that had vested interests in promoting the southern shore of the Mediterranean were blinded by self-serving priorities, a false understanding of stability, and murky connections. Hardly any debates were held on Tunisia. The only sanctions ever taken against Ben Ali's clan were raised in 2011, after the upheavals, and they concerned individuals or entities that had misappropriated Tunisian state funds.

On the southern shore of the Mediterranean, the EU and its member states too often let themselves be deceived by the pretense of economic reforms. The latter were mostly grafted on illiberal economic and political systems. One of the few, partial, on the whole skewed, and eventually misconstrued economic successes of EUROMED and ENP, Tunisia, precisely underscores this point. While Tunisia and Morocco had made the most out of the asymmetrical trade preferences initially granted by Brussels in the mid-1970s to create a clothing industry, Tunisia alone had been moving up toward more productive sectors in the electric and electronic industry, agro-industry, and services, thanks to so-called economic reforms of the second generation.

On the whole, however, the policies promoted by the Union amounted to sheer liberalization, and did not constitute a strategy per se (Ould Aoudia 2008: 91). The so-called Tunisian economic miracle of Ben Ali's years, which failed to promote employment, youth employment in particular, actually rested on corruption and the confiscation of public goods by a few. The wealth created was partly hijacked by a small clan around the president. It helped to buy a so-called social peace, and dovetailed with self-censorship, policing, and repression. Economy, politics, and policies were enmeshed, and shaped an undemocratic polity. To hail the Tunisian economic development as an "economic miracle" and as a haven of stability while turning a blind eye to repression, which had increased in the decade prior to Ben Ali's downfall—from restrictions placed on the freedom of association and freedom of the press to the systematic use of torture and the lack of independence of the judiciary—was extremely shortsighted. The European institutions and the member states chose to ignore the on-going repression, and to praise the country for its so-called economic prowess and its cooperation on the issue of border controls. The EU states geographically closer to North Africa, which have more at stake in the southern neighborhood than the Nordic members of the Union, pushed for some limited economic reforms that were not future oriented. Successive French governments were the most articulate and forceful advocates of a policy based on short-term calculations, and verging on connivance. It was Nicolas Sarkozy who initiated the UfM, which swept aside all pretense of pushing political reforms by dropping conditionality.[20]

Neither the EMP nor the ENP systematically and consistently promoted the defense of human rights in the Arab world. In spite of blatant human rights violations, the Algerian government continued to benefit from MEDA with the exception of two years, 1997 and 1998. In 2013, the European Court of Auditors harshly criticized the Commission for having pursued its programs to improve governance in Egypt, before and after the uprising, "despite the lack of progress on human rights" (European Court of Auditors 2013: point 74). The EU envisaged talks with Ben Ali's Tunisia to start negotiating an advanced status just as the regime was amending criminal law to prevent contacts between local NGOs and Europe, in July 2010. The subcommittee on human rights, democratization, and governance, which started meeting within the framework of the EU-Tunisia Association Agreement, took note of it, but negotiations proceeded nonetheless.[21] As the Euro-Mediterranean Human Rights Network (EMHRN) underlined in a report published four months before the start of the turmoil that swept over Tunisia, the EU decided to allocate 240 million euros' worth of incentives, in addition to pledges of the European

Investment Bank (EIB), for the period 2011–2013, praising excellent cooperation with a very good partner. The EU was not alone in committing this blunder. The world financial institutions did the same.

In other words, the praise and limited criticism of the Tunisian model of economic development stopped short of questioning the very nature of an authoritarian, kleptocratic, and clan-based regime. To introduce a distinction between economic reforms and political ones, and assign them different logics, is but a delusion, a convenient way to gloss over the political economy of repression (Hibou 2006). It also simply misrepresented the country's economic development. It was, after all, unemployment that brought the regime to ruins and revealed, in 2011, the wide chasm between a loathed authoritarian regime and its population. In its own interests, the EU should have called into question the nature of Tunisian economic development.

The Teddy Bear Blitz: Engaging Civil Societies

In both Tunisia and Belarus, European civil societies nonetheless played a role that the Commission and some member states supported, more in the East than in North Africa though. From early on, Europeans engaged Belarusian society. The EU funds infrastructures linking Belarus to the West, and fosters intellectual activities, promoting, for instance, EU film festivals, radio programs, and educational programs abroad.[22] A European Humanitarian University was created in 1992 in Minsk, later based in Vilnius, Lithuania, after Belarusian authorities closed it in 2006. Grants are given to students studying abroad—the University of Białystok in Poland hosts a number of Belarusian students. The Sakharov Prize for Freedom of Thought, created in 1988 by the European Parliament to honor individuals who dedicate their life to the defense of democracy and human rights, was twice awarded to Belarusian individuals or institutions, and, in 2015, the Nobel Prize for Literature rewarded Svetlana Alexievich "for her polyphonic writings, a monument to suffering and courage in our time" (Nobelprize.org).[23] After the crackdown following the elections of 2010 and the subsequent sanctions taken by the Union, Poland and Lithuania waved a visa fee for Belarusians wishing to travel to these countries—though no agreement could be reached at EU level. NGOs, such as the Polish Batory Foundation, are helping the Belarusian opposition.[24] In July 2012, a Swedish NGO launched a "teddy bear blitz" against Minsk, and dropped over Belarus teddy bears conveying a message in support of human rights, mocking the regime. Here again, however, the geopolitical turn of 2014 impacted political connections, and funds to Belarusian opposition parties seem to have dried up.

European civil societies also cultivated relations with Tunisian human rights advocates and trade unions. Thus, French trade unions and the French League of Human Rights supported their counterparts in Tunisia or Tunisians in France, which harbors a strong Tunisian community. The Tunisian president Moncef Marzouki (2011–2014) spent years in exile in France. A number of French universities established close contacts with Tunisian academics. In 2008, French trade unions of different political persuasions pulled their forces together in a remarkable and rare display of unity, following the strikes that paralyzed the mining industry around Gafsa and led to clashes between a pacific social movement and the police, resulting in arrests and deaths. Strong criticism coming from these organizations, which the French press had relayed, had previously forced the Tunisian president to postpone a visit in 1996, amid fears that he would face forceful opposition in France. Yet French governmental policy did not support these actions, to say the least.

The difference between the way the Union and, particularly, its member states repeatedly tried to craft a policy toward Belarus and their incapacity to define a coherent approach toward Tunisia before the 2011 rebellion was striking, more so, from our viewpoint, than the differences in outcomes—with Zine al-Abidine Ben Ali fleeing the country while Alyaksandr Lukashenka tightened his grip on the regime. In the case of Belarus, the Commission, some governments, and civil societies, in the East and West, coordinated their action. Conversely, the governments of France and Italy, and also of Spain in the case of Morocco, consistently pursued very lenient policies toward the southern shore of the Mediterranean and ignored civil protests on both sides of the sea (Whitney and Dworkin 2012: 7). Incoherence ensued, and the action of European civil societies, though critical, was lost in the meanders of politics.

Nonetheless, EU policies toward the Belarusian regime, be they sanctions, be they engagement, did not achieve a breakthrough. The displacement of Lukashenka can come only from within Belarus. The only hope for the EU and its members is to prepare the ground for future changes, to inform the population, to shape minds and build new elites, to foster the exchange of ideas, encourage free thoughts, and sow democratic seeds, just as Europe and the United States did during the Cold War, and later helped to further reforms in Central Europe. As one French civil servant involved in the implementation of European programs in Moldova put it, it is a bet about the future, a hope that some ideas, a few thoughts or values, will "trickle down."

The color revolutions that took place in Eastern Europe in the first decade of the millennium, and the Arab uprisings that seemed to bode well in the first years of the second decade, did not hold their promise for long. A window of opportunity briefly opened when the EU thought it could make up for its past inertia, in the southern neighborhood in particular. Yet one primary condition for the EU to exert influence is that neighboring countries turn to the EU for advice and support. However, past connivance dented the EU's credibility. Certainly the new Tunisian regime accepted EU observers to oversee elections, EU mediators to facilitate negotiations between various political actors, and EU advisers to reform the constitutional court. The EU's mediation in Libya, including under the auspices of the UN, holds promise. On the whole, however, the EU's voice and presence are hardly heard and felt. Egypt did not emulate the Tunisian regime at the time of the 2012 presidential election that brought the Muslim Brotherhood to power, and it eventually accepted a small EU observation team, in 2014, as a kind of cover-up after the military regime established it ruthless rule. Despite repression, the EU barely voices concerns, and it is doubtful that the More for More program that the EU set up in the wake of the Arab rebellions has a chance to succeed, as most regimes reject its strictures.

As often underlined in this book, democratization has to come from within. Yet many societies and polities on the surroundings are polarized, to say the least. Tunisia offers a rare case of relative consensus, in spite of increased tensions and terrorist attacks linked to radical Islam, ambiguities regarding the protection of individual rights, and the persistence of the very economic failures that triggered the 2011 rebellion. Short of insisting on democracy, which cannot be imposed from outside, the Union must nonetheless listen to civil society, and fine tune a policy of targeted and principled criticisms when laws and rights are infringed upon. Conditionality may be more effective when exercised at a microlevel, bolstered by rewards and disbursements following specific achievements, or criticisms in case of transgression. Not all the actors have to be included. Small groups of influential personalities may have an impact. When President Saakashvili closed down the independent television channel IMEDI TV in December 2007, after months of antigovernment demonstrations, the former Polish dissident and widely known editor of *Gazeta Wyborcza*, Adam Michnik, Peter Semneby, EU special representative for the Caucasus, and the French ambassador to Georgia, Eric Fournier, formally and jointly protested, so that the president eventually reopened the channel. "[The authorities] feel they are under scrutiny."[25]

However, be they at a macrolevel or at a microlevel, attempts at influencing the neighborhood, limited as they are, are threatened by one major mistake that the EU and its member states have kept committing over the past decades. They outsourced their border controls and immigration policies to the countries of the neighborhood. This means that they have to rely upon whichever government is in power, and surrender independence and principles.

5

A CRISIS IN THE MAKING?

The Refugee Crisis

> A refugee used to be a person driven to seek refuge because of
> some act committed or some political opinion held. Well, it is true
> we have had to seek refuge; but we committed no acts and most
> of us never dreamt of having any radical opinion. With us the
> meaning of the term "refugee" has changed. Now "refugees" are
> those of us who have been so unfortunate as to arrive in
> a new country without means and have to be helped by Refugees
> Committees.
>
> —HANNAH ARENDT, "We Refugees"

As of 2015, the wave of refugees who made their way to Europe reached staggering proportions. The refugees came from Europe's surroundings or from farther away, fleeing states at war, failed states, or repressive regimes. The surge in refugees in 2015 should not have come as a surprise though. The number of migrants had been rising since the beginning of the decade and the failure of Arab uprisings. Yet the Europeans did not see the writing on the wall. Instead of crafting long-term policies allowing, for instance, the resettlement of refugees from reception centers in countries neighboring the areas at war to particular locations in the EU, the Europeans did not address what was going to become a refugee crisis. Unwittingly they contributed to turning the refugee crisis into an EU crisis. The arrival of more than a million migrants in 2015 revealed multiple failures on the part of both EU institutions and national governments, in particular a lack of foresight accompanied by the incapacity of authorities to channel vast population movements in an orderly fashion. Why did the EU fail to foresee, understand, and react to this crisis in the making?

At the turn of the millennium, the EU had deluded itself with a false sense of security. It had sought to build a ring of friends who were supposed to become prosperous and more democratic, and to filter migrants coming to Europe. In fact, it hardly attempted or managed to promote democracy and prosperity to its surroundings. It is doubtful that the EU could have brought democracy to states where authoritarian regimes, based on state security apparatus, hampered democratic progress. The EU member states nonetheless entrusted the latter with their migration and border policies, violating international humanitarian laws and principles, and surrendering their own security and sovereignty. Eventually, the external border controls that the EU sought to delegate to its neighbors were not very efficient and depended on the whims of authoritarian regimes, or on the stability of governments in place.

The refugee crisis goes to the very heart of the EU, for three reasons: the cleavages it creates between member states add to those that have been dividing the EU since the early days of the Eurozone crisis; the massive displacement of populations gives rise to complex problems, sparking controversies that weaken the social and political fabric of individual member states, and feed populism and xenophobia; and it weakens the German chancellor, who has been instrumental in alleviating, if not solving, the various crises the EU is facing but now encounters domestic and European opposition for her handling of the refugee issue. Did the agreement that the EU and Turkey concluded on 18 March 2016 limit the influx of refugees, patch up differences, and reestablish German chancellor Angela Merkel's authority in the Union? After an analysis of the half-baked policies that the EU put in place over the past decades to actually delegate or outsource its external border controls to its periphery, the genesis of the so-called refugee crisis, and the solutions that the EU has been trying to cobble together, will come under focus in this chapter.

Outsourcing

In the 1980s and 1990s, the advancement of the Common Market called for the gradual abolition of internal borders between some of the EU members, and pushed border controls toward the EU's outer edge, delineating what came to be called the Schengen Area, which encompasses EU and non-EU members (Bigo and Guild 2005).[1] After 1989, the demise of communism opened up new countries that became new neighbors, and created new borders. Undocumented migrants arrived, in particular refugees from the former Yugoslavia in the 1990s (the term "migrant" applies to economic migrants, and "asylum seekers" to those who are persecuted or are fleeing war or famine: further below, the term "refugee" will be used to refer to the latter two categories for the sake of simplicity).[2] The Old Continent was graying and needed a new labor force. All this should have prompted the Europeans to adopt common border, migration, and refugee policies. Yet the EU never designed a migration policy or a refugee policy, nor did it devise a common external border policy. Instead, the following decade, which witnessed the terrorist attacks in New York and Washington in 2001, in Madrid in 2004, and London in 2005, population movements from destitute regions or war zones, and the rise of human smuggling and trafficking, well before the epochal migratory trek that started in 2015, reinforced a bias toward what has been dubbed the "securitization" of borders and boundaries, although the Europeans did not take the proper steps to enforce their security at the EU level (Bigo and Guild 2005; Jeandesboz 2007).

Patchy Measures

The EU never conceived a common migration policy. Migration policies remained a national issue, though, of course, states have to respect migrants' rights, as defined by international agreement, the right to family reunification above all.[3] When the president of the Commission, Jean-Claude Juncker, called for such a policy at the first Extraordinary Council, organized in May 2015, to discuss what has come to be known as the "refugee crisis," the heads of states and governments shoved the suggestion aside, under the pretext that migration policy was not a priority. Nor did the EU craft a European refugee policy. Certainly, attempts were made to define a uniform status for refugees, design common procedures, and determine which member state is responsible for examining the applications of those who seek refugee status, through the Dublin Convention and Regulations (respectively in 1990, 2003, and 2013) and based on international conventions (see below). The purpose of such actions was limited, however. They were meant to prevent refugees from filing claims in several member states simultaneously, and engaging in what is known as "venue shopping." The burden of examining the application of asylum seekers—and of hosting them meanwhile—falls on the country of first arrival, namely, Greece, Italy, and Spain, since most migrants cannot opt for anything else but a sea route. Though the European Asylum Support Office (EASO), an agency of the EU, was created in 2011 at the behest of the European Commission, its functions are limited, too. Within the framework of the Dublin Convention and Regulations, it gives expertise and support to member states, which have to deal with many demands.

However, this does not amount to a European asylum and refugee policy worthy of the name. The implementation of the regulations that the member states agreed upon relies upon legal, administrative, political, economic, and financial frameworks and instruments that are proper to each country in the EU, including the capacity to register refugees, host them, treat them (one hopes) with dignity, process their demands, grant them statuses that vary from permanent to temporary, and eventually integrate or reject them. For instance, the implementation of the agreement that the European Council and Turkey hammered out on 18 March 2016 depended, among other things, on whether individual member states such as Greece, not the EU, recognized Turkey as a safe third country (for refugees coming from other countries), and as a safe country of origin (for Turkish citizens who might seek refugee status). However, while the Europeans rejected an EU refugee policy, they mostly stuck to restrictive and eventually ill-conceived, national policies. Essentially they did not go beyond examining, and often rejecting, the claims of those refugees who managed to reach their borders.

Similarly, the EU never devised a European border policy. Beyond the common visa policy that the Schengen convention introduced—and that is sometimes poorly carried out, in the case of reentries for instance—there are no European customs or guards to operate controls at the EU's external borders. The European Agency for the Management of Operational Cooperation at the External Borders of the Member States (Frontex), created in 2004, was in no way intended to be a European border guard. Relying upon member states for a limited budget and limited staff, the agency's mission is to "coordinate and develop . . . European border management in line with the EU fundamental rights charter" applying the concept of Integrated Border Management.[4] It supports the national authorities of member states in registering migrants, and repelling those who are deemed illegal immigrants, sometimes saving them in the Mediterranean. The weakness of Frontex betrays the member states' will to hold on to crumbs of sovereignty, and their unwillingness to commit funds to an intergovernmental organization, even though the Commission has repeatedly called for the institution of a European border guard.

The lack of common migration and refugee policies, compounded with the lack of European control over the EU's or rather Schengen's external borders, entails adverse and paradoxical consequences because the area's external borders are difficult to control. The Schengen Area has a coastline of a little over 26,600 miles of indentations, caps, bays, and islands, some very close to the borders of Asia and Africa, where bad governance prevails, failed states proliferate, wars are waged, and terrorist networks and armies sprawl.[5] European coastlines are easy to reach and difficult to secure. Land borders, 8,190 miles as a whole, are easier to guard. For those determined to enter the EU, for better or for worse, illegal routes are the only options. The policy of relatively closed doors and open coasts also benefits smugglers who transport refugees at very high costs. Furthermore, there is no comprehensive system to track shipments and cargoes through EU ports, leaving loopholes that terrorists can exploit, according to security analysts (S. Jones 2016). This poses security risks to the EU and its member states.

The strengthening of border controls in one area diverts smuggling paths, from the southern to the eastern Mediterranean and back, and from land routes to often more perilous sea routes. After Spain struck agreements with Mauritania in 2003 and 2006 that involved, among other things, aid and joint police action to control routes, and reduced migration via the Canary Islands to a trickle, and after barbed wire began to be installed at the land border on the Evros between Greece and Turkey at the beginning of the 2010s, new routes opened up, by sea, between Turkish Bodrum and the Greek island of Lesbos, and by land, through the Balkans.[6]

Closed doors, harrowing routes, and unscrupulous smugglers imperil lives. Between 2000 and the first months of 2014 about 22,400 individuals lost their lives while crossing the Mediterranean (IOM 2014).

Certainly, Frontex has to save lives—according to international law—but it has not always done so. In 2013–2014, after 366 migrants drowned off the island of Lampedusa in October 2013, the Italian government, led by Enrico Letta, jumped in to mount a costly rescue operation, Mare Nostrum, which lasted a year, to replace the maritime missions that Frontex had organized to repel rather than rescue migrants. Assisted by Slovenia only, Rome bore the cost of the operation, €9 million a month, while the EU hardly contributed—and what it did contribute was actually drawn from the European Refugee Fund (ERF), which had been established for other purposes.

Solidarity with refugees was limited, and calls for a strategy went unheeded. In the 1990s, when Germany opened its doors to refugees fleeing the former Yugoslavia, Bonn put forth the idea of setting European quotas, according to which the newcomers would have been distributed among member states. But it did not succeed in getting the quota program off the ground. For years, too, international organizations like the High Commission for Refugees and NGOs like Amnesty International and Human Rights Watch have criticized the absence of refugee policies in Europe, advocating mechanisms that would have gone beyond the Dublin Convention and Regulations—for instance, the creation and implementation of a policy allowing safe passage for refugees, and promoting resettlement directly from refugee camps to EU member states. Resettlement can be implemented, and has been implemented by some countries, yet within limits. Countries that are far from war zones, for instance, can devise a proactive policy of resettlement. Canada implements a policy of resettlement that includes vetting, transporting, and accommodating entire families, and avoids having to reunify families and accept individuals who have not been cleared, though according to EU and human rights specialists this practice runs counter to international law. In any case, an EU resettlement policy, whatever it might be, does not prevent migrants and refugees from trying to reach the nearby shores of Europe. As seen below, the policy of relocation of refugees among member states, according to quotas, has been tentative at best. Eventually, the EU member states recoil from relinquishing what they deem to be their sovereign rights, and act according to their own needs and beliefs. In the wake of the military intervention in Libya in 2011, as thousands of migrants were trying to reach the shores of Italy, Silvio Berlusconi's government distributed visas for the Schengen Area without proper registration, and waved migrants out of the country, leading the French to briefly close their borders.

The Europeans stuck to national policies limiting economic migration. They avoided establishing common external border controls worthy of the name, and cobbled together a policy toward migrants that amounted to a patchwork of regulations and makeshift strategies. They lacked foresight and were not prepared to channel large-scale arrivals in an organized way.

Internal and External Peripheries

This patchwork of measures that fell short of innovative strategic thinking entailed consequences that most member states were trying to evade. Despite a policy of closed doors, many migrants found their way into the EU. Eventually, far from being the impregnable "Fortress Europe," which became a buzzword in the early years of the new millennium, the EU was more of a sieve. More worrying, these half-baked measures were a corollary to a deliberate policy of outsourcing the control of borders and migrants to the internal and external peripheries of the EU.

According to the Dublin Regulations, the EU member states that are the main countries of first arrival, that is, countries where migrants arrive first because they are close to Asia and Africa, have to register and examine applications. They have to host newcomers and, if necessary, repatriate them. Thus, they bear a particular burden that countries at the heart of the continent do not, insulated as they are by filtering procedures taken by the countries of first arrival—except in times of crisis. As the procedures may be long and costly, countries of first arrival bear a particular financial and social burden. In 2015, 850,000 migrants arrived in Greece, mostly to travel farther—before borders closed (see below). A rather poor country of 11 million inhabitants that has neither the personnel nor the funds to tackle a steady flow of refugees and economic migrants, Greece had to accommodate the newcomers—while, in comparison, Germany and its 80 million inhabitants struggled to receive a little over a million refugees. Hosting migrants may even chip away at the social fabric of a country like Greece, where parts of the population are no longer able to live a decent life because of austerity measures imposed in the wake of the debt crisis. Nor are the refugees' rights always guaranteed. Greece is currently in breach of international law. In 2011, the European Court of Human Rights ruled that Greece did not sufficiently heed the rights of refugees (ECtHR 2011). The Court of Justice of the European Union followed suit two years later, when it forbade member states from sending migrants back to countries where they might face "inhuman" or "degrading" treatment (Court of Justice of the European Union 2013).

To some extent, the EU tried to assuage differences between member states. In 2000, the Council of Ministers of Justice and Home Affairs created a European Refugee Fund (ERF) to improve, among other things, accommodation infrastructure and legal assistance to refugees, albeit with limited funding that amounted to €630 million between 2008 and 2013. Frontex was also supposed to help register refugees at points of entry, also in a limited way, as mentioned above. Thus the Dublin Regulations had a twofold consequence. They de facto established a two-tiered system within the EU, where countries of first arrival and core countries face different obligations and fare differently, and they could not ensure that borders would be efficiently controlled, especially in case of crises, when reception camps are overwhelmed.

The EU also deliberately externalized or outsourced its border controls to surrounding countries. It required from them to police not only their borders with the Union—at land or sea borders or at airports—but also their outer borders. It thus erected a "forward barrier" at its neighbors' outer edges. Many countries in the EU's surroundings and even farther away were asked to comply with the increasing body of laws, rules, and practices that the EU had put in place over the years. Many policies and tools were gradually invented, starting with the first readmission agreements that were concluded bilaterally in the 1990s between an EU member and a third, non-EU country. Germany and Poland were the first to sign such an agreement, requiring from Poland, then a non-EU country, to readmit nationals or citizens from other non-EU countries who had crossed its territory and illegally entered Germany.[7] Such agreements between the EU or individual member states of the Schengen Agreement and so-called third, or non-EU, countries were systematized, compounded by, (1) the deployment of immigration officers and the transfer of administrative know-how and equipment (surveillance equipment, for instance) to the outer borders of the EU, first implemented in the 1990s; (2) the adoption of sets of rules as of 2002; (3) the imposition of the Schengen *acquis* on candidate countries; (4) cooperation with Frontex to pursue so-called return operations to repel—and sometimes save—migrants, especially in the Mediterranean; and (5) the adoption of less formal, and more flexible, modes of arrangements, before the major migratory crisis of the mid-2010s questioned or upended some of these practices (Coleman 2009; Jorry 2007; Cassarino 2010).

Candidate members have to respect the Schengen regulations before joining the EU and well before becoming part of the so-called Schengen Area. The Union also increasingly imposed the adoption and respect of migration policy provisions on third countries that seek Association or Cooperation Agreements. Conditionality is accompanied by financial and technical incentives to help candidates and associates comply and to alleviate the task of their having to closely control their borders, both with the EU and with their non-EU neighbors. In some cases, requirements for local and regional cross-border traffic have been eased in order to allay the disruption created by the constitution of a Schengen "paper wall" at the EU's borders, for instance, between Hungary and Romania after the former joined in 2004, three years before the latter, or at the border between Poland and Ukraine, or Poland and Kaliningrad.[8] Visa procedures for nationals of these countries were facilitated. Commercial concessions, trade incentives, and the prospect of a free trade area (FTA) or so-called deep and comprehensive free trade areas (DCFTA) are also meant to entice non-European countries to follow suit.

Nonetheless, this policy of externalization placed the onus of border controls upon non-EU members, European neighbors, and Europe's neighbors, who were supposed to verify documentation, including visas that the EU requires, prevent illegal immigration, and deal with asylum seekers and migrants entering their territories. If they undersigned readmission agreements, they committed themselves to take in all those who entered the EU illegally through their territories. In a way, they became security portals. To escape this quandary, the countries surrounding the EU increasingly turned to their own neighbors to sign readmission agreements, Ukraine with Russia, Morocco with sub-Saharan countries, a geography that may vary according to the redirection of migration routes. They created what Sandra Lavenex dubbed a ripple effect (Lavenex and Uçarer 2004; Cassarino 2015). As border controls were pushed outward, the EU became surrounded by a series of outer borders, like concentric circles.

Contrary to what some analysts have suggested, the EU not only triggered a process of deterritorialization. It also reterritorialized. Certainly, borders controls have been deterritorialized, since checks take place in countries farther away, at airports, in harbors—though they are also performed within borders, at the Gare du Nord in Paris, for instance, when boarding the Eurostar (Bigo and Guild 2005; Jorry 2007). Yet at the same time, the Union restructured the territories on the continent and its wider periphery, creating rings of territories with which it entertained various legal, institutional, and political ties, and to which it exported different types of governance in disconnected ways. To some extent, it reproduced the policy of forward defense that characterized the Cold War era. NATO devised a forward defense to protect the alliance by waging or threatening to wage war well beyond its borders. Similarly, "forward security" was supposed—is supposed—to prevent migrants from reaching EU territories. The difference, however, lies in the fact that NATO, including its European members, was protecting Europe, while the EU is outsourcing its border controls. To that extent, the EU is more akin to the Austro-Hungarian Empire, which entrusted communities on its periphery, like the Zadrougas in Croatia and Slavonia or the Haiducs in Transylvania, with its defense against Turkish incursions (Nouzille 1991).

This policy on the part of the EU amounted to a "policy of remote control," as Virginie Guiraudon (2003) wistfully put it, from which the members of the Schengen Area expected to benefit. Outsourcing was to supplement the patchy controls that were operated by Schengen members. It was to reduce the costs of detention and repatriation of illegal migrants. It was a way to keep "illegals" at bay, that is, individuals without proper documents, whose claims EU governments and many in the public did not want to examine despite international conventions. It prevented oversight by national parliaments or the European Parliament (Cassarino 2010: 183; Lavenex 2006). Yet it entailed dire consequences. While the EU imposed more or less stringent conditions on future candidates and neighbors who had to implement Schengen rules and regulations, it discarded the higher principles of solidarity within the area, and solidarity with the refugees whose rights are to be heeded. The EU "schengenized" its policy toward its neighbors, and placed itself in the hands of governments, inside or outside the EU, some of them authoritarian, who were or are both unwilling to cooperate and willing to pressurize the EU.

Schengenization and the Loss of High Moral Ground

The main purpose of forward border controls by proxies, combined with the policy of cross-border connections through EMP, ENP, and their avatars, which was analyzed in the previous chapter, was to stabilize the borders and frontiers of the EU. Stability has always been a quandary that most empires faced, especially land-based empires, which had to secure borders and boundaries, as they grew more vulnerable with each expansion. Such control has been key to the expansion of empires, and to their rollback as well. Eventually, the EU came up with the same design that former empires had invented. It created boundaries *and* borders, concerned as it was—and is—by stability and the need to prohibit unwanted crossings and illegal flows. To stabilize its marches, east, south, and even north, the EC/EU had to anchor its neighbors, new and old, and breathe stability and prosperity into them, while preventing instabilities from reaching or overrunning it. It wanted to export stability, not to import instability. It tried to surround itself with a "frontier," in other words, not a borderline but an in-between, a *limes*, or marches, like those that formerly protected the periphery of the Roman Empire or that of the Central European empires, from Brandenburg and Krajina to Ukraine, which allowed connections *and* control at the same time (Maier 2006; Christiansen, Petito, and Tonra 2002: 391–393).[9] Blurred and hard borders together helped to create a belt shielding the Union from the outside world, from the *leones*, the lions, of medieval maps.[10] They devised graded boundaries.

On paper, the logic was compelling. In reality, it was faulty. It relied on the willingness of neighboring countries to abide by EU rules and policies. The EU was not necessarily the more potent partner, however, notwithstanding its structural power and policy of incentives. Neighboring governments, authoritarian or not, did not appreciate the lack of reciprocity, and deemed the compensatory offers too puny. To protest against the policy of securitization that the EU was trying to impose, some of the Arab leaders whom the EU called upon to enforce its forward security stayed away from the 2005 Barcelona conference, which was supposed to mark the tenth anniversary of the launch of the EMP with a statement on the fight against terrorism. The EU and its member states were in the position of supplicants that the neighboring governments exploited for their own sake. In the first decade of the new millennium, Colonel Gaddafi obtained funding from the European Commission in return for keeping migrants at bay, but the EU was hardly in a position to verify the conditions under which they lived. In 2009, Gaddafi obtained from Silvio Berlusconi, the Italian prime minister, $200 million a year over twenty-five years, which was supposed to finance infrastructure investments in Libya in return for reining in migration. This was followed by a similar deal with the European Commission in 2010. Gaddafi could pay stately visits to Rome, Paris, and Brussels and pitch his tent in front of the Elysée Palace (Human Rights Watch 2009; European Commission 2010a). Since the outbreak of the war in Syria, the EU has faced a similar quandary, playing into the hands of the Turkish government, as analyzed below.

The pact was devilish. The EU member states entrusted the surveillance of their own borders to nondemocratic, repressive, and sometimes murderous regimes, which could not be relied upon. Hence, they had to turn to other means. They constructed barriers, material and immaterial, paper walls and forbidding gates on land, and sent patrols to roam the Mediterranean Sea and repel migrants there. They required visas that governments at war with their own populations most probably do not deliver. They built fences, the equivalent of America's Rio Grande, around Ceuta and Melilla, the Spanish enclaves in Morocco, along the Eurostar route on the continent and in Great Britain, at the Greek and Bulgarian borders with Turkey, and, as of 2015, at the Hungarian border with Serbia and Croatia. In a number of cases, the EU's funding helped to build fences. Thus, Bulgaria started building a fence to protect its border with Turkey and deter illegal crossings in 2013 at the same time that the ERF was granting the latter €750,000 designated for refugees and €13 million in external border funding (European Commission, DGSs Migration and Home Affairs 2015).[11]

Democracy was lost in the meanders of outsourcing. The aim of controlling borders clashed with the claim to create cross-border interconnections, and conditionality became a tool to transfer border controls to neighboring countries instead of promoting democracy, human rights, and the rule of law there. Certainly, as seen in the previous chapter, other reasons concurred to gloss over democracy, but the fact is that the ENP became "schengenized." And not only did the EU and its member states come to rely upon regimes that were not democratic in nature, but they also disregarded the rights of migrants in two ways: they entrusted migrants to nondemocratic regimes, and they prevented them from reaching the shores of Europe, in obvious contradiction to international conventions that give refugees the right to illegally cross borders to flee persecution and war, and to humanitarian laws that require all to respect human life. Both citizens of neighboring countries and refugees were the first to be affected by the EU's lack of principles. In 2013, in Lampedusa, Pope Francis condemned the "globalization of indifference" toward the death of migrants. The Union had lost the moral high ground (Pope Francis 2013). And not only was its policy destructive; it turned out to be ineffective.

Displacement and Dislocation

In 2015, the number of refugees coming to the EU increased dramatically. That year 1.3 million migrants—economic migrants, refugees, and asylum seekers—reached the EU. More than a million arrived in Germany alone, and almost half a million applied for asylum, while Hungary registered the highest number of applications per inhabitant in the first half of the year (European Commission 2015a; Eurostat 2015; BAMF 2015).[12] Over 3,700 lost their lives at sea during roughly the same period (IOM 2015). The wave of new arrivals that reached the EU as of 2015 was not unpredictable. Since the end of the USSR, the Union had witnessed several peaks of migration: in the 1990s, when the Yugoslav federation broke up violently; at the turn of the millennium, especially in the wake of the wars in Iraq and Afghanistan; and in the second decade of the new millennium, with the decomposition of the Libyan state, the civil war in Syria, increasing violence in Iraq, Afghanistan, and Pakistan, a brutal regime in Eritrea, to name only a few countries where life has become harrowing, as well as in conjunction with the war in eastern Ukraine. Since the beginning of the Arab rebellions, the number of migrants has increased year by year.

The European border agency Frontex estimated that in 2014, 280,000 undocumented migrants crossed the external borders of the EU, up from 100,000 in 2010, and 140,000 in 2011 (Frontex 2015: 12). In 2014, 122,000 Syrians already constituted the biggest group of refugees coming to the EU, while about 14,000 Ukrainians applied for asylum there, ranking fourteenth behind other nationalities and stateless individuals (European Commission 2014b). The predicaments that confounded the

Union as it scrambled for solutions were predictable, too. Certainly, migration reached unprecedented proportions. Yet beyond the disintegration of states on Europe's surroundings, what has come to be called a "refugee crisis," and which is a migrants' crisis, was also an EU crisis insofar as it laid bare the lack of foresight and the unpreparedness of the Union and its member states, the lack of connections in a complex patchwork of partial and dysfunctional policies sketched over the past decades, and the discrepancy between international laws that require states to heed the rights of refugees and the policies of states themselves. All this eventually revealed the Union's incapacity, political, administrative, economic, and social, to deal with major influxes of populations over a short period of time. The EU member states contributed to the crisis through their uncoordinated policies or lack of policies, and their diverging conditions and calculations.

Aporia

It is true that states are constrained by an aporia, which arises from a clash between the moral imperative to protect refugees, "the right to have rights," as Hannah Arendt put it, embedded in post–World War II international laws, and national political obligations, considerations, and limitations (Arendt 1949: 34). The 1951 Convention Relating to the Status of Refugees, its 1967 expanded version, the New York Protocol, and the European Convention of Human Rights constrain the sovereignty of states. They give refugees rights, such as the right to cross borders illegally—and migrants also have rights, for instance, regarding family reunification. Certainly, according to Article 2 of the Convention Relating to the Status of Refugees, refugees have to respect the constitutional order and laws of the states that accommodate them—for instance, they have to register with the authorities once they have crossed borders. In practice, however, to what extent do refugees' rights dovetail with the obligations that fall upon states to preserve their constitutional order?

Governments, including EU governments, have to control their borders for the sake of maintaining order and ensuring the security of their citizenry. The preservation of peace, order, and security, and the protection of persons and property, are part of states' and governments' functions and obligations. Yet the definition of order and security is political and varies according to governments and majorities. In other words, it is open to various interpretations. It depends, among other things, on very practical short-term and long-term challenges, and on the way they are appreciated. Among these are the capacity to register and accommodate newcomers, to know who they are and why they fled their countries—that is, to distinguish between refugees and economic migrants, a status that is sometimes difficult to determine, and those who come or come back to Europe to sow violence—the necessity to teach migrants a new language, match their skills with vacancies in the economy, and integrate them, although some may fear a dilution of their identity and religion, and even hold very different views on gender relations, harbor prejudices toward Jews, or disregard the constitutional and legal requirements of the countries where they settle.[13] In short, integration is a two-way street. It relies upon the capacity and willingness of refugees to integrate into European societies, and the capacity and willingness of the latter to open up to them. All this is rendered difficult by the gap between liberal societies and the conservative background of some of the migrants, or between conservative societies in Europe, especially in Eastern Europe, and the rejection of Muslims; by the EU's economic travails; by the success or failure of previous integration policies; by attempts by radical Islamists in the EU to reach out to newcomers, especially those who are most vulnerable; and by the repercussions of wars and terrorist actions that affect and traumatize refugees, influence European public opinion, and boost political parties that exploit feelings of insecurity.

German president Joachim Gauck, a former Lutheran pastor, attempted to balance moral and political requirements when, at the World Economic Forum in Davos in January 2016, he underlined that "some, among the migrants, have not adopted all the fundamental principles that Europe cherishes. This is true in particular of some who come from Muslim countries or are of Muslim origin and do not share our views regarding the role of women, tolerance, the place of religion or our constitutional order"; and called for limiting migration: "A strategy that aims at limiting migration may even be morally and politically necessary to preserve the state's ability to function. It may be required in order for a majority to welcome refugees. To that extent, limiting numbers is not unethical *per se*: it helps to maintain acceptance. Without acceptance, a society is not open, nor is it willing to embrace refugees" (Gauck 2016).[14]

In short, moral imperatives and international obligations clash with national conditions, historical and political experiences and self-representation, institutional, economic, and societal resilience, and resources, depending on the number of newcomers that each country attracts. Consequences for domestic polities, policies, economies, and societal fabrics are difficult to assess. Massive new arrivals—the "refugee crisis"—stir strong feelings, and foster intense political debates. The policies to be followed eventually are a matter of political judgment. Answers are to be found only in an imperfect, unstable, and constantly changing equilibrium where moral imperatives have to be balanced against political constraints and practice. They create fractures within and between European societies and polities, fractures in which individual fates hang in the balance.

The Ides of August

Compounding this aporia, the mechanism of registering migrants broke down at the turn of the 2010s. After the ECtHR had ruled that the Greek government and institutions were not respecting the rights of refugees, other EU member states stopped deporting to Greece the refugees who had first landed there. In other words, the Dublin Regulations were suspended as early as 2011, as far as repatriation to Greece was concerned.

Yet neither the increase in the number of migrants nor the partial breakdown of the so-called European refugee policy triggered concern or raised alarm at the highest level of decision making in the EU and in most capital cities. The plight of refugees, Syrians in particular, in the Middle East should have led officials to conclude that they would seek a passage to Europe and, most probably, arrive in a country, Greece, to which the Dublin Regulations no longer applied. Agencies such as Frontex, cells such as the High Level Working Group on Asylum and Migration, created in 1998, international organizations, think tanks, and NGOs that gather intelligence, evaluate risks, and make forecasts certainly made proper assessments. But they did not attract the attention of decision makers. Information, a precious source of power, is often not shared. And it can be lost in the meanders of multiple crises that heads of states and governments have to confront. When asked why foresight had been glaringly missing in the years before 2015, an official from an important EU member state admitted that it is "difficult to do multi-tasking in times of crises." An EU high official retorted, however: "If it ain't, broke don't fix it!"[15] One would rather say: "If it ain't totally broke . . ."

The refugee crisis that turned into an EU crisis resulted from a series of decisions taken by individuals, administrations, and governments, which interfered and interacted with one another, creating ripples and waves from Syria to Turkey, from Greece to Germany, and back to the Middle East, the Balkans, and the EU. The cost of hosting migrants was becoming too high for certain countries in the Middle East. Five countries of the Middle East—Iraq, Turkey, Lebanon, Jordan, and Egypt—which for different reasons are fragile societies, harbored about 4 million Syrian refugees in 2015 (Amnesty International 2015). The help that the EU granted them was paltry, leading to a rapid deterioration in the living conditions of refugees. In spite of the fact that Turkey accommodates the greatest number of Syrian and Iraqi refugees—over 2 million—the EU allocated it only €44 million since "the beginning of the (current) crisis," according to the ECHO agency, while Ankara claimed to be spending €2 million a month (European Commission, Humanitarian Aid and Civil Protection 2015).[16]

Because of dire economic straits, and of the presence of important minorities—Palestinians in Jordan, for instance—host countries hardly offer refugees the prospect of integration. Lebanon has not set up camps, to discourage Syrians from staying. Refugees' rights were sometimes denied. Thus, Turkey does not extend the status of refugees to individuals from countries that are not European—as the New York Protocol requires—though it recognized a temporary status of refugees in 2014. One should underline, however, that while life may be difficult in Turkey, in particular for employed and underpaid children who feed their families, a number of Syrian entrepreneurs have also set up booming companies thanks to the lack of red tape. In any case, while Syrian and Iraqi refugees often stayed either in their country at war, as IDPs, or in neighboring countries, waiting for better times to return home, 2015 destroyed whatever hope remained, as extremist groups such as ISIS and Al Qaïda tightened their grip on the Middle East, and Russia started massive air operations in Syria targeting moderates' and civilians' positions rather than those of Islamist radicals. Facing a grim future, larger numbers of Syrians left for Europe.

While refugees packed to find a better life on the Old Continent, Turkey and Greece were the first barriers to fall. Turkish authorities let migrants depart from or cross Turkey without much supervision. Newspapers close to the government announced that Europe had to be "flooded" with refugees (Karagül 2015).[17] According to some European and Turkish observers, Ankara may have even intentionally eased departures to Europe in order to put pressure on the EU, and assuage criticism of Turkey's leniency toward ISIS, and hostility toward Syrian and Turkish Kurds. Meanwhile a myriad of individuals, including smugglers and passport forgers, contributed to the exodus from Turkey. Later in the year, at the other end of the continent, at the border between Russia and Norway, the Russian authorities also made a U-turn, and allowed into Norway undocumented refugees or refugees allowed to stay in Russia. They did the same at the border to Finland.

On the other hand, Greece, which had been severely castigated for its treatment of refugees, was not ready to jump in to guard the EU's borders, because of both principles and calculations. The new government that was elected in January 2015, a coalition of the left-wing party Syriza and the national conservative and populist Independent Greeks (ANEL), led by Alexis Tsipras, decided not to deport to their countries of origin those refugees who had not applied for asylum but who belonged to categories that needed protection—a measure EU member states were starting to implement, too, complying with international rules. More surprisingly at first, in addition Greece refrained from building up capacities, on the islands in particular, where scores of refugees were stranded. As it was facing a massive influx of migrants, Athens could have requested emergency support from the EU. However, it did not. Support might have entailed the dispatch of personnel who would infringe upon Greek national sovereignty, and material help for refugees might have stirred resentment in the Greek population, which had become embittered by years of austerity.

Whatever reasons may have led the government to shun help from the EU, as Angeliki Dimitriadi put it, "[it] abandoned the Greek islands to the NGOs."[18] This is only understandable if we surmise that Athens wanted to compel the EU to revise the whole mechanism that places on Greece—and a few other states—the onus of guarding the EU's borders. Building up capacity and facilities, and detaining economic migrants and asylum seekers in pre-removal centers, as the previous government had, would have been tantamount to supporting the so-called common refugee policy—which it later did. Also the government may have wanted to use the crisis as a bargaining chip to obtain more help from the EU to meet the heavy financial and societal costs of the migrant influx, and to ensure that it had room to maneuver in negotiating with international and European institutions regarding the financial and economic terms of a settlement in the Eurozone.[19]

While some transit countries on the Balkan route between Greece and the other EU countries started opening up their doors, Germany became, with Sweden, Austria, and Hungary, a magnet for refugees, the first three because of their generous asylum policy, the last because it was one of the main points of entry into the EU once the Balkans had been crossed. At the beginning of 2015, the German Federal Office for Migration and Refugees (Bundesamt für Migration und Flüchtlinge, BAMF), an agency of the Ministry of the Interior, decided to streamline the procedures for asylum seekers from Syria, Iraq, and Eritrea, because of their large numbers, because, as they were fleeing countries at war, their case was relatively clear, and because of a lack of means and a considerable backlog in the treatment of claims over the years. All this again played a role when on 21 August the BAMF ultimately stopped enforcing the deportation of Syrian refugees to the country of first arrival. Greece had contributed not only to the dysfunction of Dublin and Schengen, but also to the dramatic deterioration of the situation in Syria, and the costs and inefficiency of deportation ruled out any other policy. The BAMF merely formalized what had become a rule and a reality over the previous years. From then on, Germany opened its door to refugees and made it much easier for Syrians, Iraqis, and Eritreans to obtain asylum. The decision was an internal administrative decision. The German chancellor gave it a face and a voice.

Angela Merkel defended the decision to "suspend Dublin," and made the case for welcoming the refugees. She gave Europe a voice, the voice that the Arab rebels should have heard early on in 2011. On 31 August, while conceding that some confusion reigned, Merkel made a forceful statement reiterated in the months that followed: "We can do it" (Wir schaffen das). A few days later, Germany and Austria embraced the refugees who had remained behind as Hungary closed its borders.[20] We can only speculate about the reasons for the German chancellor's decision. Those who recalled the removal of barbed wire along the Hungarian-Austrian border in May 1989, leading to the liberation of Eastern Europe and the reunification of Germany and indeed of the continent, were shocked to see another Hungarian government erecting a fence. The chancellor referred to a "humanitarian imperative," an expression that her close confidant Peter Altmaier, head of the Chancellery and minister for special affairs, also used. Merkel further recognized that those EU member states where refugees first set foot, Greece essentially, could not be left alone to deal with a massive influx of newcomers. The decision was part of an attempt to refurbish Germany's image, which had been tarnished by the government's proausterity policy toward Athens. The widely circulated and influential newspaper *Bild* started the campaign "#welcomerefugees" to rebuild Germany's credit among EU members. Other reasons stemmed from longer-term calculations. In 2014, the chancellor had hailed Germany as *Einwanderungsland*, a country of immigration and diversity, to counter adverse demographic trends and the declining workforce there.

Domino Effects

The BAMF's decision, triggered by individual and political decisions in the Middle East, Ankara, and Athens, had immense repercussions in the Middle East, the EU, and individual member states. A few days later, the European Council on Refugees and Exiles posted the decision, making it accessible to a wider public in the Middle East (AIDA 2015). The trail of refugees increased over the latter part of the summer, in the autumn and winter, and well into the following months, covering half of the continent. Some of the consequences were worrying. Before the terrorist attacks in Paris on 13 November 2015, where individuals originating from Europe posed as Syrian refugees, and well before the violent and sexist incidents that a month and a half later marred New Year's Eve in a number of German cities, where scores of individuals of North African background harassed women, panic started gripping public opinion and public authorities in Europe.

First, capacities were rapidly overstretched. In Germany, despite the commitment and support of many persons and institutions, NGOs, football clubs, companies, cities, regional and national governments, the lack of administrative personnel, of the BAMF in particular, budget cuts, mismanagement, and the sheer volume of refugees coming in strained individual and collective resources.[21] As early as September 2015, the liberal president, Joachim Gauck, admitted: "Our capacities are limited"; and, a month later, the open-minded and pro-European managing director of the BDI, Markus Kerber, criticized the naïveté of those who believed that refugees could rapidly find employment (Gauck 2015; Kerber 2015). In November 2015, the Swedish Migration Agency declared it could no longer offer accommodation to all newcomers. Unease spread in Austria. However, the countries that suffered most from the massive arrivals were those between the Aegean Sea and the Austrian border. Greece had to register, host, and wave hundreds of thousands of migrants across its northern border before the latter's closure (see below). Farther north, Macedonia, the fourth poorest country in Europe, with only 2 million inhabitants, one of the five Balkan states outside the EU, experienced a daily inflow that rarely fell below 2,000 between August 2015 and February 2016, when borders were closed. None of the transit countries had the means to face a migratory wave of such magnitude, even those countries that, like Slovenia, had first embraced the newcomers with great sympathy.

Second, with this flow of people came disorder and dissatisfaction. Among the million refugees that Germany received in 2015, German officials surmised that about 200,000 individuals were unaccounted for. Similar concerns were raised in other countries, in Norway, for instance, a member of the Schengen Area that lost track of 1,500 individuals.[22] To borrow the words of officials or former officials, Germany had "lost control," and so had other countries. While xenophobic groupings or political parties stridently castigated Chancellor Merkel for her policy, doubts and criticism emerged from the midst of German and European societies and elites. Indeed, reactions were mixed, ranging in the summer of 2015 from outright welcome in Sweden and Austria, a country of choice and a country of transit, to hostility, in Hungary particularly. They varied over time, too, as the number of refugees swelled. Criticism became more strident in Sweden and even more so in Austria, where consensus frayed, the chancellor came under increasing attack, and a member of the right-wing party, the so-called Freedom Party of Austria (Freiheitliche Partei Österreichs, FPÖ), was almost elected president in May 2016.

Third, as EU member states started scrambling for solutions to control their borders and maintain a semblance of order, it became increasingly difficult to maintain cooperation and unity within the Schengen Area, and in the Balkans as well. Instead, EU member states and non-EU Balkan states engaged in a game of blaming and shaming other governments for their allegedly uncooperative behavior. Having amplified if not triggered the crisis in the summer of 2015, the German chancellor was held responsible for the chaos that gripped the Balkan states, from Greece to the Western Balkans.[23] She had claimed: "We can do it." Yet whom did "we" refer to: to the Europeans or to the Germans alone? The German chancellor may have assumed that other European countries would emulate her policy. In any case, she glossed over the consequences that massive transit would entail, especially for the poorer Balkan countries, EU members or not—as she had earlier done when deciding, in 2011, to gradually close down all the nuclear plants in Germany, a measure that had immediate repercussions on the country's southern neighbors. Greece also came under scrutiny. It was repeatedly criticized for lax controls that magnified the migratory wave, while in turn Athens reproached the EU for failing to fulfill its pledges of assistance (European Council 2016).

In the following months, domino effects occurred in reverse. In the fall and winter of 2015, border controls were reinstated. Germany was one of the first countries to reestablish border controls at the Austrian border in mid-September, at a time when about 13,000 migrants were reaching Munich every day. Fences were erected in Europe to organize an orderly passage, at the Austrian-Slovenian border, for instance. For the first time since 1958, the Nordic countries reintroduced border checks, disrupting smooth interconnections in the Danish-Swedish Øresund region, one of the fastest-growing areas in the EU. By March 2016, seven members of the Schengen Area, Austria, Belgium, Denmark, France, Germany, Norway, and Sweden, had reimposed controls on some or all of their borders with other Schengen states. Though allowed by the Schengen regulations, temporary reinstatements of border controls might bring about the demise of an area without internal borders, were they to last, and incur dramatic economic, financial, and even political costs.

Not only were border controls reinstated, but borders also closed. Hungary erected fences in the summer of 2015. Central European countries started shutting their borders. However, the situation was tenser in the transit countries of Central and Southern Europe, most of which do not belong to the EU and the Schengen Area. Their southern neighbors followed suit to avoid becoming dead ends on the migrants' journeys to nowhere. On 18 February 2016, the Austrian government vowed to limit to 37,500 the number of asylum seekers it would accept that year, leading its southern neighbors, Slovenia, Croatia, Serbia, and Macedonia, to tighten the screws. On 24 February 2016, the Austrian government convened a summit with nine Balkan states, excluding Greece and other EU countries, and restricted access to their territory to Syrians and Iraqis only. Considering Greece a weak link that did not properly filter migrants and distinguish between economic migrants and refugees, some governments toyed with the idea of ring-fencing Greece, or even ejecting it from the Schengen Area. Actually, the closure of the Macedonian-Greek border practically isolated the southernmost member of the EU. With some 50,000 migrants stranded there, Greece threatened, in the words of the minister of immigration policy, Ioannis Mouzalas, to "become a cemetery of souls" (Byrne and Robinson 2016).

Greek Woes and Turkish Whims or European Solutions?

However, the Commission and the European Council, which, more than the Council of the Ministers, has become the locus of decision, sought tirelessly for European solutions, most of which were hardly innovative. The chancellor herself had been relatively consistent since the crisis started raging—though she increasingly stridently vowed to contain the number of refugees (see, e.g., Bundesregierung 2015a, 2015b). Certainly, measures were taken at the national level, which the EU had to allow. The EU condoned the temporary restoration of border checks under EU law, and sent border guards to help countries like Slovenia and Macedonia. Simultaneously, EU governments lowered the minimal common standard allowance that refugees are granted, limited family reunification, and barred migrants from certain places that they do not consider at risk, such as North African countries and a number of areas in Afghanistan.[24]

More innovatively, in September 2015, the Council adopted legally binding decisions, which should have been applied to the EU as a whole. These decisions "established a temporary and exceptional relocation mechanism for 160,000 applicants in clear need of international protection from two Member States under extreme pressure Greece and Italy" to other EU members (European Council Decision 2015a, 2015b). The principle of relocation was endorsed after a vote in an Extraordinary Justice and Home Affairs Council, in September 2015, a rare occurrence indeed, since decisions are mostly consensual in the Council (European Commission 2015b). Four EU member states, the Czech Republic, Hungary, Poland, and Romania, opposed the compulsory system of repatriation, while Finland abstained.[25] Despite its opposition, Poland accepted the majority view, but backed away after the election of a Conservative government. However original the relocation scheme was, its implementation relied on EU-wide cooperation that was glaringly missing. By mid-March 2016, only 937 people had been relocated, thirty of them to France (European Commission 2016).[26]

In the absence of EU solidarity regarding internal border cooperation and relocation, a plan that started being hammered out in the fall of 2015 aimed at strengthening the external borders. Frontex saw its budget increase from €94 million in 2014 to €142 million in 2015. In April 2015, it launched a CSDP military operation EUNAVFOR MED, Sophia, to pursue vessels suspected of human trafficking in the Mediterranean, while a NATO Standing Maritime Group was deployed to patrol the Aegean Sea, as of February 2016, and provide Frontex with information on suspicious activities (Leggeri 2015; NATO 2016).[27] Actually, a NATO operation proved to be necessary to balance Greek and Turkish concerns over a border mission in the Aegean Sea. Yet this was a far cry from the European external border guard service that the Commission had repeatedly called for. Hence, once more, the makeshift solutions that the member states turned to primarily revolved around the gatekeepers.

Greece, the main point of entry since the early days of the refugee crisis, attracted not only criticism from the EU, international organizations, and NGOs, regarding poor refugee care—and also lax control, as far as the EU was concerned—it also received attention and help to improve its capacities. The Commission earmarked €700 million over three years to provide food, shelter, and sanitation—sending humanitarian aid to other transit countries as well—and the EU member states committed 4,000 specialists to serve in the reception and identification centers (RICs), the so-called hot spots, on the islands and the mainland to register migrants and tackle the backlog.[28] Nonetheless, improvement was slow to materialize, and the refugees face appalling conditions in the reception centers, which are practically akin to detention camps. Compounded with the closure of its northern borders, the country itself is confronted with "a political crisis in which the EU and the overwhelming majority of EU member states have abandoned Greece," as François Crépeau, the UN special rapporteur on the human rights of migrants, contended in 2016 (United Nations Human Rights Office, Office of the High Commissioner 2016).

Because of the slow progress at the EU's internal borders, some officials, the German chancellor first and foremost, surmised that to dry up quickly, migration had to be tackled upstream, in Turkey essentially, Syria's largest neighbor and the main point of departure of most migrants over the past years. In November 2015, the EU agreed to a €3 billion help package to Turkey, the opening up of new chapters in the accession negotiations, regular high-level political meetings, and the progressive liberalization of its visa policy toward Turkish citizens, in return for Turkey's readmission of illegal migrants and reception of refugees (European Council 2015). The agreement had a high price. The German chancellor had to whittle away principles and turn a blind eye to the nature of the Turkish regime. She paid a visit to Ankara, in October, at a very conspicuous time. The Commission had delayed the publication of a very critical yearly country report on Turkey, elections were to take place in Turkey in November, and President Erdoğan was lashing out at democracy and ridiculing the EU. Not all in the Union were ready to grant Turkey a key role that gave the regime the upper hand in the negotiations.

The agreement, however, remained a dead letter till 18 March 2016, when Angela Merkel and her Turkish counterpart, Ahmet Davutoğlu, hammered out a somewhat different version.[29] In return for accepting all migrants that Greece sends back, Syrians and non-Syrians, that is, those who would easily receive refugee status and those whose application would more likely be rejected, the EU pledged to resettle Syrians directly from Turkey to EU member states on a one-to-one basis, capping, however, the number of resettlements at 72,000, though the German chancellor had repeatedly rejected setting an upper limit (*Obergrenze*) in her own country. The EU doubled the sum to be allocated to Ankara in order to meet the needs of migrants in Turkey, provided that the country heeds their rights according to international law, and ensures them decent conditions. Yet the agreement struck on 18 March did not grant the Turkish government everything it asked for. Though membership negotiations were supposed to be "re-invigorated," Turkey did not meet the conditions necessary to open up new chapters except for one on financial and budgetary matters, or to allow full visa liberation. The EU's policy of visa liberalization toward any country requires the fulfillment of technical and political criteria. In the case of Turkey, visa-free travel to the EU, promised in the March 2016 agreement, was conditional upon an overhaul of antiterror laws that restrict press freedom. However, the Turkish president flatly refused. Last, EU's financial help has to be traceable, a reason the Commission intended to direct it through UN agencies and NGOs, whereas the strong, sovereign Turkish government insisted on being the direct recipient. In this case the Commission and the Council did not seem willing to flout technical conditions—all the more so since visa liberalization might increase the number of newcomers and stir concern in certain segments of the public and political parties.

Yet as in the past, the Commission and the Council disregarded higher principles. EU member states can send migrants back to Turkey only if the latter is deemed a safe third country for the migrants who are returned—that is, if the latter are granted all basic human rights, including extended protection, access to legal counseling, and the right to file asylum applications. The Law on Foreigners and International Protection, which was adopted by the Turkish parliament in 2013 and came into force in 2014, guarantees all these rights, yet its implementation falls short of all legal requirements, national and international, because of lack of capacities and experience, and because of past practices that endure. According to Orçun Ulusoy, a human rights lawyer, "Turkey is not a safe country for migrants, asylum seekers, and refugees and will not, at least in the near future, provide sustainable and durable shelter for the people fleeing from their countries to save their lives." Ankara has even returned Syrians to their country of origin in contravention of international law (Ulusoy 2016; Amnesty International 2016).

Generally speaking, the Turkish judicial system, which has not been overhauled despite serious shortcomings, the increasingly authoritarian turn of the regime, its ambiguous policy in Syria, and the abrupt end it put to the negotiating process with the PKK, rekindling a disastrous civil war in the east of the country, do not substantiate an EU policy that relies upon Turkey to cater to the needs and interests of refugees, nor to those of its own citizens—hence, it is not a third safe country of origin, nor is it safe for its own citizens. As the well-known Turkish liberal thinker Soli Özel wryly put it, "The EU has betrayed its own principles. The refugee crisis basically showed [that] when expediency demands it, hypocrisy is the rule, and commitment to principles is rather the exception"; Özel then added: "We [i.e., Turkish liberals] are on our own" (quoted in D. Jones 2015).

Hence, the EU and its member states face criticism that they have proceeded with mass expulsions of potential asylum seekers, in full contravention of international law. In May 2016, a Greek appeal committee objected to the return of a Syrian national to Turkey, which it deemed an unsafe country. As for the EU member states, they might once more default on hasty promises made on their behalf. Considering the past record of relocation from Italy and Greece to other member states, the resettlement program from Turkey to the EU that the 18 March 2016 agreement foresaw might never be implemented. For all these reasons pertaining to the evolution of the Turkish regime and the absence of principles and solidarity among EU member states, the agreement is as impractical as it is illegal with respect to international law. However, as always, other routes open up. Arrivals to Italy have soared again since the beginning of 2016, leading Rome to call for EU agreements with African governments, including the fragile national unity government in Libya. Indeed, the Libyan route is particularly frightening, not only for migrants but also for EU citizens and governments, since Daesh can make profits from trafficking. Once more, we see that the Europeans have chosen a short-term fix in lieu of a long-term strategy. A policy of resettlement pursued at the beginning would have provided a better outcome.

As shaky as it is, the March 2016 agreement sent a signal to those ready to pack. The number of arrivals considerably declined in the following weeks and months. Meanwhile, the agreement does not stand alone. Other policies are being put forth or implemented. Upstream, the EU or EU member states negotiated—or will negotiate—agreements with countries of departure, some of them at peace yet in need of development, such as Mauritania, which underwrote the aforementioned agreement in Spain, or Nigeria with which the EU Commission plans to start negotiating, and some of them at war. At the November 2015 EU-Africa summit, held in Valletta, Malta, the EU vowed to stabilize and pacify countries to restrict if not eradicate migration. However, the EU's record in contributing to the development of African countries is not particularly impressive (Balleix 2010). The EU also contends that countries at war should be pacified. Yet the semblance of negotiations over Syria, the success of which neither the Syrian regime nor its Russian and Iranian allies probably want, will not convince the population to stay. Considering the EU's limited capacity to influence its neighbors and countries farther away, the Union and its members should primarily work on what they theoretically can master, that is, common border policies, which the Commission and a small number of politicians in certain countries are calling for. The institution of a common border guard controlling the EU's external borders, decent reception camps, and a common EU asylum policy might, however, require a number of years before member states agree and implement, if at all.

Meanwhile, the agreement between the EU and Turkey laid bare the differences between the member states, as well as between the Commission and the German chancellor. Certainly, the EU-28 managed to reach a compromise, as they did during the Yugoslav Wars, to preserve a semblance of unity. They rallied behind Germany's chancellor, Angela Merkel, after having watered down some of her concessions toward Turkey. However, her decision to push for an agreement with Turkey bruised many in the Commission and the Council. These dissensions add up to the rifts that divide EU member states—and the states of the Balkans, some of which are candidate countries. Indeed, they reinforce cleavages that have emerged over the years: between proausterity governments and countries that suffer from the Euro crisis, and between governments in the East that criticize Germany's Russia policy and its refugee policy and those that follow Germany's lead somewhat more closely. In this crisis, Merkel has lost some of her aura and influence for having imposed policies or solutions repugnant to many.

This crisis, which undermines solidarity between member states, demonstrates the paralysis of EU institutions and national governments and gnaws at the democratic fabric of Europe. The EU is in a quandary. On the one hand, close as Europe is to continents wrecked by wars, failed institutions, and authoritarianism or tyranny, it is, more than other regions in the world, confronted with the demands of thousands of refugees knocking on its door. On the other hand, the EU and its member states are almost completely lacking the paraphernalia that would allow them to proceed with an orderly reception of migrants. They lacked the foresight and the will to go beyond the institution of the Schengen Area and the Dublin Regulations, which could not properly function without common migration, refugee, and border policies. Instead, they relied upon their internal and external periphery. The latter, Turkey in particular, professes to implement deals on its own, illiberal terms. The former, Greece first and foremost, runs the risk of slipping into utter despair. Paradoxically, however, the southern countries of first arrival seem so far somewhat more impervious to the success of populism than do countries that lie at the geographic or political core of Europe. There, from Hungary and Austria to France and countries farther north, the refugee crisis latched onto previous discontents that the estrangement of the political class, the economic destabilization of the working and middle classes, and conditions particular to each country—liberalization in the absence of sound institutions in Hungary, corporatism in Austria, or economic decline in France—had stoked for years. All this combined to nurture a deep resentment toward established parties and EU institutions. The refugees are paying the price.

6

COMPETITIVE DECADENCE?

Russia and the EU

A perverse dialectic sets in. Interdependence hinders the complete
severance of ties and prevents autarkic isolation. On the other hand,
however, this very interdependence entails vulnerabilities which can
fire back in case of sanctions.

—PIERRE HASSNER, "Feu (sur) l'ordre international?"

Under Vladimir Putin, Russia has become one of the most serious geopolitical challenges that the EU and the United States have to confront.[1]
Russia's annexation of the Crimean peninsula and interference in eastern
Ukraine signaled, in 2014, a turning point in the Kremlin's foreign policy, just as its military intervention in Syria demonstrated its recklessness,
in bombing moderates and civilians, and its determination to assert and
expand power.

Nonetheless, in the 1990s and early years of the new millennium, the
Kremlin had displayed an apparent willingness to cooperate with the
United States and the EU, intertwined with episodes of confrontation
and blatant violation of commitments. In the 1990s, Russia seemed on its
way to join the liberal, democratic world. Association with NATO, and
membership in the WTO, were on the map. Demanding that Russia "be
recognized as a full-fledged European nation," Boris Yeltsin (1997) even
went so far as to say: "We also are prepared to join the European Union."
The suggestion was fleeting. Membership in the EU was hardly realistic,

for good reasons. Russia, a huge geographical landmass, is too vast. Since the first decade of the new millennium, however, as Vladimir Putin's rule became domestically more ruthless, and externally more aggressive, the Kremlin has mounted increasing and ominous challenges to the very principles on which the international order, and, in particular, the European order and the EU, are based. Yet it is also chipping away at the solidarity of the EU insofar as the Russian regime finds support and fulcrums within the Union despite its aggressive policy to the east and the southeast of the continent. Why so? What are these challenges? Is the EU, together with the United States, responsible for having missed the opportunity to embrace Russia? Or did it simply misunderstand the strategic implications of its policy vis-à-vis a state that has increasingly come to challenge Western order and values? And what are the implications for the Union and its members?

With the demise of communism, both Russia and the EU confronted similar problems. Both had to adjust to the fall of the USSR. The EU had to embrace new democracies that counted on Western help to revamp their economies and polities, and on Western support to escape Moscow's grip. The tasks Russia had to tackle appeared even more daunting. The whole country had to invent a new economic and political system, and transform itself from empire into state. It had to delineate new borders, physical and psychological. Willy-nilly, it had to recognize new sovereign states that it had formerly controlled. It had to forgo assets in territories lost, gas and oil pipelines, industrial and nuclear plants, and military bases, while thousands of its former citizens were now stranded in new states. It had to invent a new script for a territory, still the largest in the world, yet deprived of what it considered its cradle, "Kievan Rus."

Hence, the relations between the two entities were encumbered by the need not only to devise new common borders or to grant a status to Russians stranded in new countries, but also to invent new relations with one another in a world in which Russia had to shed its imperial claims, and which bore the West's imprint—a Western order that Russia's smaller neighbors yearned to join.[2] As some Western analysts and officials, and many Russians, pointed out, the Europe and the West that Russia encountered in the 1990s were overbearing. Yet a renegotiation of this order would not have brought about significant changes, if only because it had to be grounded in international law—in other words, only a democratic

Russian regime could fully adhere to the principles upon which the existing European order was predicated.

This chapter will consider the lackluster policy the EU invented to try to embrace a Russia whose ordeal it did not fully understand, the backseat the EU took while NATO enlarged before it did, and the way it allowed its huge neighbor to use and misuse European weaknesses, before turning to Russia's revision of the post–Cold War and even Cold War order and the battle of Ukraine, which have unfathomable consequences for Europe. While EU-Russia relations will be at the center of this chapter, the role of NATO and that of the United States will, of course, be taken into consideration.

A Bigger Poland?

In the early 1990s, relations between Russia and the Union—or the West, generally speaking—were based partly on illusions on both sides, and partly on Western recognition that the way forward portended trouble. Having done away with communism and the Soviet empire, having put an end to the Cold War and the threat the USSR represented, and having unilaterally discarded a number of nuclear weapons in the 1980s and the 1990s, the new Russian leaders expected to be helped by the West. What they had not abandoned, however, was the thought or delusion that their country was still a great power. Russian illusions also nurtured or echoed Western ones. The new Russia that the first years of Yeltsin's presidency ushered in seemed to herald democracy, a market economy, and the rule of law. Yet Western hopes for a free and democratic Russia embedded in a new world order, and a new European "security architecture," were tainted with fear stirred by Yeltsin's increasingly erratic behavior. Russia was perceived as "a special mix of acute short-term problems and glorious long-term prospects" (Haukkala and Medvedev 2001: 25). Above all, officials, particularly in the United States and in Germany, were wary of the weaknesses and unpredictability of a country that had suddenly shed its empire. In her seminal book on US-Russia relations, Angela Stent quotes an official of George H. W. Bush's administration who contended that "dealing with a wounded rival was just as complex as dealing with a strutting one" (2014: 7).

To mitigate Russia's hardship, the West offered the newcomer membership in the international organizations it had invented after World War II, and tried to adapt to the new context. On the basis of the Helsinki Agreements of 1975, the Charter of Paris for a New Europe, which most European governments, Canada, the United States, and the Soviet Union signed in 1990, laid down the principles of a new European order to replace the bipolar system of the Cold War and turn the former CSCE into a permanent organization, the OSCE, that was to oversee treaties and commitments. NATO incrementally opened its door to Russia, displaying a lack of grand strategy as it ratcheted up its offers in ways that echoed the tentative opening up of the EU to the CEECs.[3] Russia also acceded to the IMF and the World Bank in 1992. Russian leaders held meetings with the G-7 from 1994 onward, and formally joined the group in 1997 before being expelled in 2014 as a result of its intervention in Ukraine. It became a member of the Council of Europe in 1996.

Certainly, doubts lingered concerning Russia's credentials as a market economy and as a democracy. John Major, the British prime minister, and Helmut Kohl, his German counterpart, were not favorable to Russia's formalized membership in an enlarged G-7—Russia had to wait a few years to be invited by Tony Blair. A group of eminent lawyers who reported on Russia's applications to the Council of Europe also concluded that it did not meet the standards expected from members (Bernardt et al. 1994).[4] Nonetheless, Europeans and Americans rewarded Russia before Russian leaders delivered. The country had to be welcomed and integrated, not isolated or shunned as Germany and Russia had been at the end of World War I. Western leaders, and public opinion in certain countries, in Germany particularly, were fully aware that "the Soviet Union remains the only empire in European history to fall other than in the convulsions of war or violent revolution. It did so, by and large, 'gracefully'" (Andréani 2010: 238).

The EU also tried to embrace Russia. It put on the table a Partnership and Cooperation Agreement (PCA), signed in 1994, borrowed from the European agreements that were concluded at the same time with the CEECs. The PCA created a political dialogue between the Union and Russia, involving biannual summit meetings of the Russian and the EU presidencies, a cooperation council at ministerial level, and a cooperation committee made up of the European Parliament and the Russian Duma.

It granted Russia the status of most-favored nation, with a significant proportion of Russian goods entering the Internal Market under the EU's Generalized System of Preferences (GSP), which was actually reserved for developing countries. Though painstakingly economic and very technical by nature, the agreement was also political, yet mainly unbalanced in that it did not treat Russia as an equal.

First, Russia did not get all that it asked for—for instance the status of a market economy, which it acquired only in November 2002, and a free trade area, to which the Russian government attached great importance. The latter is not within reach, as the two partners have very different standards and rules of governance; Russia did not join WTO before 2012, and since then it has been its worst offender. The PCA further reflected a variety of opinions, interests, and policies inside the EU, where southern countries were cautious in opening up their markets. Second, Russia was expected to adopt EC legislation, and the Commission included a suspension clause, were Russia to violate human rights and democratic rules. After Russian negotiators insisted that such a clause smacked of inequality, the EU mellowed and agreed to discussions each time a case might trigger suspension.

Through commercial intercourse, the extension of norms and standards, and a rhetoric of shared values, the EU purported to anchor democracy in Russia. Yet it never figured out how to balance equality and requirements—equality between the EU and Russia, and the requirements the EU meant to impose on Russia. Nor did Russia, whose government did not shy away from contradictions. It benefited from specific provisions reserved for developing countries while claiming to be a world power. Russian legislation incorporated elements of European legislation, albeit very selectively, though the regime rejected European norms as an imposition (House of Lords, European Union Committee 2008: 35; Bordachev 2003: 52).

Eventually, conditionality remained weak, and EU member states fairly meek. No sooner had the PCA been signed than the first war against Chechnya broke out in December 1994, delaying the PCA's implementation till 1997. The word "sanction," however, was not uttered. When the second war against Chechnya was launched in 1999, the foreign ministers meeting on 24 January 2000 agreed on sanctions that both the Commission and the General Secretariat had recommended, though stressing their lack of leverage. As Vladimir Putin took over from Boris Yeltsin, the same heads of state and government who had agreed to punish Russia paid their due respects to the incoming president.

On the whole, the PCA was a mere exercise in technicalities, some of them not negligible. Financial and technical help was put forward. TACIS, superseded by ENPI in 2007 and ENI in 2014, espoused the same guidelines as PHARE with more than €2.7 billion allocated between 1991 and 2006 in areas such as legal, administrative, and judicial reforms. It sought to involve Russian regions, local management and civil society, through the Democracy program, for instance (Delcour 2002).[5] When the PCA was put on hold, it was the only EU policy on offer. The EU was also instrumental in helping Russia and other states that had formerly belonged to the USSR to decommission nuclear weapons and production centers, destroy chemical weapons, and initiate the industrial transformation of former military cities.

All this could hardly conceal the lack of originality of the Union's policy vis-à-vis Russia. The Commission's approach was bureaucratic and cautious, and member states did not push for a policy worthy of the name, cultivating, as we will see below, their own relations with Russia, and jealously protecting their own remit. However, by the mid-1990s, it dawned on them, on Germany and France in particular, that a strategy had to be devised. By May 1999, at a summit in Cologne, the EU heads of states and governments adopted a Common Strategy on Russia—followed, six months later, by one on Ukraine (European Council 1999a).

Indeed, a strategy was a dire need. At the beginning of 1996, the liberal minister of foreign affairs, Andreï Kozyrev, had been replaced by Yevgeny Primakov, who insisted on reconstructing Russia's power and standing in the world.[6] Two years later, the financial crisis hurled Russia into economic and social chaos.[7] In May 2000, a new Russian president had been elected. After the chaotic last years of Boris Yeltsin's presidency, his chosen successor, Vladimir Putin, promised to restore order, to the relief of Russians and Westerners alike, and vowed to embrace Europe. In a famous speech delivered in front of the Bundestag, the German National Assembly, on 25 September 2001, Putin professed that Russia had made Europe its choice. A strategy was also necessary because the EU was about to include former Soviet satellites and republics, triggering protests from the Russian government, which in February 2004 refused to include the ten new members of the EU in the PCA, arguing it was losing exporters, clients, and subordinates—as it would do in the case of Ukraine, years later, when the EU was about to sign an Association Agreement with the latter in 2013.

Yet the strategy adopted in 1999 was a strategy in name only, a catalogue more than a strategy (Haukkala and Medvedev 2001: 65). An EU policy vis-à-vis Russia was still conspicuously missing. To assuage Russia over enlargement, the EU invited it to join the ENP. This turned out to be a diplomatic faux pas. As a former empire, a pole on the European continent, a country that yearned to regain its standing in the world and assert itself in the neighborhood, Russia could not be treated just as *any* in-between country. After all, the Union could also be called Russia's neighbor. The Kremlin turned down the offer.

In lieu of neighborhood policy, the EU and Russia devised the so-called Four Common Spaces, in May 2003, in St. Petersburg.[8] The Union was still trying to ratchet up its offer, still seeking to extend its norms and standards to Russia, but it had to scale back its ambitions. The first blueprint called for compatible rules and regulations; the final one, in 2003, for an open and integrated market only. Eventually, the Four Spaces, "a monstrosity of bureaucratic boredom," as Lilia Shevtsova wryly remarked, fell short of innovation and imagination (Shevtsova 2010: 216). The scheme was once more an enumeration of projects, from programs tailored for small and medium enterprises to sludge incineration in St. Petersburg.

The EU still sought to accommodate the Kremlin—up to a point. In June 2004, two years after the EU recognized Russia as a free-market economy, and a month after both issued a joint declaration addressing Russia's concern over enlargement, the Union demonstrated support for Russia's protracted accession to the World Trade Organization (WTO). In 2002, in parallel with the accession negotiations between Lithuania and the EU, an agreement was reached on transit conditions for Russian citizens traveling to and from Kaliningrad.[9] A few years later, in May 2006, visa facilitation and readmission agreements were concluded at the EU-Russia summit in Sochi, and came into force in 2007. In the two latter instances, Russia first put forth radical demands, claiming rights of transit through Poland and Latvia as well as Lithuania, asking for the extension of a visa-free regime for the Russians of the entire Kaliningrad region, and calling for a visa-free regime for Russians, before agreeing to less.

Who Lost Russia?

In its relations with Russia, the EU certainly lacked imagination—as did the United States. With the blessing of the Council, the Commission borrowed the recipes that it had applied in the neighborhood. It meant to institutionalize relations with Russia, based on a belief in shared values and a common future, and treated Russia as a junior partner that had to adapt. Only slowly did it realize that the Russian regime was not the partner it had imagined, and that increasingly it was becoming very difficult to deal with.

Certainly, one should bear in mind that since the demise of the Soviet Union the Russian government has never stopped being unpredictable, unreliable, and rogue in its dealings with its smaller neighbors, former republics, or satellites. Already in the 1990s, it had imposed trade sanctions on various neighbors and complained over the conditions of Russians in the Baltic states. It waged two wars to regain Chechnya, in 1996 and in 1999. At the OSCE conference in Istanbul in 1999, it promised to withdraw its troops from the two Georgian provinces of Abkhazia and South Ossetia and from the slice of Moldova beyond the Dniestr, Transnistria, but never abided by its commitments. In 1999, Russian troops made a curious and aborted attempt to overtake Western troops and seize the Pristina airport, in Kosovo, to steer the course of the war with Serbia. Yet, though grudgingly, Russia did choose to cooperate with the United States and the EU over the former Yugoslavia, and in the "war against terrorism." In 2001, Moscow welcomed Lord Robertson, the secretary-general of NATO. Pragmatic cooperation, whatever the expression meant, considering the glitches, became the new motto.

Nevertheless, divergences and discords became more palpable with the new millennium and Vladimir Putin's first, second, and third administrations and his stint as prime minister.[10] Threats, rhetorical or real, started punctuating the regime's discourse and policy, beginning with Putin's famous address to the annual international security experts' meeting in Munich in February 2007; the suspension in 2007 of Russia's participation in the Treaty on Conventional Forces in Europe (CFE), which had been signed in 1990 to put a ceiling on conventional troops on the continent, and later its withdrawal in 2015;[11] the cyberattack against Estonia in April 2007; the war against Georgia in August 2008; its characterization of NATO as a threat to international security; its hike in military expenditures as of 2012; its clamp down on Western-funded NGOs, as Russian citizens were demonstrating against Putin in 2011 and 2012; its blockade in the UNSC of Western proposals regarding Assad's regime in Syria after the start of the civil war in 2011; and finally its stealthy interference in Ukraine starting in 2014, and its massive interference in Syria in 2015 and 2017. All this boded ill for the future of EU-Russia and US-Russia relations.

Certainly, Moscow went on cooperating on such issues as the fight against terrorism, the war in Afghanistan, and, to some extent, on sanctions against Iraq and Iran, though not on Syria, and, in 2010, it ratified the Strategic Arms Reduction Treaty (START) that it had concluded with the United States to reduce strategic nuclear weapons. Yet with the involution of the regime, Russia's foreign policy became mostly noncooperative and difficult to fathom. It looked as if Vladimir Putin was launching a formidable challenge to establish Moscow as a veto power or a spoiler, a world power, and increasingly a counter-pole to the West.

It does not fall within the remit of this book to ponder at length the reasons that have guided and continue to guide Vladimir Putin's foreign policy. Others, specialists in Russian affairs, have done that well, linking in particular foreign policy to the nature of the regime, which some have characterized as fascist, or mafia-like, and to the tensions between so-called Westernizers and Slavophiles or Eurasianists. Nor is it our purpose to slip "into the head of Vladimir Putin" (Eltchaninoff 2015). Suffice it here to say that the post-Soviet regime never reconciled itself with the idea of a bygone empire. Though Boris Yeltsin vowed "to rid [Russia] of its imperial mission," Vladimir Putin is famous for having bemoaned, in 2005, the "major geopolitical disaster of the century," the "collapse of the Soviet Union," whose fate was intimately linked to that of many "left outside the Russian territory," and certainly to his own life (Yeltsin 1994: 115, quoted in Åslund 2013: 3; Putin 2005). Eleven years earlier, in 1994, the little-known former KGB officer and aide to the mayor of St. Petersburg had already lamented the loss of territories, "which historically have always belonged to Russia," and, in the year 2000, the newly elected president complained again about the great catastrophe (Ash 2014; Putin 2000).

In this respect, two facts stand out. Domestic politics and foreign policy are closely intertwined. Nurturing a siege mentality and the twin myths of humiliation and encirclement is a ploy essential to preserve the regime. As a corollary, the Kremlin is mounting a formidable challenge against the West and what it represents, in particular democracy, liberalism, and open societies. Rather than "faking" Western democracy, the Russian regime "disqualifies" what it calls a weak and decadent West, as Marie Mendras astutely put it (Krastev 2007, 2008; Mendras 2008). As examined in the latter part of this chapter, Ukraine epitomizes this twin concern.

This ideological brew is supposed to appeal to all those "post-Soviets" who bewail the loss of past times, and the demise of a greater Russia. It aims at reviving ties that bind beyond borders, turning to the Orthodox Church and comforting with passports those who have lost their nationality. This has sometimes been dubbed "soft power." It is in fact a hardball game, a fierce battle for influence that entails force if need be. And it is about establishing spheres of influence under the pretext of defending Russians abroad. It is about the control of policies and narratives in the neighborhood, in Europe, and farther away.

The Myth of Broken Promises

In this context, the regime's discourse about Russia having been humiliated in the years following 1989–1991 deserves particular attention, as it weighs heavily on the relations between Russia and the West at large. The Russian regime has created a powerful narrative of Western lies and broken promises, and stirred a controversy even among Western diplomats and intellectuals. Did George H. W. Bush, his secretary of state, James Baker III, and Chancellor Helmut Kohl extend to the Russian leaders a verbal promise not to expand NATO or to deploy NATO troops beyond the pre-1989 demarcation lines, as some politicians, civil servants, and academics contend (Matlock 1995; Baker 2002; Goldgeier and McFaul 2003: 183–185; Sarotte 2009; Stent 2014: 36–38; Braithwaite and McNamara, quoted in House of Lords, European Union Committee 2015: 35)? In his memoirs, Mikhail Gorbachev is ambiguous, but in an interview in 2014, he clearly denied that any promise had been made not to expand NATO farther east (Gorbachev 1996: 528–529; 2014). Western leaders, such as George H. W. Bush, his national security adviser, Brent Scowcroft, James Baker, and diplomats also deny such a promise was made

(Zoellick 2015a; Ischinger 2015). In 1990, NATO enlargement was not on the table, since the Warsaw Pact, its counterpart, still covered Eastern Europe. The only commitment that was made was to refrain from stationing NATO forces, weapons, or bases in eastern Germany. NATO's enlargement may have breached the spirit, if not the letter, of the 1990 Cold War settlement (Andréani 2010: 241). Nonetheless, Moscow had the opportunity to voice discontent when Russia joined the Partnership for Peace (PfP) with NATO in 1994, and when the NATO-Russia Council was constituted in 2002. Boris Yeltsin acquiesced to NATO's enlargement, but disagreement was also aired against what Yevgeny Primakov called a "big mistake, possibly the biggest mistake since the end of the Second World War" (quoted in Mankoff 2009: 166).

This begs two remarks. First, the Western allies, the United States above all, had to make an inconvenient choice between heeding the concerns of a seemingly humbled former superpower and supporting the new democracies of Central and Eastern Europe, which could not be left in an uncomfortable in-between situation, so close to their former dominator. The new democracies needed guarantees. Russia needed consideration. The West made the mistake of not understanding Russia's thirst for certainty and recognition, real or instrumentalized. However, it could not let down the new democracies and allow the Kremlin to rewrite the rules of the game at the cost of smaller states. As German defense minister Volker Rühe said in 1993, "We cannot save reform in Russia by placing reform in Central and East-Central Europe at risk" (quoted in Stent 2014: 38). In any case, NATO forwent a significant and permanent stationing of troops on Russia's borders in an agreement with the Kremlin from 1997, and troops were absent—aside from bilateral agreements and limited use of facilities—till 2016 when NATO members started deploying manpower and material in Eastern Europe.

Actually, Russia was not threatened by NATO's successive waves of enlargement. It is difficult to understand how the population of the biggest country in the world, which comprises eleven time zones and dwarfs most of its neighbors, may feel encircled. Yet it cannot be denied that the American administrations and EU governments took unilateral steps, from the strikes against Serbia in 1999 to the recognition of Kosovo in 2008, from Washington's withdrawal from the Anti-Ballistic Missile (ABM) Treaty in 2002, to facilitate the deployment of missile defense capabilities in Europe, to the war against Saddam Hussein's regime in Iraq beginning in 2003 and the decapitation of Gaddafi's regime in 2011. Some decisions may have been right; others, terrible mistakes. Some, such as Kosovo's recognition, were taken after long, convoluted negotiations with Russia. Others ignored Moscow. In any case, they bolstered the Russian government's argument that Russia was left out of security arrangements. This is certainly true, but the Russian government never offered any counterproposal.

This is precisely the second remark that the debate on "broken promises" calls for. No Russian government made any meaningful effort to rebalance by peaceful means what it perceived as asymmetry. Certainly, before and after the war in Georgia, in June 2008 and in April and November 2009, President Medvedev and his government pleaded for a new security system encompassing the whole continent (Medvedev 2008). The proposal was, however, unpalatable, too vague for the West in terms of substance, and too crude in terms of intention, since it would have loosened ties between the United States and the Old Continent. Instead the so-called Corfu process was set up to improve the efficiency of the OSCE, the sole security organization that could pretend to span the continent, but it never materialized, as the Kremlin did its best to paralyze it. All other attempts to reformulate the rules of the game that the West had devised were made in defiance of international law, and increasingly relied on force.

The discourse on "broken promises" is part of a wider narrative to cow the West and mesmerize spirits in Russia. It is selective at best. Vladimir Putin superbly manipulates feelings, blending personal sufferings, the humiliation of people losing their status and bearings in the 1990s, and the political hiccups of the so-called democratization and liberalization process of the Yeltsin years with the loss of the empire, while at the same time glossing over the sufferings and destruction that the Soviet Union had wrought. The discourse is unbalanced as well. The Kremlin orchestrates an anti-Western campaign while commentators in the United States and the EU openly debate the West's responsibilities. Last but not least, it is bitterly ironic that the Kremlin managed to orchestrate such a powerful narrative, echoing Germany's humiliation after World War I, whereas the West, the Germans and the Americans in particular, was wary of nurturing a Weimar syndrome (Zoellick 2015b).

Wahlverwandschaften, Passions, and Interests

Till the war in Ukraine, the EU was deeply divided over Russia, and divisions still furrow the Union, though member states aligned themselves behind Chancellor Merkel's policy after the annexation of Crimea. Of course, geography and history shape representations. Well before 2014, Russia was resented and feared by its closest neighbors, while farther away, in other European countries, it conjured up a promising Far East and sometimes resonated like a close relative. History, affinities, passions, and interests subliminally define intellectual discourse and public attitudes. In the Baltic countries, 9 May 1945 is a day of sorrow, as the president of Latvia Vaira Vike-Freiberga daringly recalled in Moscow, in 2005, at the ceremonies commemorating the sixtieth anniversary of the end of World War II, which Paris and Berlin happily celebrated with Russia. For the past two centuries, the France of Voltaire and Diderot cultivated a sustained interest in Russia, and found in it an ally against Germany. In the twentieth century, the mighty communist parties of France and Italy flirted intensely with the Soviet revolutionaries. Yet French and Italian curiosity pales in comparison with German affinities for Russia, for no other country in Europe entertains such a rich, complex, and ambiguous relationship with Russia.

German-Russian relations have a long and convoluted history, from the numerous German city planners, craftsmen, officers, and diplomats who served successive czars to the upheavals and abominations of the twentieth century, the complicity between two outcasts and two great powers that aspired to influence and recognition in a Western-dominated world, and the enmity they entertained till the very bitter end. The Treaty of Rapallo that the two post-World War I pariahs signed in 1920, the drilling of German troops in the USSR at a time when Berlin was forbidden to rearm, the Molotov-Ribbentrop Non-aggression Pact in 1939, the battles and extermination campaigns that decimated populations in the "blood lands" of Europe, the fall of Berlin at the hands of Marshal Zhukov in 1945, the loss of Eastern territories and the flight of Germans from the advancing Red Army, the carving out of what was to become the GDR, anticommunism and *Ostpolitik*, none of this suffices to represent all the strands of German interest in and passion for things Russian (Snyder 2011).

So-called *Wahlverwandschaften* (selective affinities) refer not only to literary encounters but also to the complicity between two cultures, thought to differ from Western civilization, to borrow from the distinction between *Kultur* and *Zivilisation* that Germans and Russians drew. The war that Nazi Germany waged on its Eastern front was far more destructive than the war in most parts of Western Europe, a mayhem for which many Germans still entertain a guilt tainted with awe for the Red Army, which devastated, looted, and raped Germany. East Germany, on which the USSR imposed its regime, harbored the last reform-minded communists in the Soviet-dominated countries, as communism alone defined its identity, while a nonnegligible part of the German population toyed with the idea of a third way between East and West, and some of the West German pacifists from the 1950s to the 1980s fell prey to Soviet manipulations. And though anticommunism shaped public discourse and political behavior and policies in West Germany, pragmatism, interests, and sometimes fascination led West Berlin and Bonn to open up a dialogue with East Berlin and Moscow to soothe the fate of divided Germany, and induce communist governments to relax their grip. Nevertheless, some of the very architects of *Ostpolitik* forgot civil societies in Eastern Europe. Herbert Wehner, for instance, a member of Willy Brandt's Social-Democratic Party, scolded Solidarność in the 1980s for challenging Moscow and "rocking the boat."[12]

Reunification strengthened affinities. As one intellectual underlines, it was as if Germans marveled at the fact that Russians did not expect repentance and concessions.[13] Certainly, respect was paid to those Eastern European societies that fought for freedom. Yet Moscow's consent mattered most, and Mikhail Gorbachev became Germany's hero. Reunification also nurtured further rapprochement, as both countries were undergoing profound transformations, compounded by anti-American resentment rampant among parts of the German intelligentsia and the political establishment, left and right (Stelzenmüller 2009). The consolidation of German-Russian ties also unfolded against the backdrop of a lingering blindness to the fate of the smaller countries in the in-between. All those strata of history and memories nourish romanticism and confusion, and betray the fascination and admiration, mixed with contempt and awe, that Germans nurture vis-à-vis Russia. All this shaped German attitudes toward Russia.

German public opinion has nonetheless displayed little sympathy for Vladimir Putin and his policies, especially since the turn of 2004, Mikhaïl

Khodorkovsky's imprisonment, or the assassination of journalists. It has become increasingly critical of the regime (Adomeit 2014; Köcher 2014; Le Gloannec 2007). Polls taken after Russia's annexation of the Crimean peninsula, in the midst of the Kremlin's subversive actions in eastern Ukraine, showed that 55 percent of the German public deemed Russian policies dangerous, while 76 percent thought that German-Russian relations were at risk (Köcher 2014; Infratest Dimap 2014, 2015). After the downing of a civilian flight over Ukraine in July 2014, 52 percent of Germans interviewed favored robust sanctions, while 39 percent opposed such a move (Klimentyev 2014).

Even more remarkable was the amazing mobilization of intellectuals, journalists, historians, and sociologists, who raised their voices against an army of sycophants, so-called *Putinversteher* (Putin sympathizers), trolls, and disinformation professionals. A series of blatantly biased talk shows on ARD, one of Germany's major TV channels, and a petition more sympathetic to Russia than to Western policies, prompted blame from historians such as Karl Schlögel, an Eastern Europe and Russia specialist, and Heinrich August Winkler, most famous for his four-volume magnum opus on the history of the West (Schlögel 2014; Winkler 2015).

Paradoxically though, a sizable segment of the German public, 49 percent—more in the east than in the west of Germany—want their country to be neutral, and advocate a policy of "equidistance" between Russia and the United States (Köcher 2014; Infratest Dimap for ARD; Jungholt 2014).[14] In spite of the uproar following the invasion of Ukraine, and the criticisms of intellectuals, the battle of ideas and the battle for minds are far from over. More than a battle of ideas, one should rather speak of manipulation of information and facts to confuse citizens, skew perceptions and shape political events. In 2016, for instance, a sizable contingent of Germans who had emigrated from Russia organized vocal demonstrations after allegations that a German-Russian girl had been mishandled by refugees, and the Russian foreign minister went so far as to take up her cause.

Some of the political, intellectual, and business elites in Germany also remain ambiguous. Though Chancellor Merkel could hardly conceal her distrust of the former KGB spy in Dresden, three former chancellors, Helmut Schmidt, Helmut Kohl, and Gerhard Schröder, moved by different concerns, expressed understanding for the Kremlin's policy, its annexation of Crimea, and resentment over the West's so-called broken promises, against the backdrop of estrangement from the United States, linked with the intrusiveness of American surveillance and spying in Germany.

Compounding affinities and influence, interests that bind German companies to Russian ones are numerous. Up to 2015, Germany was Russia's third market, after the Netherlands, which imports twice as much from Russia as Germany does, and China. Germany is Russia's main provider after China. It accounts for about 20 percent of EU-Russian trade. Yet Russia ranks as only the eleventh commercial partner of the EU. With less than half of Germany's imports to and exports from Russia, France lags behind Germany, China, the Netherlands, and Italy, and in relative terms, Russia's main partners are former Soviet republics or satellites, or small trade-dependent Western European states (European Commission, Directorate-General for Trade 2013). On the whole, Russia accounts for only a small percentage of the imports and exports of Germany, France, and Italy. Yet the latter have woven strong ties with Russia. Total, Renault, Schlumberger, and BNP in the case of France, ENI—Gazprom's first client—Finmecanica, and Alenia Aeronautica in the case of Italy, and Germany's E.ON Ruhrgas, Siemens, Hochtief, Mercedes, BMW, and Volkswagen, among others, are all present in the Russian market, which is vital to them. Some German sectors and companies specifically depend on the Russian market, for 350,000 jobs total in 2014, before sanctions were raised against Russia (BDI 2014: 14). In the first decade of the new millennium, these extensive ties led the German government, and later the European Commission, to try to devise a policy of influence through interdependence, a policy that might have succeeded had the Kremlin been genuinely interested in introducing reforms.

Modernization without Liberalization

After it became obvious that the Russian regime was tightening its grip in 2004–2005 onward, the EU abandoned its mantra of shared values and replaced it with pointed, albeit meek, criticisms of human rights' violations. Yet an overarching framework was missing. The German government devised it. Paris and the Commission followed suit. Engaging Russia was the name of the game. More than other governments, the German and the French governments had been forthcoming toward Russia, accepting, for instance, the Kremlin's objections to NATO's immediate enlargement to Ukraine and Moldova in 2008. Engaging Russia meant, domestically, helping it to modernize, and internationally, turning it into a responsible stakeholder. In both cases, Germany and France were seizing what they considered to be overtures coming in particular from President Medvedev. More than his overbearing prime minister, the president called for modernization, seemingly suggesting that this could lead to respect for the rule of law, and democracy. Medvedev also echoed previous Russian attempts at modernizing with Western—German—help, in particular under Peter the Great.

Making the most of a closely knit network of interests and passions, of knowledge and tight connections, the German government shaped a policy of *Annäherung durch Verflechtung,* rapprochement through interrelations. This smacked of the *Ostpolitik* of the 1970s, when, with France trailing behind, Germany devised its own version of détente, and sought to change the Soviet Union, the nature of its regime, and its international behavior by *Wandel durch Annäherung* (change through rapprochement). The new *Ostpolitik* placed modernization at its core. Yet coined by the foreign minister of the grand coalition in Berlin (2005–2009), Frank-Walter Steinmeier, it was much more modest. Though requiring increased transparency and lawfulness in business practices, it did not boast about infusing Western values. In any case, as in the 1970s, it was the German government that forged a policy vis-à-vis Russia. As a French analyst put it, "The Germans connect the dots; the French do not."[15]

This prompted the EU to follow suit. Previous EU policies had failed. They had not succeeded in convincingly embracing Russia as "one of us" while trying to impose conditions on it. Conversely, the Russian regime was not cultivating democracy and a market economy. Rather it was transforming itself into a rent-seeking oligarchy, fostering conflicts in its surroundings. The renewal of the PCA stalled in 2007, when Poland and Lithuania blocked negotiations, to retaliate against Russian stoppage of oil deliveries to Lithuania and import of Polish meat—though negotiations resumed in 2008 before being upended by Russia's intervention in Ukraine. The Common Strategy had petered out, and the Four Spaces were not holding their promises. In quest of a new policy, "engagement through modernization" seemed to entail promise. It might have fostered modernization, promoted economic interests on both sides, and sown the seeds of law and freedom. On 1 June 2010, at an EU-Russia summit meeting at Rostov-on-the-Don, both partners agreed upon a partnership for modernization, and bilateral partnerships were signed with individual member states on specific issues. Germany, for instance, cooperates with Russia on energy efficiency, health care, logistics, training, and commercial law.

Modernization, however, was no panacea. Short of reforms, what remained were isolated technological projects, such as the so-called Russian Silicon valley, Skolkovo, and limited undertakings, which could not kick-start the modernization needed. As one author put it, "However important in Russia, no number of commissions, working groups, orders and regulations even with budget allocated to their implementation can produce the miracle of modernization" (Larionova 2010: 40). In other words, the Russian regime conceived modernization as a makeshift for reforms, as the Soviet regime had in the 1960s. It kept relying on energy: in the mid-2010s, gas and oil revenues represented 50 percent of Russia's revenues (EIA 2014). The gas industry accounted for 5.6 percent of Russia's GDP, probably unofficially more (Globalsecurity.org 2012). The pillar of a "Gazpronomy," it has become a tool in the hands of the Kremlin to make political inroads in the EU (on Gazpronomy, see Shevtsova 2007: 141).

Divide and Rule

Gazprom relies on European buyers. It sells most of its production to Europe and about 60 percent to the EU. In the latter part of the first decade of the new millennium, roughly 40 percent of Gazprom's entire profit was generated by exports to Germany and Italy. Conversely, in 2012, Germany imported 37 percent of its gas from Russia, and Italy 29 percent, without, however, depending much or solely on Russian sales for their gas import, let alone for their energy mix (EIA 2014).[16] Furthermore, Gazprom needs to access Western financial markets, investments, and technologies in order to exploit new fields, for instance, deep-water gas fields, lest they remain inaccessible, or to develop liquefied natural gas (LNG). This endows Western economies with a crucial advantage that has come to the fore in the mid-2010s when the West barred the export of spe-cific technologies to Russia after the latter invaded Ukraine.

Nevertheless, Russia also benefits from a particular advantage, that is, the constitution of a political-energy complex, as one formerly spoke of a military-industrial complex in the USSR. The Kremlin used Gazprom as a tool to pursue a systematic policy that established Russian dominance in certain EU member states or in the "shared" neighborhood—and it still does. Hence the so-called overall interdependence between seller and buyers that some Western experts extolled did not do justice to the many intricate asymmetries, which created imbalances playing into the hands of one party, the more centralized and opaque one: Russia (Mandil 2008).[17]

The Fuel of Division

Gazprom, a heavyweight in the Russian economy in spite of a fake, Potemkin-like liberalization, owes its European dominance partly to the vagaries of history and geography, and partly to a systematic policy of control.[18] His-tory and geography placed Russia and Gazprom, as the successors to the Soviet Union and to the Soviet Ministry of Gas Industry, at the center of a network linking Central Asian gas producers and the Russian state, a pro-ducer and transit route, to Eastern European states that are both transit routes and consumers, and to the processors, distributors, and consumers in Central and Western Europe.

In the late 1960s and in the 1970s, the USSR started exporting gas to Austria, Germany, and Italy, as an extension of its deliveries to Central Europe. Two decades later, it began moving downstream to sell added-value products to West European markets. The first joint venture between the German oil and gas company Wintershall and Gazprom, Wingas, was created in 1993. Building upon this foundation, Gazprom, or the Kremlin, developed a strategy that seemed carefully designed and imple-mented over the years to take control of transit routes, and buy shares in a number of companies operating gas pipelines, hubs, storage facilities, and distribution in the former Soviet republics and satellites, the Bal-kans, and the EU. To pursue its strategy, it sometimes resorted to dubious intermediaries and deals (Łoskot-Strachota 2009: 22; Eyl-Mazzega 2010; Hyndle-Hussein 2014).

The expansion of westward exports and of downstream investments had a commercial rationale at first. The prices on the international market were higher than on the domestic and Eastern European markets, where prices were subsidized, and investments in value-added products brought better returns than the sale of gas at the borders of importing countries (Stern 2005: 127). The logic changed after the demise of the USSR, when the former Soviet republics and satellites became independent. According to Vladimir Milov, a former deputy minister of energy who resigned in 2002 and became a fierce critic of the government's energy policy, the Soviet Union had been "seeking effective monetarization of its . . . natural gas reserves," while Russia wanted to "establish . . . [its] economic and political domination in Europe" (Milov 2008: 6).

Domination or influence took different forms. The size and degree of dependence of foreign markets on Gazprom, and the political relations governments entertain with Russia, endow the Kremlin with different types of leverage on its surroundings and on the EU. Gazprom retains a monopoly in its former republics and satellites, outside or inside the EU, and decides upon the price. A graph published in 2013 revealed that Belarus paid then the lowest price, and Ukraine, Poland, and Macedonia the highest (Gawęda 2013; Tagliapietra and Zachmann 2015; Nemtsov and Milov 2008: 23). Economic geography alone hardly explained the differences. Political reasons did. In 1992 and 1993, the Kremlin avowedly linked the reduction of gas supplies to the Baltic states to the status of Russian civilians and military there. As far as Ukraine is concerned, Gazprom diminished its gas deliveries in 1993, prior to discussions over the stationing of the Russian fleet in Sevastopol. Some of the most contentious disputes between Moscow and Kiev involved the cut-off of deliveries to Ukraine in 2006, in the winter of 2009, and after the start of the Russian subversion of Ukraine and the decision, taken by the Kremlin years earlier, to build new transit routes bypassing the former Soviet republic, to increase its leeway (Socor 2009; Eyl-Mazzega 2010).

A number of governments of these captive markets have tried to free themselves from Gazprom's grip. As of 2014, Lithuania anchored a floating liquefied natural gas (LNG) terminal in the port of Klaipeda. Baptized Independence, it provides the Lithuanian market with 20 to 25 percent of the gas it consumes, and sells small quantities to Estonia. Even President Yanukovych, supposedly Moscow's ally, repeatedly tried to loosen the noose and approached Western companies to invest in shale gas, even though he also toyed with the idea of selling part or all of the Ukrainian GTS to Gazprom.

Conversely, the Kremlin cajoles allies. It granted the government of Viktor Yanukovych low gas prices when the latter agreed to renew the lease of the Sevastopol naval base in 2010. In Southeastern and Central Europe, Gazprom struck advantageous deals. Some governments in the EU have been keen on nurturing close relations to the Kremlin and to Gazprom, in particular the government of Viktor Orbán. Austria, Bulgaria, Croatia, Greece, Hungary, Serbia, and Slovenia all signed agreements with Russia to build South Stream, a gas pipeline that would have connected Kazakhstan and Russia to Southern and Southeastern Europe, up to the hub of Baumgarten in Austria. This project successfully prevented the construction of Nabucco, the pipeline that the European Commission had been advocating to circumvent Russia.[19]

Not only has the Kremlin been leaning on the internal periphery of the EU, but it has also acquired influence over core states such as Germany, Italy, Austria, and France, where certain sectors and companies depend on Gazprom and Russia for supply security, benefits, and employment. Actually, big gas companies in the EU are Janus-like multinationals, former public utilities still looked upon as national champions though they follow the logic of their own economic and financial interests, whereas Gazprom is a global conglomerate working for the sake of a regime. As national champions, they can bring pressure to bear upon their respective governments and shape their governments' policy toward Russia. These companies have sometimes become objective allies of Gazprom, accentuating the fragmentation of the EU, which plays into the hands of the Kremlin.

The construction of Nord Stream across the Baltic Sea encapsulates the Kremlin's strategy of "divide and rule," pitting Germany's sectorial and national interests against Ukraine and Poland. The gas pipeline started operating in 2012, circumventing the two eastern countries to ensure direct delivery of Russian gas to Germany. German companies were—and are—following a commercial and financial rationale, and do not heed the geoeconomic and geopolitical concerns of neighboring governments wary of losing transit fees or facing unexpected cut-offs in Russian deliveries. Yet the German government that signed the basic agreement with its Russian counterpart in a publicity stunt in September 2005, a few days before the German elections, should have.[20]

The Commission Strikes Back

Until the first decade of the new millennium, the EU tried to engage Russia in multilateral frameworks that it devised or helped to devise: through the PCA, which included a vague wording on energy cooperation; through an EU-Russia "energy dialogue" launched in the year 2000, which called for legislative "approximation," the opening up of markets, and improvement in investment climate; and through the creation of an early warning mechanism, following the gas dispute between Russia and Ukraine in 2009, that was never triggered. The Union also prompted Russia to join the Energy Charter Treaty, which was signed in 1994 and came into force four years later, to break the mold of bilateral relations (Energy Charter Secretariat 2004: 44). Fearing that it would have to open its pipelines to third partners, the Russian government never ratified it, and withdrew its signature in July 2009, a few months after a confrontation with Kiev, three months after it aired an international counterproject to the charter, as vague as the Medvedev security plan, and two weeks after the signing of the now-defunct Nabucco Inter-governmental Agreement. Moscow signaled it would abide only by Russian rules.

The heteroclite nature of the EU energy market, an aggregation of national markets and companies of various sizes, power, and influence, further weakens Western Europe's clout. Decision making is split between the Commission, that is, the Energy, Competition and Trade Directorates-General (DG), and governments and companies. The functioning of the energy market, supply security, energy efficiency, and the promotion of renewables fall within the remit of both Commission and member states. However, the EC obtained some competences over the years, in particular regarding cross-border energy infrastructure (Trans-European Networks, TENs) and environmental policies. The fact that the European market must be treated as a single market constrains energy companies in the EU. Last, the Commission has also been able to wrest power for itself, in particular in alliance with new member states. In any case, qualified majority voting is the rule, which increases the Commission's clout.

In parallel, though lacking external energy competences, the Commission acquired a key external role, though tampered with or even hampered by member states and companies. Not only does the Commission derive power from the very existence of the Internal Market and the regulations that bind all the economic actors, including foreign ones present in this market. It also seeks to export to its neighborhood regulatory norms and practices through policies and programs, in particular through the Energy Community and the Energy Community Treaty it started signing in 2005 with neighboring countries, chipping away at Russia's dominance in these countries.

This has a bearing on Gazprom. First, the constitution of a common energy market requires that all members, actors, companies, and consumers in the EU and in the Energy Community have equal access to deliveries through third party access (TPA), banning the old practice of Gazprom, which forbade the resale of gas to third parties. After the annexation of Crimea by Russia in March 2014, Slovakia and Ukraine concluded a deal under EU supervision to redirect, through reverse flows, limited quantities of the gas that Bratislava purchases from Gazprom. Second, the Commission questioned Gazprom's price policy within the European market. In the fall of 2011, it launched the first stage of an antimonopoly inquiry against the Russian company, echoing similar inquiries into EU and non-European corporations, and, in 2012, it opened a formal investigation at the behest of Lithuania, which pays the highest price of all European Gazprom clients (European Commission 2012a). After several years of the initial probe, the Commission raised legal charges against the Russian company in 2015, potentially adding to the sanctions undertaken by EU governments against the Kremlin in the wake of the Ukrainian crisis. Third, the so-called Third Energy Package adopted in 2009 imposed unbundling, that is, the separation of energy production and transmission systems, and dismantling of vertically integrated companies that cover the whole range of tasks from exploitation of resources to retail sales. Fourth, legal tenders have to be publicized and transparently awarded, and swapping shares is not allowed in order to undercut corruption. Consequently, the Commission required from members and neighboring states that they revise their bilateral agreements with Russia that infringed these rules. States in the Balkans were and are particularly concerned. This led the Kremlin to discard South Stream in 2014, with a good deal of bravado.

However, the Commission often collides with the defense of national or sectorial interests of member states, which the Kremlin instrumentalizes to override the general European interest (Hanson, in House of Lords, European Union Committee 2008: 53). Unbundling, for example, met the fierce criticism of Berlin and Paris in particular, which espoused the staunch opposition of their national energy champions. Bluntly put, Russia stealthily sat at the decision table in Brussels. A compromise was finally reached: without insisting on full unbundling, the Energy Package required the independence of national regulators and the creation of an Agency for the Cooperation of Energy Regulators. The Energy Union, to which Jean-Claude Juncker and Donald Tusk, respectively president of the Commission and president of the European Council, gave shape in 2014, remains relatively puny (Fischer and Geden 2015). In the case of the reciprocity clause, dubbed "Lex Gazprom," Article 11 of Directive 2009/73/EC stipulates that it is up to member states to decide whether they allow investments by a vertically integrated third-country company. The Commission has only a consultative power. One of the most far-reaching proposals, the centralized gas purchase by EU authorities, has also been discarded on the ground that it infringed anticartel laws and smacked of politicization, as Berlin and Paris contended. Nonetheless, small, pragmatic steps such as reverse flows and the construction of transnational grids show a way forward. Will, however, the Commission be determined enough to apply market rules to the Russian-German Nord Stream II agreement? In any case, as seen below, economic weapons do not seem to be able to measure up to military weapons.

The Battle of Ukraine

For years, Ukraine has been one of the major obstacles preventing Gazprom from controlling all transit routes toward the EU. Whoever was in power, protégé or opponent of the Kremlin, Kiev refused to sell Ukrainian infrastructures to Gazprom, though President Yanukovych almost accepted.[21] Twice it reasserted its independence: in 2004, when Ukrainians protested against rigged elections that President Putin had sought to manipulate, and in 2013–2014, when they took to the streets again, and overthrew Viktor Yanukovych, who, under Russian pressure, had refused to sign an agreement with the EU. The first revolution died of internal contradictions and incompetence, which the Kremlin certainly stoked. The Kremlin's answer to the latter was more dramatic. It invaded part of the country by stealth and force.

As early as 1995, Ukraine had insisted on EU membership, which the reluctant European public and some equally reluctant EU member states dismissed as unachievable or undesirable. The Kremlin, however, could not afford to lose Ukraine. Much has been written on historical and cultural connections between Ukraine, the cradle of Kievan Rus, and Russia. On the eve of Ukraine's revolution and invasion, Vladimir Putin recalled with a tinge of passion and nostalgia the blood ties linking Russians and Ukrainians while a somber-looking Ukrainian president, albeit officially allied with the Kremlin, stood by (RIA Novosti 2013). Interests also mattered, such as access to the southern seas, oil and gas reserves off Crimea, and underground gas storage facilities, built when the country was part of the USSR. Ukraine is an important transit route for gas and oil, though Moscow has built pipelines to bypass it, as mentioned above. It is also likely that more or less murky political and economic networks straddle the border.

To define Ukraine as constitutive of Russian identity and interests depends, however, on Russia's political makeup and aims. Were a democratic government to take hold in Moscow, the definition of Russian identity and interests would probably be different. From the perspective of a regime bent on cementing its power, Ukraine is a frontier and barrier against Western influences and democratic contamination. For Vladimir Putin, to "lose" Ukraine portends the subversion of empire and power. As the Bulgarian analyst Ivan Krastev shrewdly put it, the 2004 Orange Revolution that ousted Moscow's candidate, and brought into office a kind of democratic regime, translated into Putin's "9/11" (Krastev 2005). It was later echoed by demonstrations in Moscow in 2011–2012, and in Kiev in 2013–2014. The downfall in February 2014 of Viktor Yanukovych, however duly elected in 2010, rattled the Kremlin.

Since the demise of the Soviet Union and the creation of a largely symbolical Community of Independent States (CIS) in December 1991, successive Russian governments have relentlessly invented institutions to draw Ukraine into an economic and political union. A toothless free trade area was signed in 1994, and a customs union with Belarus and Kazakhstan concluded in 1995, which Kyrgyzstan and Tajikistan later joined. It was with Vladimir Putin, however, that the contours and content of a so-called union comprising Russia, Belarus, and Kazakhstan started taking shape, a Eurasian Economic Community in 2000, and a Eurasian Customs Union

(ECU) in 2010. Comprising these three members, they were to be the first step toward a much more ambitious project, a Common Economic Space in 2012, and the Eurasian Economic Union (EEU) as of 2015, endowed with a Commission and a court. As the Kremlin tried to enroll new states, Ukraine would have been its crown jewel.

After the Orange Revolution, which had brought about a messy, conflict-ridden, not entirely democratic, and certainly corrupt yet relatively open regime, Brussels signaled its readiness to embrace Ukraine, albeit cautiously. Ukraine had joined the WTO in 2008, and was offered an Association Agreement including a DCFTA in 2007. The Kremlin did not show much concern then (House of Lords, European Union Committee 2015: 53). Vladimir Putin did not mention Ukraine in the biannual EU-Russia summit, a high European civil servant recalls, while his foreign minister, Sergei Lavrov, complained once or twice. Nonetheless, as the date approached for the treaty to be signed at the Eastern Partnership summit in Vilnius, in December 2013, the Kremlin began exerting massive pressure on Kiev. It launched a trade war against the country in July 2013, barring the import of many products, from steel pipes to chocolate (Åslund 2013). The "chocolate war" was by no means a sweet one. In parallel, the Russian authorities tried to lure their Ukrainian counterparts with the prospect of lower gas prices and a $15 billion loan, which Kiev could not obtain from the IMF without groundbreaking reforms.

Russian pressures and incentives compounded the political costs of the Association Agreement and the DCFTA. Not only did the agreement require the adoption of far-reaching economic reforms, and EU norms, it also insisted on free and fair elections, the reform of the judicial system, and the liberation of political prisoners. Yet reforms were hardly acceptable to a kleptocratic and corrupt regime in dire straits. On 23 November 2013, the Ukrainian government announced that it would not sign the DCFTA. A few weeks earlier, the Armenian president had also abruptly backed down from an agreement with the EU. Only Moldova and Georgia initialed the agreements at the Vilnius summit. This volte-face set off demonstrations that never stopped till blood was shed in Kiev on 21 February 2014, when the regime evaporated within hours, leaving behind, shattered and in shambles, a wrecked economy and a cleaved society. After Yanukovych's demise, the interim government signed the Association Agreement with the EU, and a few months later, in June 2014, the newly elected government of Petro Poroshenko underwrote the DCFTA.[22]

The Ukrainian government had misunderstood the writing on the wall. Like its Belarusian counterpart, it tried to navigate between East and West, and assumed that it could stifle popular yearning for Western standards, and a better and dignified life (Razumkov Centre 2013a, 2013b). Meanwhile, the tug-of-war between Moscow and the EU resulted from the pursuit of mutually exclusive aims, which both parties couched in technical terms. The Russian regime argued both that the ECU would bring Ukraine more economic advantages than a costly DCFTA, and that association with the EU would damage the EEU. All Western experts agree that DCFTAs involve short-term losses because they require vast economic restructuration, but will foster competition in the mid- and long term. A DCFTA would prompt Ukraine to diversify, increase standards to access the largest world market, and improve the investment climate, while the ECU would merely provide short-term relief to an embattled government and a sinking economy, hamper the modernization of an economy that would have to go on relying on energy, agricultural resources, and outdated industrial production, and leave it to Russia's whim to manipulate the terms of deliveries and imports (Movchan and Shportyuk 2012; Movchan and Giucci 2011; Åslund 2013; De Souza 2011; European Commission 2012b, 2014b).

As to the second argument, it is true that Ukraine could not both increase customs duties, as required by the ECU, and lower them within the DCFTA. On the whole, EU and EEU standards may prove incompatible, all the more so as some EEU members have not joined the WTO (House of Lords, European Union Committee 2015: 66). Discussions between the ECU, that is, Russia, and the Commission on such questions might have eased differences—and such discussions actually started *after* the invasion of Ukraine. Yet technicalities were not at the center of the dispute. Rather, the future orientation of Ukraine was at stake (European Commission 2014b). The incompatibility between the two Unions was political.

This is what most in the West misunderstood, at least till December 2013, when they still believed that Kiev would sign the agreement in Vilnius. The analyses that came from the High Representative and from the Commission ignored the political stakes. A few understood the stakes but were not able to attract attention at the highest level. The Polish foreign minister, Radosław Sikorski, was one of the very few to fear Kiev would tighten the screws. Absorbed as they were by the turn of events in Syria, most EU governments, however, considered the DCFTA routine.

Even then, they did not deem it necessary to "sell" it, in particular to ease restructuration and reforms—a pattern one finds in other neighboring countries. Meanwhile the EU member states keen on embracing Ukraine may have intentionally ignored the political implications that could scare those closer to the Kremlin. While for a long time both the Russian government and the EU did not spell out, or did not want to understand, the implications that the Association Agreement and the DCFTA had for Moscow, the Kremlin seized the initiative in the summer of 2013. It framed the battle over Ukraine. It framed it as a zero-sum game, DCFTA vs. ECU, EU vs. EEU, them vs. us. Not even then, however, did the EU conceive a counterstrategy.[23] It might have raised the quotas of goods imported from Ukraine to offset losses resulting from the embargoes, as it later did when Russia forbade the import of Moldovan wine. Instead, it merely softened its demands for political reforms, choosing to focus on the liberation of Tymoshenko, as controversial as she was.

Some events were certainly unpredictable: the Maidan demonstrations, for instance, the use of force, and Viktor Yanukovych's flight. Yet borrowing Christopher Clark's metaphor, the House of Lords contended in its excellent report that the EU "sleep-walked" into the crisis (House of Lords, European Union Committee 2015: 6; Clark 2012). The EU ignored geopolitics. When some did take note, however, in Central and Eastern Europe in particular, they glossed over it lest Western European governments withdraw their offer. There was no strategy, no prevention. Eventually, Russia imposed its choice: the return of power politics. Certainly, the Commission did not bear the sole responsibility for this dramatic failure. As Jean-Luc Demarty, the director-general for trade, underlined, the trade agreement with Ukraine "was not something decided by obscure trade officials: it was an initiative that was taken with the unanimity of member states at a metapolitical level" (quoted in House of Lords, European Union Committee 2015: 63). The EU and its member states erred collectively.

The Battle of Europe

Having failed to prevent Ukraine's turn to the West, the Kremlin countered, in May 2014, by launching the Eurasian Economic Union with Kazakhstan and Belarus. Yet without Ukraine, it was a "union minus."

Moscow went on applying pressure on Kiev, threatening it with gas cuts, and retroactive increases in prices that added to the country's debt burden. More ominously though, it upped the ante after Yanukovych's fall, and resorted to military threats, infiltration, and intervention. It did not recoil from pursuing what came to be called a hybrid war. It applied old and new instruments, deploying troops and organizing military exercises at the Russian-Ukrainian border, stealthily sending mercenaries, unmarked soldiers, special forces, and military intelligence, transferring sophisticated weapons to Ukraine, and launching cyberattacks and disinformation campaigns against a country it knew well. It engineered the secession of Crimea in March 2014, and fomented rebellions in the east of the country. All of this sent ripples farther west into the Union's neighborhood, the EU and the transatlantic alliance.

The year 2014 and the battle over Ukraine marked a watershed in relations between Russia and the West. With hindsight, the war over Georgia looked like a rehearsal of the battle over Ukraine, testing the Europeans' and Americans' will or unwillingness to defend the EU's neighborhood. Yet both wars also differed in means and scope. While in 2008 the Kremlin resorted to disproportionate violence against Georgia, in 2014 it displayed caution *and* audacity in the use of multifarious tools and nefarious proxies (Independent International Fact-Finding Mission on the Conflict in Georgia 2009; Bērziņš 2014). And more than the war against Georgia, the Russian intervention in Ukraine marked a revision of the post–Cold War and even Cold War orders, defined by a number of international covenants, treaties, and agreements to which the Soviet Union and Russia had subscribed.[24] Russia reneged on its international commitments and violated the international rules on which the international order is based. The battle for Ukraine was the battle for Europe.

For some time, the West's answer was subdued because of the Union's division over its eastern neighborhood and over Russia. Yet as the battle over Ukraine intensified, opposition subsided. It slowly dawned on most Europeans that the Kremlin was pursuing what gradually seemed to be the *Reconquista* of Ukraine. The Western answer was two-pronged, involving sanctions against Moscow and military support to Eastern European NATO members while launching and pursuing negotiations with Russia. After the annexation of Crimea in March 2014, the American administration and the EU raised sanctions targeting individuals close to Vladimir

Putin. Following the crash of a civilian airplane shot down over rebellious territory in July 2014, and the massive incursion of Russian soldiers in eastern Ukraine a month later, both the American administration and Europeans hardened their stance. Further waves of sanctions, decided in July and September 2014, hit large-scale investment plans, and prohibited the export of goods and services in the energy, financial, and defense sectors—followed by some Russian countersanctions. Never before had the EU taken robust sanctions against Russia. Certainly, some had been raised when the second war against Chechnya was launched in 1999, albeit limited and immediately rescinded as Vladimir Putin took over the presidency. After the war in Georgia in 2008, sanctions were swept aside. Hence, sanctions in 2014 marked a break with the past, commensurate with Russia's offensive.

A military buildup within NATO underpinned the sanctions. At the NATO summit held in Newport, Wales, in September 2014, the heads of states and governments decided to set up a strong rapid reaction force (RRF) to be deployed within forty-eight hours. After the Obama administration announced in February 2015 that it had quadrupled its military spending in Eastern Europe, the NATO defense ministers agreed to boost the RRF, and to install command-and-control centers in Latvia, Estonia, and Lithuania, as well as in Poland, Romania, and Bulgaria, and antimissile sites in Romania and Poland. Materiel is to be prepositioned, infrastructure enlarged, and exercises conducted, and troops are deployed, a commitment reasserted at the July 2016 NATO summit in Warsaw. Bilateral agreements between NATO member states compound NATO undertakings. Troops are to rotate. At Newport, Chancellor Merkel, who promoted the RRF in which Germany actively participates, opposed the permanent deployment of NATO troops on the territory of new members, arguing that this would contravene the 1997 NATO-Russia agreement. During the Cold War, the stationing of NATO soldiers on German soil had constituted the ultimate protection against a Soviet invasion, the trip wire that would have triggered war and, hence, prevented it. The measures taken should compensate for the lack of permanent deployment.

On the other hand, the West, the Europeans primarily, launched negotiations. During the winter of 2013–2014, European politicians flew to Kiev to convince the leadership to relent, just as the Lithuanian and Polish presidents had done at the time of the Orange Revolution. After blood was shed in February 2014, the German, Polish, and French foreign ministers tried to convince the old guard to bring about changes, though Viktor Yanukovych's flight caught them unawares. The German chancellor spent a considerable amount of time speaking with the Russian president, and within the so-called Normandy format, involving Ukraine, Russia, France, and Germany, that emerged from the D-Day celebrations in Normandy in June 2014, she encouraged the parties to the conflict to sign, in September 2014, the so-called Minsk I Protocol, and in February 2015, a Minsk II agreement.[25] Both agreements called for a cease-fire, the monitoring and surveillance of the Ukrainian-Russian border, and decentralization of power in Ukraine. Minsk II entailed far-reaching concessions to Russia, including the drafting of a new constitution for Ukraine, devolution of power and the holding of elections in the rebellious areas of Donetsk and Luhansk, the resumption of social transfers from Kiev to the rebellious areas, and provisions that were impossible to implement, such as respect for the Ukrainian-Russian border.[26] At the time of writing, none of these provisions have been implemented, and some of these might never be, such as the restoration of Ukrainian sovereignty in the eastern part of the country. However, a cease-fire has held more or less since September 2015.

Pursuing this twin policy of strength and negotiations, reminiscent of the dual-track approach devised in the 1960s toward the USSR, which aimed at rearming and devising a new strategic concept while opening up channels of communication, Chancellor Merkel has played a crucial role in inflecting US policies, shaping EU actions, and rallying Germans and Europeans behind her. She backed military reinforcement, short of permanent deployment that might have fostered escalation, which she carefully avoided—even though the Kremlin had violated the European order and the 1997 NATO-Russia agreement. She imposed sanctions while having to reconcile very different interests and diverging viewpoints both within Germany and within the Union. In Germany, she is constrained not only by public resistance to the use of force, but also by her partner in the grand coalition, the Social-Democratic Party (SPD), which sometimes harbors strange sympathies for the Kremlin, and the business community. She is further bridled by some of her partners in the European Council. In June 2014, the Austrian president, Heinz Fischer, met with Vladimir Putin, and Austria's main oil and gas company, OMV, signed a contract with Gazprom. Yet France under President Hollande stood together with

Germany, in spite of strong pro-Russian, and even Putinophile, undercurrents in the establishment. It agreed to cancel the delivery of two Mistral-class amphibious assault ships, agreed upon by former presidents Nicolas Sarkozy and Dmitri Medvedev.

Nonetheless, the postponement of Minsk II encapsulates the lack of blatant success of Western policies. On the one hand, the Kremlin has suffered some setbacks: it has lost the minds and hearts of Ukrainians, at least in the western part of the country; the economy bears the burden of sanctions, compounded by the fall in energy prices and Russia's shortsighted reliance on natural resources; and without Ukraine the EEU remains puny. A year of negotiations between Brussels, Kiev, and Russia instigated by Berlin, and supported by the president of the Commission, Jean-Claude Juncker, to synchronize the DCFTA with EEU ended in a stalemate—though the door is not closed. The DCFTA entered into force in January 2016 while the Russian authorities scrapped its FTA with Ukraine.[27] On the other hand, Vladimir Putin has not suffered from being a spoiler on the world scene, as some in the West contended, but rather basks in the sun of regained strength. He has managed to split Ukraine. Before the war, eastern Ukraine did not aspire to join Russia, it merely wanted to cultivate ties with it (Razumkov Centre 2014; Pew Research Center 2014). The war and the intense propaganda eastern Ukraine is subjected to, as well as Kiev's mistakes, may have deepened the rift with western Ukraine. Meanwhile, though force mesmerizes spirits in western Ukraine, a very low intensity conflict bleeds Kiev financially, and destabilizes it politically, stoking dissensions between oligarchs who fund pro-Ukrainian militias in the East, and reformers who want to eradicate corruption.

While a cease-fire hardly holds, Moscow reignites conflict and tensions at will while pressuring Ukraine economically and financially. Before a round of Normandy negotiations, in February 2016, combat escalated in Ukraine—and Syria—and Russia engineered surprise maneuvers in the Black and Caspian Seas. Combat resumed in the winter of 2016–2017. As in Georgia, Russian forces and authorities hold the ground so that they can devise the rules of the game to lull the Europeans into lifting sanctions through negotiations.

In the tug-of-war between the West, particularly the EU, and Russia, Vladimir Putin has consolidated his own position, at least as far we know. The myth of "the besieged fortress," and the "restoration" of Russian "grandeur" thanks to the annexation of Crimea and the "defense" of Russians abroad, boosted the president's standing among Russians. Vladimir Putin may not be invincible: he may have wanted to invade greater swaths of Ukrainian territory, and he may have sent Russian planes and troops to Syria partly to compensate for the absence of overall victory in Ukraine and economic woes in his own country. However, compensation alone does not account for the systematic expansion of Russian raw power to its west and south. The military buildup, which started at the beginning of the decade, the scope and breadth of military exercises at the country's western and southern borders, dangerous incidents caused by military planes violating NATO members' air space, an increasing presence in the Baltic and Black Seas, all point to a strategy of air and sea denial, designed to evict the Atlantic alliance from Russia's doorstep.

This lays bare Western weaknesses. Though sanctions hold at the time of this writing, cracks have appeared within the EU and within countries. For instance, as German companies and politicians advocate the construction of Nord Stream II, and companies such as the Deutsche Bank skirt sanctions against Russia, Berlin may be accused of applying double standards by the Italian government, which also seeks privileged ties with Moscow, or by the governments of Poland or of the Baltic countries, which resent Angela Merkel's opposition to the permanent deployment of NATO troops on their territory. To that extent, the West's belated decisions to prop up NATO members hardly paper over critical deficiencies undermining Western defense.

Russia's buildup must be considered within the broader framework of a policy of gradual penetration and undermining of the West, and of the EU in particular, some aspects of which were analyzed in this chapter, and which goes well beyond military and economic ventures. It is also about ideological invasion and denial. All this is beginning to be documented (e.g., Reitschuster 2016). Moscow musters financial and intellectual resources to reach out to parts of the elites and public opinion in EU member states. Funding of political parties, and corruption, seem to belong to the Kremlin's arsenal. Media and the Internet disseminate targeted information and disinformation. Putin's supporters are to be found in different parties and countries: from Germany's social democracy, whose former chancellor Gerhard Schröder approved the construction of

Nord Stream I just before losing the national elections in 2005 and taking up a position at Nord Stream, or extreme-right European Patriots Against the Islamisation of the West (Patriotische Europäer Gegen die Islamisierung des Abendlandes, Pegida), who coined the motto "Merkel to Siberia, Putin in Berlin," to traditional conservative or right-wing parties in Hungary, Italy, and France, where Victor Orbán, a former flamboyant critic of Soviet occupation, Silvio Berlusconi, a three-time prime minister of Italy between 1994 and 2011, and Marine Le Pen, president of the National Front, who contracted a credit with Sberbank, partly owned by the Central Bank of the Russian Federation, and subjected to EU sanctions, all admire the strong man in the Kremlin—at a time when a new American president shows a strange inclination toward the Russian regime. While all or most countries in the Union may be affected by this hybrid campaign, one stands out, Germany, where disinformation has been particularly multifaceted, leading a number of commentators to ponder Vladimir Putin's aims and suspect an attempt to destabilize the chancellor. After all, as Lenin is supposed to have asserted, "he who controls Germany, controls Europe."

CONCLUSION

Can the EU Survive in a Postliberal World?

Things fall apart; the centre cannot hold;
Mere anarchy is loosed upon the world,
The blood-dimmed tide is loosed, and everywhere
The ceremony of innocence is drowned;
The best lack all conviction, while the worst
Are full of passionate intensity.

—WILLIAM B. YEATS, "The Second Coming"[1]

An era of anarchy emerged in 2014–2016, compounded by nationalism, populism, and authoritarianism. It was rooted in a culture of xenophobia, resentment, and identity politics, and in the rejection of globalism, trade agreements, international institutions, supranationalism, and perceived interference from outside, which nourish renewed violence, domestic and international. The transgression of European borders, invasions and wars, policies of brinkmanship, disinformation campaigns and manipulation of facts and minds, worldwide shifts of tectonic plates, and, not least, the rise of terrorist attacks, involving sometimes a very limited number of casualties but striking enough to awe people who fear that "terrorists are among us," have disrupted the relative peace that prevailed in Europe for a few decades. Russia's invasion of the Crimea in 2014 and the violation of international covenants, the refugee crisis that reached a peak in 2015, displayed the EU's lack of foresight, and gave some European governments and societies a pretext to close borders and minds, and, in 2016, the British referendum on EU membership, which demonstratively opposed the free movement of people and rejected anything that smacked of infringement on sovereignty, all marked the end of an era, against the backdrop of rising illiberalism in Europe and elsewhere, from Turkey to the United States.

For the first time since the fall of the Berlin Wall, countries in Europe's surroundings are ablaze, from Libya to Syria, while, from the Baltic states to Moldova, European countries increasingly denounce Russia's pressure—though a few countries, members of both EU and NATO, turn to Russia rather than looking to the West. Instead of building a "ring of well-governed states," heralded by the ENP and the ESS, the neighborhood has turned into "a ring of fire," as former Swedish foreign minister Carl Bildt wryly put it in a speech delivered in 2015.[2] For the first time in decades, Europe and the EU are threatened from within, not only by radical Islamists but also by an extreme right that undermines democracy. Never before has the contempt for democracy, the rule of law, and the rights of individuals fallen on as propitious ground as it does now in a number of EU states and societies. For the first time in Europe since the Second World War, democracy, the glorious horizon of progress that the "end of history" epitomized, is not taken for granted any more. For the first time in almost seventy years of existence, the EC/EU is a source of rejection more than of attraction to citizens and countries from inside and outside, except for the citizens of poor and corrupt countries on the continent, who want to overhaul governance at home, and for destitute immigrants desperate to reach the shores of Europe.

This begs a remark. The manifold crises that buffet the world echo and amplify one another, and resonate with Europe's domestic woes, debilitating the Union. Till 2014–2015 the EU's failings and failures were considered in isolation from other developments. In the preceding years, the EU had been increasingly looked upon as the weak link in the Western world. Britain's unexpected decision, in 2016, to pull away from the EU against its own interests, the patent rise of populism in the United States, punctuated by the emergence of the Tea Party and the election of Donald Trump as president in 2016, and the entrenchment of authoritarianism on the EU's periphery, east and south of Europe, and farther away, have dissipated the illusion of what might be called Europe's "reverse exceptionalism": the EU's woes are also those of the liberal world. Yet they feed on evolutions proper to the EU and to its member states.

Continent by Default set out to scrutinize the EU's decades-long achievements, such as the consolidation of democracy in candidate countries, the use of conditionality to press reforms on them, and the invention of policies toward neighboring countries to lock them in and pacify the continent and its surroundings. Leaving aside cases such as the constitution of an EMU in order to concentrate on the logic of expansion, this book has provided a grid to understand the EU's policy of building a continent and organizing its surroundings to entrench stability and democracy, a policy that, however, sometimes glossed over democracy for the sake of stability. It has offered keys to understanding the limits and faults of such a policy. On the eve of this new era jolted by unpredictable Brownian movements, when, losing its relative stability and unity, Europe is becoming increasingly fragmented in an increasingly fragmented world, it is time to draw the balance sheet of half a century in which the EU has acted as the organizing pole on the continent and in its surroundings. And it is time to chart the future of Europe, if it is indeed possible not to lose one's bearings in an era of unpredictability.

The Dialectics of Fragmentation and Unity

Over centuries, fragmentation and disunion had been Europe's hallmark, a source of woes and throes that threatened to engulf the continent and drag it into irrelevance after the twin suicides of two world wars. The creation of the European Communities/European Union was an attempt to introduce some unity into Europe's political patchwork, and peace through partnership where there was almost none. It was a means to tame fragmentation, not only between members but also between an ever greater number of members, as the EC/EU proceeded to expand beyond its original borders. *Continent by Default* focuses more or less on the decades that the fall of the Wall ushered in, even though the earlier decades, of the EC's/EU's inception, serve as a backdrop to understand later developments. The fall of the Wall, in 1989, and the demise of the USSR, in 1991, opened up a new space east of the continent and heralded an exceptional era. The retreat of the Soviet empire was relatively graceful by historical standards, and a new peace order superseded the balance between two nuclear super-powers, the United States and the USSR, that had shaped Europe's fate for almost half a century. The Cold War, now past, was masterfully closed when Western, liberal institutions, which had shown resilience and effec-tiveness in preserving democracy and prosperity in the Western world, expanded to embrace the eastern part of the continent.

Now that Europe was free, it had to become whole. The reunification of Germany through the incorporation of the former GDR, the expansion of NATO, the enlargement of the EU, and the Charter of Paris, which turned a process, the CSCE, into a Pan-European organization, the OSCE, followed by a number of agreements with Russia, dovetailed with one another. The challenge was now to devise what came to be called the "architecture" of the continent, that is, to cover the latter with an institu-tionalized order. In this construction, the United States played a key role as the dominant power in Europe, the "indispensable power," the only country capable of stopping an aggressor, in the former Yugoslavia, for instance, and of extending its protective wing, NATO, over the continent. Other actors and institutions notwithstanding, the EU played a key role in reorganizing the continent and cementing the European peace. Once Mikhail Gorbachev bowed out and agreed to a settlement that primarily George H. W. Bush and Helmut Kohl skillfully devised, the EU looked like the "other indispensable power" on the continent, well into the new mil-lennium. Taken together, these Western institutions devised a democratic continent that Russia would not or could not offer.

Of all the institutions that could help organize the continent—NATO as a military organization to defend Europe and provide security, the OSCE, and the Council of Europe, both intergovernmental institutions that promote civil, human, and minority rights—the EU was the only body to pool sovereignty, laws, and policies to give the liberated countries road maps toward democracy and the rule of law, to anchor democracy in states and societies that aspired to join the ranks of European democra-cies, replace authoritarian structures with democratic ones, restore pri-vate initiative and public trust, and maybe transform political behaviors. It was also the only body that could influence neighbors and encourage democracy beyond borders, and open an immense market to all neigh-bors, Europeans and non-Europeans. It seemed the most appropriate of all organizations to offer a full-blown blueprint for most of the continent. From the Balkans, where, together with the international community, it established protectorates, to Central and Eastern Europe and Turkey, where it embraced new members and candidate members, from northern Africa to the Middle East, where it sought new neighbors and backed up the United States in the Palestinian-Israeli conflict, the EU extolled and expanded its rules and role (see chapters 1–3). It became a model and an anchor.

Enlargement was the tool, but for a long time it was neither a policy nor a strategy. In the first decades of its existence, the European Community/ies had grown, from six to nine and twelve members. From its inception, it had never stopped enlarging. "In the beginning was enlargement" (chapter 1). Enlargement had remained limited though, in both its geographical scope and its strategic ambitions. At that time, the USSR covered more than half of the continent, halting the EC's expansion, had the latter wanted to expand. Yet the EC's aim was not to expand but merely to respond to applicants who sought association or membership because of the EC's comparative advantages, economic or political. The EC had no geostrategic pretensions beyond its own borders, and a strategy was absent.

Though enlargement had never been conceived as a policy, it became one, by default more than by design, incrementally and almost incidentally. As the EU gradually, and sometimes grudgingly, offered membership to new democracies, it transformed foreign countries into "similars" to fit into a union of democratic and prosperous states and societies. Enlargement served as a makeshift foreign policy, a foreign policy that became domestic insofar as it resorted to a repertoire of domestic policies instead of foreign policy instruments, and insofar as it contributed to shape very intrusively the domestic policies, and even skew the polities, of applicants. Enlargement also provided a matrix for policies toward the neighbors, that is, those who were not to join the EU, sooner or later. As the Union came to embrace the whole continent and its surroundings, south and east, it devised a neighborhood policy, and a policy vis-à-vis Russia, that borrowed from enlargement, yet remained short of membership, that is, a policy that was limited in aim and scope (see chapters 4 and 6). Thus, enlargement became a kind of "one-size-fits-almost-all" policy by default. Like the British Empire, a wider Union arose in a "fit of absent-mindedness." Indeed, remarkable achievements often occur in reaction to outside circumstances and opportunities, be they political, technological, social, or economic, that actors, private or public or both, perceive and exploit to pursue their interests—hence, reactivity, a policy of reaction rather than prevention, and incrementalism, a policy of small steps, may not be the signature of the EU alone.

At the turn of the millennium, enlargement and its by-products, the neighborhood policy in particular, looked like tremendous achievements, culminating, in 2004, in the inclusion of ten new members, the adoption of the European Neighborhood Policy (ENP) and of the Four Spaces linking the EU and Russia. A kind of hubris was floating in the air. Close to being united, though not meant to become a United States of Europe, the EU looked to some analysts like the new hegemon in lieu of, in place of, the United States. It appeared to be the superpower in the making that Johan Galtung had envisioned in the 1970s. Eight years later, however, at the time the Union was awarded the Nobel Peace Prize, the aura of success had dissipated. Concerns and disquiet, which had already been in the offing a few years earlier, were looming large in some capital cities and among the wider public in most member states. How could hubris and celebration so quickly go awry?

Expansion fed fragmentation. The larger the Union, the higher the number of members and the number of neighbors there were, the more complex an overall pattern became, the more regional poles it drew in, the likelier it was to fall prey to subregional interests, affinities, and alliances. Fragmentation grew. This reverberated in the vocabulary around the EU. The notion of "periphery" emerged in political and analytical discourses, sometimes in jest, as the designation of PIGS suggested; the PIGS—Portugal, Ireland, Greece, and Spain—were considered faulty countries, and were held responsible for the EU's flaws. Some of the first studies to recount and account for the plurality of political cultures, in Greece or Romania, were published at the time when the economic crisis erupted. In other words, the emergence of new, diverse challenges tore away the veil of unity. Worse, they even reinforced some fault lines as crises resonated with one another.

The so-called refugee crisis, for instance, weakened Greece, a country that had already borne the brunt of the economic, monetary, and bank crises (see chapter 5). For a number of years, Greece had been one of two or three member states mainly, if not solely, responsible for the EU's refugee policy as a whole. As a so-called country of first arrival, according to the definition of the Dublin Convention, it had to readmit refugees who had first set foot in Greece and had, therefore, to apply for refugee status, yet had moved on to other states that are party to the Convention. As long as the number of arrivals was limited, so was the country's burden, financial and economic, administrative and political. With the surge that started in the first half of the 2010s and reached unprecedented levels in 2015, it became a burden difficult to shoulder—all the more so as Greece itself sagged under exacting austerity measures. Rigorous enforcement of the Dublin Convention was intended to restrain the number of refugees that reached Germany, and reduce the financial, economic, social, and political price that the latter had to pay. Certainly, Germany was contributing to the rescue of Greece's budget and banks. Yet Greece was contributing the lion's share to the refugee crisis.

On the other hand, Europe's difficulties were benefiting Russia in many ways. The number of Syrian refugees surged in 2014 and 2015; Syrians were fleeing not only ISIL but also the massive pounding of the civilian population, in particular as of September 2013, when Moscow committed air-borne force to support Bashar al-Assad, and boost its presence in the country. The destruction of Aleppo was crucial to keep Assad in power and Russia in place. Concurrently, Russia's intervention sent tens of thousands on the road to Europe. This movement in turn nourished resentment in some of the countries refugees were crossing and boosted the appeal of populist parties—in government in Hungary, for instance, or in the opposition from Austria to England—which rode the antirefugee wave. The refugee crisis weakened the fabric of democratic societies and, indirectly, refurbished the image of authoritarian regimes in Moscow, Ankara, and Budapest. Unity fell apart—and with it the security of the continent.

Geopolitics and Power Politics

Paradoxically at first sight, the EU had wanted to foster security without having a security policy. Unity was the key to security, the unity of all against one another and of all against others. After the two world wars that they had unleashed, the Europeans discarded war as an instrument of international relations and wanted to turn their back on power politics—an action they could afford, as the United States had taken it upon itself to defend Western Europe. Yet the Europeans were, nonetheless, working at constructing an area of peace. The European project was very much a political one, and a geopolitical one. The EC/EU was to bar war in Europe and create peace by pooling sovereignty, laws, and resources. Law, not war, was to rule the Communities and later the continent. For centuries, thinkers like Montesquieu, Benjamin Constant, Auguste Comte, Henri de Saint-Simon, and Joseph Schumpeter conceived of a world where trade and commercial relations would supersede war and glory, where the requirements of the former, based on trust, reciprocity, and predictability entrenched in a peaceful and law-based environment, would sound the death knell of martial virtues. A bourgeois world of civil values was supposed to replace a heroic past (Hirschmann 1977; Aron 1959). The EU was to embody those "normative" or "postmodern" virtues—though the EU is not as normative, nor even as postmodern, that is, postsovereign, as often contended. The EU was to offer the certainty that "peace and trade provide a better return than war and looting" and that "democracies are in the long run more stable than dictatorships" (Cooper 2005: 25; see chapter 1). And it was to export its vision to its surroundings.

In other words, Europeans were not turning their back on geopolitics. Geopolitics never went away (Mead 2014).[3] They were turning their back on power politics, in Europe above all (chapter 3). The ESS, a paltry document published in 2003, a nice "first try" that remained without proper follow-up, captured that lack of firm understanding of power politics. European societies, European polities, and EU institutions had and have, on the whole, difficulties coming to terms with power and violence. Some European countries fought wars in Asia, or in Africa. And still do. When a military operation was set up to, at first, protect the Libyan population and, eventually, bring down Colonel Qaddafi's regime in 2011, the EU as such stood aside, while ten European countries, the French and the British primarily, led or took part in the international coalition. In 2013, the French president signaled his willingness to protect the civilian population and, later, to direct strikes against the Syrian regime that targeted civilians, while his allies, American and British, backed away. A year later, an international coalition comprising the French, the British, and six other European countries led, or supported, the strikes against ISIS in Syria—and some of them, the strikes in Iraq. The EU does not do wars, though it has been able to send small military missions, limited in scope and aim, to faraway countries—well beyond the geographic and intellectual ambit of this book. When, on the EU's borders, the former Yugoslavia descended into chaos, most Europeans refrained from intervening. Very few, the British, the Dutch, and the French, dispatched combat troops to Bosnia-Herzegovina.

Instead of making war, maintaining, or seeking to maintain, security boiled down to a series of techniques (chapter 3). Designed to bring enemies together and to pacify minds, the "Irish tool kit" that the Commission conceived with the European Council's approval was transplanted to Cyprus, Israel, and Palestine, and, farther away, to the Caucasus, though without much success. To succeed, reconciliation required a parallel track: a political agreement or, at least, the agreement to hammer out a political solution. In Northern Ireland, the agreement concluded in 1998 has held ever since because of the democratic environment—despite past setbacks, and the future difficulties that Brexit promises. Conversely, multiple cleavages, economic, political, religious, and linguistic, oppose Israelis and Palestinians, Greek and Turkish Cypriots, Abkhaz and Georgians, and fuel conflicts that, at least on Cyprus and in Georgia, a patron, Turkey or Russia, stokes from outside. As an advocate of reconciliation through cooperation, as a promoter of a policy, the ENP, designed to meticulously cultivate the seeds of democracy and prosperity, the EU misunderstood the nature of power and the economic and political foundations of authoritarian regimes in its surroundings—then as now.

For a long time indeed, the neighborhood was unsettled and unsettling. Authoritarian governments too often maintained an artificial peace, depriving civil societies of their most fundamental rights. Relieved that authoritarian or dictatorial regimes controlled migration flows with an iron fist, the EU mostly ignored the latent or seething unrest that was taking hold of Europe's surroundings. On the continent itself, it was taken off guard by the implosion of Yugoslavia, as of 1991–1992, though the dissolution of the federation had been in the making for at least a decade, and a number of experts had warned against some of the measures that inevitably spelled violence. War and genocide came back to haunt the continent. Srebrenica, where Muslim men were massacred in July 1995 under the passive eye of European peacekeepers, epitomized the weaknesses, errors, and crimes of an EU engrossed in its own travails, and of Europeans who had taken leave of international politics. Having pretended at first to maintain or restore a Yugoslav peace, the Europeans had to call in the United Nations—and the United States. For the first time, China, a permanent member of the UNSC, legally exercised control over European affairs. As Pierre Hassner kept repeating in the 1990s, working on Europe's architecture while Rome burned seemed a mere exercise in futility.

East and southeast of the continent, two states, Russia and Turkey (chapters 2 and 6), also posed a challenge to the EU. Though differently, both faced the difficult tasks of shedding the vestiges of empires. How would Turkey and Russia, two staunch advocates of unqualified sovereignty, fit into the Union, a constellation of states that, albeit reluctantly, mutualize their laws and policies? How would Turkey behave as member of the EU while its troops occupy Cyprus, a sliver of EU territory? How did it reconcile the necessity to abide by EU's rules while negotiating with Brussels from a position of strength? The EU and the member states should have devised strategies specific to each case. Though Russia's membership was practically ruled out, Russia, a European power, had to be embraced. The challenge was to define institutions, formal or informal, in order to anchor it in Europe short of enlargement. In the 1990s, there was a policy, or rather a vision. Fearing a repetition of history and the resurgence of "Weimar," a code word for Germany's debasement after World War I and its descent into Nazism, the German chancellor, for instance, advised Germany's allies not to humiliate Moscow. Together with the American president, George H. W. Bush, and other leaders, Helmut Kohl opened the doors of international organizations to Russia, and his government compensated its Soviet/Russian counterpart for withdrawing from reunified Germany.

Nonetheless, European leaders and institutions were caught off guard when in Turkey and Russia the fledgling process of democratization that seemed to take off at the turn of the millennium ground to a halt a few years later, and made way in both countries for a combination of personal rule and arbitrariness, corruption and the restriction of civil liberties. The evolutions in Ankara and Moscow differ from one another, and bear very different consequences, domestically and internationally. Turkish society and polity are increasingly cleaved, and dominated by a process of "sultanization," that is, the ever more authoritarian and personal rule of Recep Tayyip Erdoğan, who wants to don the mantle of Ottoman history. What the former prime minister and current president of Turkey is launching against segments of his own population is a *Kulturkampf*. Yet Erdoğan does not openly confront the West. It certainly would not be a propitious time to do so. Turkey needs Western support in its multifarious war at its eastern border, while in a tug-of-war against the West it needs the Turkish Cypriot government, though the latter seems to be evading Erdoğan's grip as it seeks to reunify with the RoC. Instead of confronting the West, Erdoğan turns his back on the West, and scorns the EU.

By comparison, Russia poses a danger not only for its people but also for the EU and for the West. It is already undergoing a process of Weimarization, if one is to believe Mikhail Kasyanov, former prime minister under Vladimir Putin. It is threatening countries and peoples. Outside of its borders, the Kremlin resorts to hybrid wars that combine old tactics and new techniques: delivery of conventional weapons, cyberattacks, massive disinformation, and reliance on proxies, unmarked soldiers, trolls, or sycophants, with the so far rhetorical threat to use nuclear capabilities, massive deployment on Western borders, and "near misses" in airspace. Russia is possibly the most massive *and* insidious threat posed to the Union and its members. Farther south, Islamist terrorist networks represent a less powerful but symbolically more frightening threat, as they build bridges between alienated youth in our societies and extremists who pervert Islam and wage a total war against those who do not share their distorted creed. Yet both Russia and ISIS in the Middle East similarly cast into question borders that the West drew and the international community condoned. In the Middle East, in 2014, ISIS symbolically and actually trampled the border that the Sykes-Picot Agreement of 1916 had drawn in the sand to mark the boundary between Syria and Iraq. Farther north, in 2014, Russian troops, mercenaries, and material were smuggled into Ukraine, despite the fact that Moscow had recognized the country's sovereignty through international agreements.

In other words, Russia and ISIS ignore borders, material or virtual, and they reject the West and what it stands for. Some governments and some individuals or groupings are impervious to Western influence, and to the values that the West extols. Thus, even though wealth acquired in times of peace is more durable than wealth acquired through conquest, as the latter may prove to be a mere illusion, militants and mercenaries prefer heroic virtues to civil and civilian values, and ways of life or sources of revenue that are both immediate and off the track of bourgeois life (Angell 1910).[4] Similarly, autocrats cherish hoarding power and riches, and personal rule is to them of greater value than democracy and rights. Heroes and hoarders have little in common with the contemporary West—and little in common with parts of the population they dominate or pretend to represent. Like mercenaries and militants, they manipulate the people, and cast the passions of those who are suffering from downward mobility and loss of dignity in a powerful narrative of national misery and greatness. To that extent, their language and methods resonate with those of populists in Western societies.

To some extent, the West contributed to the return of power politics—even though it did not always understand the nature of the authoritarian regimes that were taking hold in Moscow and Ankara or grasp the essence of radical Islamism. In the past decades, the West had not shied away from double standards. It heralded norms that it did not heed, and disregarded, for instance, societies and individuals in the Mediterranean basin while calling for the respect of human rights. It lacked coherence, mainly at its neighbors' expense: it intervened in Libya, and remained mostly absent from Syria. Primarily, it undermined the institutions it had built after World War II, which had been regulating the international order since then, and it did so because it bypassed them when acting unilaterally. From the 2002 abrogation of the antiballistic missile treaty that condoned parity with Moscow to the military intervention in Libya, which ended up toppling Muammar Qaddafi amid Russian and Chinese denunciations, and boosted centrifugal tendencies in the country, the West took steps without heeding Russia's claims, or pretending to do so. Last but not least, the financial and banking crisis that originated in the United States and the EU, and the ensuing complex crisis, which is chipping away at the economic, political, social, and even cultural substance of European societies and polities, seem to vindicate all those who castigate Western weaknesses, and feed into Western self-doubt and self-retreat.

Can the EU Recoup Its Influence?

It is necessary for the West, for the EU in particular, to ponder its mistakes, an exercise that goes far beyond apportioning blame. The West and the EU must avoid providing their critics or opponents with ammunition. More important, while power politics, and its success or failure, are the only criteria that matter to the enemies of democracy and liberalism, liberals and democrats also have to measure up to moral requirements. Consequently, making mistakes often means for the West losing the moral high ground. This is particularly damaging for the EU, as moral principles lay at the very core of its construction. The EU was built around an idea, that of securing peace in a union of democracies. Culturally diverse, it lives on as an idea. This raises important questions: Can the EU still survive as an idea in a world of populist tactics and national withdrawal? What are its chances of recouping influence? Several scenarios are possible.

It is difficult to imagine the demise of the EU. As the European Communities/Community/Union emerged over the years, they wove together multiple political, economic, and legal ties, interactions, and entanglements, like so many layers of deposit in a riverbed, or so many wires intertwined with one another. Though the EU's Common Market remains fragmented in many ways, though incoherence blurs or thwarts attempts at a common foreign and security policy, the members of the EU have over the years spawned a specific body of laws, rules, and policies, and implanted them in the national systems of the member states. Hence, as highlighted in the reflections and negotiations over Brexit, it will be extremely lengthy, costly, and pernicious to sever ties and separate layers—one reason, albeit tenuous, why Brexit might not happen.

Furthermore, as *Continent by Default* has shown, the EU still exerts an attraction on countries or regions of the periphery, by offering them, mostly unwittingly, a specific added value. These are poor, small or large, but nonetheless weak countries that want to partake in Europe's prosperity and pursue the European way to democracy—Georgia and Ukraine are obvious candidates; and small and rather rich and democratic states that belong to a larger union or federation and yearn for independence, such as Catalunya and Scotland. Leaving Ukraine aside, the EU might increasingly become a union of small states, rich or poor, that call for the EU's support to sustain their independence and/or implement Western strategies to entrench democracy and prosperity. In a more distant future, one might even envisage an EU x.0, a patchwork of diverse territories linked to the EU, where London and Northern Ireland, for instance, would belong to the EU while also part of the UK and/or the Republic of Ireland. More than ever, the EU would resemble empires of the past, characterized by multiple and overlapping allegiances.

Legally and politically, these two types of applicants, those who have been part of federations or unions that were in the EU and those states that are fully newcomers, differ from one another. Enlargement to the former might be inevitable because these newly independent states would have already conformed to EU policies, laws, and rules for a number of years. For them, becoming an EU member might be a matter of a few years only, even though resistance might hamper political steps that would seem to condone secessions. As far as newcomers are concerned, enlargement is not an option that the EU should lightly consider. As a matter of fact, with enlargement came increased diversity, and greater difficulties in devising a common policy, toward Palestine and Israel, for instance, or toward Russia. Thus the EU has to avoid dealing too soon with a new candidate country such as Serbia, for instance, which has too often departed from EU policies toward Russia on the question of sanctions, and entertains connections of all sorts with a country that some consider "Serbia's protector." Upon coming into office, Jean-Claude Juncker, the president of the European Commission, declared a five-year moratorium to give the Union some breathing space in order to work out some of the differences between countries and fix some of the woes from which it suffers (Juncker 2014b).

Conversely, the EU would be in dire straits if it were to lose those large states that are more or less democratic, prosperous, and in any case indispensable because of their political, historical, and financial weight—in other words, countries that can carry the EU or by leaving it debilitate or annihilate it. Brexit, for instance, has raised questions not only about the place of the UK in Europe and the world, but also about how Brexit will affect European citizens and governments, in particular as regards electoral behavior. In the wake of Brexit, a number of populist leaders in those countries that underwent national elections in 2017, the Netherlands, France, and even Germany, rejoiced over the results of the British referendum, as it tarnished the image of an everlasting, ever enlarging Union. At the same time, however, as the complexity of a divorce and a deal between the UK and the EU emerges, the number of those who, in the UK, still favor leaving the EU has dwindled, according to some opinion polls—even though, on the whole, the country is rather unlikely to change tack and espouse a pro-EU policy: as mentioned in chapter 2, the UK has always looked for special treatment that it never achieved. Europe-wide, the percentage of those who oppose the EU has decreased, and at some of the large pro-EU demonstrations that took place after the referendum, in the UK in particular, "Love for the EU" popped up as a slogan (WIN/Gallup International, in *Les Echos* 2016). Who would have thought that an acronym, an organization much decried for its technocracy and bureaucracy, would inspire love?

Meanwhile, France's departure from the EU would be both more straightforward and more dramatic than Brexit. Though French politicians and citizens have always displayed ambiguity and skepticism toward the EU, France's role in the creation of the Communities, and in the advances of the EC/EU toward an "ever closer union," through the EMU, or CSDP and *l'Europe de la défense*, would deprive the Union of one of its historical prime movers, and it would also deprive Germany of an ally and a counterweight. To that extent, France's departure from the Eurozone and from the EU, which the president of the extreme right National Front (Front National, FN), Marine Le Pen, calls for, would spell the end of the EU. The EU might live on as a Union of northern states, echoing the *kleindeutsche Lösung* of the nineteenth century, yet it would be as different from the EU as the *kleindeutsche Lösung* was from what would have been a *großdeutsche Lösung*, encompassing not only the German federation but also the Austrian empire: limited to few like-minded members, economic satellites of Germany.

In a way, the two options envisaged here, option "EU x.0" and "the dissolution of the Union," are located at each end of a spectrum dotted with in-between, mixed, fuzzy options. The EU may live on and still fulfill some of the purposes that have been assigned to it, or it might live on but change beyond recognition, and discard any major role. In any case, one should bear in mind that even though the French presidency evaded the leader of the Front National in May 2017, extremism and populism will not disappear, as their causes will survive. In the years to come, Europe will still be characterized by a divide between the super-rich and a population that suffers from downward mobility and lack of social recognition and moorings. Marine Le Pen or her successor will have to wait till 2022. Each election then will be like a roller coaster, arousing hope and despair in a number of countries. Citizens in Europe will probably send mixed messages, some of which might be contradictory and vary from country to country. In 2016, a majority of Austrian citizens elected an independent as president of the federation, yet they are likely to favor the so-called Liberal Party of Austria (FPÖ), a nationalist party, to lead future governments. Authoritarian leaderships have taken over government and state in Hungary and Poland, whereas Romanian citizens, supported by European institutions, put their corrupt leadership under pressure. The EU may become a kaleidoscope of moving constellations, unstable but not necessarily doomed to failure.

To ensure the survival of the EU, or of a revamped EU, encompassing the main founding states and a number of smaller countries, the Union will have to deliver—since it relies more on an allegiance through efficiency than on emotional links. The EU will have to discard policies whenever it does not or cannot deliver, rethink in particular its CSDP because political cultures, regarding, for instance, the use of weapons, are so different. It will have to further common projects that do not bear the roaring and misleading title of "common policies," and concentrate on those that prevent pernicious influences or actions linked to or supported by foreign governments or nongovernmental actors from spreading into the EU, in the area of coordinated counterinformation, for instance. Beyond practical achievements, the EU and EU member states will have to stand up to their principles, in two ways. It is a delusion to believe that Western, in this case European, ideas will be emulated and need not be defended— or supported. To be emulated, ideas have to be defended, starting at home. The Europeans will have to rebuild democracy inside the EU, instead of conniving with authoritarian leaders to undermine it, and to turn the EU and the EU member states into a paragon of democracy and liberalism. And they will have to firmly defend democracy abroad.

In this respect, the Union has capabilities, or, rather, it has an advantage that accrues from its very weakness: its diversity. Out of necessity the EU should make that a virtue. The diversity of its political cultures must be reckoned with. The Union has to rely upon it and tap it to regain influence. Since the early years of the new millennium, formats of various kinds, bilateral or multilateral, networks of heads of states and governments, foreign ministers and EU institutions, have addressed various issues, according to personalities, interests, and talents, the added value they bring, or the necessity of accommodating nonstate actors that pursue specific interests. This can be time-consuming, though small formats also allow quicker steps.

This diversity should be pursued, more openly, more systematically, and more broadly. Companies in particular should be included, for instance, on major issues such as an energy union, in order to tie their interests in more closely and to tame them or entice them to cooperate. Alliances should be struck more widely with civil societies. One of the main lessons that can be drawn from the 1970s and 1980s, the high times of the CSCE, is that governments, civil societies, and some of the first NGOs worked, more or less, together. In spite of all the glitches and contradictions, this was Europe at its best. The EU must be vigilant at home and innovative abroad when standing up to its values. What is at stake is a battle of words and a battle of worlds.

ACKNOWLEDGMENTS

My thanks go to the institutions that supported my work: CERI and Sciences Po (Paris), where I have been working for many years, and their directors; the Woodrow Wilson International Center for Scholars (Washington, DC), where the project was conceived; and the Nobel Institute (Oslo), where it was completed.

Thanks also to a number of officials, diplomats, civil servants, representatives, members of NGOs, researchers, journalists . . . , who agreed to share their thoughts with me (their titles and functions omitted here): Mika Aaltola, Martti Ahtisaari, Gilles Andréani, Michel Antoine, Pavlos Apostolides, Claude-France Arnould, Ronald Asmus, Carl Sverker Åström, Olaf Bachmann, Erkki Bahovski, Peter Balasz, Kakha Bendukidze, Jörg Bentman, Bénédicte Berner, Christoph Bertram, Vladimír Bilčík, Joachim Bitterlich, Bo Anders Bjurner, Agneta Boman, Jakub Boratyński, Jean-Louis Bourlanges, Rodric Braithwaite, Véronique Bujon-Barré, Vincenzo Camporini, Didier Canesse, Walter Carlsnaes, Anibal Cavaco Silva, Jacek Cichocki, Robert Cooper, Brian Crowe, Marta Dassù, Jacques Delors, Pavol Demeš,

Kemal Derviş, Thanos Dokos, Tobias Dürr, William Ehrman, Atila Eralp, Oded Eran, Gérard Errera, Philippe Errera, Steven Everts, Henriette Faergemann, Caroline Ferrari, Mark Fischer, Eric Fournier, Roland Galharague, Jaime Gama, Geneviève Garrigos, Carlos Gaspar, Thornike Gordadze, Heather Grabbe, Charles Grant, Jeremy Greenstock, Catherine Guicherd, Fernando Andresen Guimaraes, Rolf Gustavsson, Hans Gutbrod, Antonio Guterres, Hansjörg Haber, Hiski Haukkala, Harry Helenius, Seppo Hentilö, Janos Herman, Gunilla Herolf, Jörg Himmelreich, Zoltán Horváth, Douglas Hurd, Panayotis Ioakimidis, Jaakko Iloniemi, Gints Jegermanis, Maurits Jochems, Peter Jones, Sven Jürgenson, Boaz Karni, Andres Kasekamp, Kirsti Kauppi, Iris Kempe, Keti Khutsishvili, Kimmo Kiljunen, Suat Kınıklıoğlu, Matthew Kirk, László Kiss, Beata Kołecka, Heinrich Kreft, Jean-Claude Lallemand, Eneko Landaburu, Angus Lapsley, Elisa Launey-Rencki, Lotte Leicht, Georg Lennkh, Bernardino León, Mark Leonard, Bruno Lété, Pierre Lévy, Kadri Liik, Barbara Lippert, Jens Lorentz, Viljar Lubi, Hans-Dieter Lucas, Ulrike Lunacek, Jari Luoto, Markus Lyra, Monica Macovei, Michael Matthiessen, Markus Meckel, Marko Mihkelson, Eric Millet, Hughes Mingarelli, Antonio Missiroli, Pierre Mirel, Pierre Morel, Arkady Moshes, Henryka Moszicka-Dendys, Nils Muižnieks, Pauline Neville-Jones, Robin Niblett, Tom Nijhuis, Ghia Nodia, Eva Novotny, Piotr Nowina-Konopka, Bálint Ódor, Hanna Ojanen, Alar Olljum, Ziya Öniş, Sean O'Regan, Soli Özel, Žaneta Ozoliņa, Kaspars Ozoliņš, Andrejs Panteļējevs, Roland Paris, Ioan Mircea Paşcu, Zsolt Pataki, Quentin Peel, Errki Pennamen, Marc Perrin de Brichambaut, Mats Persson, Rosario Puglisi, Oliver Rentschler, Xavier Rey, François Rivasseau, Christian Rivet de Sabatier, Magnus Robach, Romaric Roignan, Alexander Rondeli, Toms Rostoks, Pascal Roux, Maria van Ruiten, Lars Ryding, Kimmo Sassi, Axel Schäfer, Daniel Schek, Joscha Schmierer, Andreas Schockenhoff, Henning Schröder, Daniela Schwarzer, Francisco Seixas da Costa, Stefano Silvestri, Aleksander Smolar, Teresa de Sousa, Gerfried Sperl, Carina Stachetti, Constanze Stelzenmüller, Angela Stent, Jan Stora, Walter Stützle, Etienne Sur, Paweł Świeboda, Heikki Talvitie, Pirkka Tapiola, Sylo Taraku, Jan Techau, Teija Tiilikainen, Roberto Toscano, Laurent Toulouse, Jan Truszczyński, Loukas Tsoukalis, Sinan Ülgen, Frank Umbach, Justin Vaïsse, João de Vallera, Álvaro de Vasconcelos, Nina Vaskunlahti, Hubert Védrine, Pierre Vimont, Pekka Visuri, Peter Volten, Martin Vukovich, Alexandre Vulic, James de Waal, Stephen Wall, William Wallace, Veronika Wand-Danielsson,

Michael Webb, Simon Webb, Detlef Weigel, Nicholas Whyte, Rob de Wijk, Andrew Wilson, Patrick Wouters, Temuri Yakobashvili, Alexandros Yannis, Wojciech Zajączkowski, and Salomé Zourabichvili.

I also thank colleagues and friends, Nilgün Arısan-Eralp, Henri Barkey, Hamit Bozarslan, Frédéric Bozo, Antonela Capelle-Pogacean, Angeliki Dimitriadi, Virginie Guiraudon, Riva Kastoryano, Arndt and Barbara Freytag von Loringhoven, Luis Martinez, Marie Mendras, Samuel and Sherrill Wells, and many others on both sides of the Atlantic; two knowledgeable and helpful librarians at CERI, Dorian Ryser, and first and foremost, Sylvie Haas; successive research assistants; and my students over the years.

All helped me further my research and thinking about the European Union. However, I am responsible for the interpretations I give. Following the wish of certain interlocutors, quotations are not attributed. Interviews are not quoted but included in the analysis.

I extend my profound gratitude to those who opened their doors, in particular Marie and Catherine Mendras and their family, Marie-Aimée Mornay, and Eva and Wolfgang Schenk, as well as to Françoise Mereyde, Thierry Bouillet, Niels Brion, and the whole team of the AHP, to whom I owe so much.

Cynthia Cohen deserves a particular place: she taught me the skills required to address a British and an American public, and knew how to support and soothe me in dire times through her immense wisdom. So does Pierre Hassner, with whom I learned so much over all these years; Edvard Munch, whose paintings inspired some of my rewriting; and my dear daughter, Elisabeth-Kyrà, who radiates strength and joy, though she came to hate this book that consumed my time—a cosmopolitan and a European, to whom this work is dedicated.

NOTES

Introduction

1. The Treaty of Rome, formally known as the Treaty Establishing the European Economic Community (TEEC), was signed on 25 March 1957 by Belgium, the Federal Republic of Germany, France, Italy, Luxembourg, and the Netherlands and came into force on 1 January 1958. It established the European Economic Community (EEC) on 1 January 1958. The Maastricht Treaty, formally the Treaty on European Union (TEU), which was signed on 7 February 1992 and came into force on 1 November 1993, turned the European Economic Community into a European Union. The Treaty of Lisbon, or treaty on the functioning of the European Union, was signed on 13 December 2007, and came into force on 1 December 2009. Henceforth, I use the term "Community" (or the acronym EC) when referring to the European institutions prior to 1993, and "Union" (or EU) for the period after the Maastricht Treaty came into force. "EC/EU" will come up when referring to periods of time both before and after 1993. The term "Communities"—plural—refers to a whole series of treaties instituting, first, the European Coal and Steel Community (ECSC), signed in Paris on 18 April 1951 by France, Germany, Italy, and the Benelux countries, which came into force on 23 July 1952; the Treaty founding the European Atomic Energy Community (EAEC, or Euratom), signed on 25 March 1957, which came into force on 1 January 1958; as well as the aforementioned EEC. All merged in 1967. The name and the adjective "European/s" will refer to the citizens of either European countries, inside and outside the EU, or EU member states (in which case it would be more appropriate, yet somewhat awkward, to speak of EU-ropeans: the context will help determine the meaning of the adjective/noun).

2. According to the Rome Treaty, the Commission had the competence to negotiate and conclude agreements, with states, with unions of states, or with international organizations and to advise the Council on these matters. Article 224 left a door open insofar as it called upon member states to consult in case an international crisis might arise affecting the Common Market.

3. The Treaty Establishing the European Defence Community, which would have created a European army, was signed in 1952, but the French National Assembly rejected its ratification in 1954.

4. The Federal Republic of Germany is often characterized as a *Macht wider Willen*, a reluctant power. See Hacke 1993.

5. When referring to official denominations, I use the English spelling used in the documents of the EC/EU.

6. *Universitas* (Latin) means "universe" or "world."

7. See chapter 6.

8. Of course, the distinction between the EU and its member states is relevant—especially when it comes to foreign policy, which is both the remit of the Council (of the High Representative and also of the Commission or even the European Parliament) and the ambit of member states. This is why the interaction between EU institutions and member states, as part of the institutions and as independent actors, is crucial. Here, however, I do not look at the way these "independent" actors are influenced and shaped by EU institutions and intergovernmental interactions—increasing analysis is devoted to this question, which this book does not address.

9. Following the Hungarian historians István Bibó and Jenő Szűcs, one might add that Central European states, particularly Hungary, were and still are wavering between East and West.

1. In the Beginning Was Enlargement

1. This offer was never replicated in any other association treaty, except in those dubbed "European agreements" with Central and Eastern European countries.

2. The word "wave" describes the fact that hardly any country applied without being followed by others. Denmark, Ireland, and the UK joined in 1973. Greece applied in 1975 and joined in 1981, followed by Portugal and Spain, which applied in 1977 and joined in 1986. This may be called the second wave of enlargement, while the third wave of applications encompassed Austria in 1989, Sweden in 1991, and Finland in 1992, all joining in 1995. Cyprus and Malta submitted their applications in 1990, Hungary and Poland in 1994, Bulgaria, Estonia, Latvia, Lithuania, Romania, and Slovakia in 1995, the Czech Republic and Slovenia in 1996. Cyprus, the Czech Republic, Estonia, Hungary, Latvia, Lithuania, Malta, Poland, Slovakia, and Slovenia became members of the EU in 2004, Bulgaria and Romania in 2007. One may speak here of a fourth wave of enlargement, Romania and Bulgaria making up, in a sense, a fourth and a half wave. Norway is an odd man out. Having withdrawn its application in 1962, it applied twice in 1967 and in 1992, but each time the citizens rejected membership by referendum. Switzerland refused to join the European Economic Area (EEA), established in 1994, which encompasses the European Free Trade Association (EFTA, made up of Iceland, Liechtenstein, Norway, and Switzerland) and the EU, and establishes the free movement of persons, goods, and services within the area. EEA member states have to adopt relevant EU legislation without being part of the EU decision-making process. Having rejected the EEA, Switzerland suspended membership negotiations with the EU. Next to Morocco, whose application was presented and rejected (on the grounds that Morocco is not European) in 1987, Turkey is another odd case: it applied in 1987 and is still not a member (see chapter 2). These so-called waves, leading up to the "big bang " in the first decade of the new

millennium, have given way to a case-by-case approach, for reasons to be examined in subsequent chapters. Croatia applied in 2003 and joined the EU in 2013; Macedonia applied in 2004, but Greece blocked the opening of negotiations that the Commission had recommended. Montenegro applied in 2008 and Serbia in 2009, at the same time as Iceland. Negotiations with Iceland were suspended by Reykjavik after the April 2013 elections, the result of which was interpreted as a vote against the EU. Negotiations with Montenegro and Serbia started, respectively, in 2012 and 2014. Bosnia-Herzegovina applied in 2009, as did Albania. Together with Kosovo, these three states are considered potential candidates, that is, as having a European future. Having joined the EEC as part of Denmark, Greenland left it in 1985 after gaining home rule and is one of the EU's Overseas Countries and Territories. The Faroe Islands, also a self-governing territory in Denmark, was never part of the EEC. Andorra, Monaco, San Marino, and the Vatican have specific links with the EU.

3. Following the last successful British bid, it took Stockholm twenty years to apply, for a variety of reasons.

4. Established in 1994, the European Economic Area (EEA) provides for the free movement of persons, goods, services and capital within the Single Market of the European Union (EU). It encompasses three of the four member states of the European Free Trade Association (EFTA), Iceland, Liechtenstein, and Norway, and the EU.

5. As a member of EEA, Finland had already adopted the *acquis communautaire*, the whole body of laws and regulations that candidates have, among other things, to incorporate, and quickly became a member of the EU in 1995, after having applied in 1992.

6. There is a profusion of academic literature on this topic, including Marxist approaches (Wallerstein 1974 and 1980 etc.), the theory of *dependencia* (Cardoso 1969), and the analysis of structural economic dominance (Perroux 1948).

7. This approach in terms of core-periphery has subsided with successive enlargements, and it has not been further developed to conceptualize the relations between countries *inside* the European Union. Decision makers and analysts as well must have surmised that belonging to the EC/EU implied the disappearance of a core and a periphery. The travails of the euro are bringing this approach back to the fore.

8. See Article 237 of the Treaty of Rome (1957), subsequently Article 49 of the Treaty of the European Union (TEU) (Maastricht, 1993), and unchanged by the Lisbon Treaty (2009). The second paragraph of Article 237 reads as follows: "The conditions of admission and the adjustments to this Treaty necessitated thereby shall be the subject of an agreement between the Member States and the applicant State. This agreement shall be submitted for ratification by all the Contracting States in accordance with their respective constitutional requirements."

9. German political discourse put a high premium on *stability*. Three Stability Pacts have been concluded in Europe, all three initiated or co-initiated by a German government: the Stability Pact that the French, followed by the Germans, put forth in 1994 and which led to the conclusions of treaties between Hungary and its neighbors to cement good-neighborly relations; the Stability Pact for South and South-Eastern Europe, devised by Germany in 1999 to foster reconciliation and peace after the wars in the former Yugoslavia; and the Stability and Growth Pact adopted in 1997 to complete the Economic and Monetary Union.

10. This probably gives a fuller account of the decision making than, for example, the concept of "rhetorical entrapment," as judicious as it is (Schimmelfennig 2001).

11. Point 18: "Ce sont ces autres aspects, non géographiques, qui donnent sa signification au mot 'européen' dans le texte de l'article 237."

12. Point 20: Il faudra aussi se demander si, outre les conditions géographiques et économiques, la structure politique du pays en question n'en fera pas un corps étranger à la Communauté." Translation of this quote and subsequent quotations from this report is my own.

13. Point 24: "Il faudra se demander si . . . la structure politique du pays en question n'en fera pas un corps étranger dans la Communauté"; point 25: "Les États dont les gouvernements n'ont pas de légitimation démocratique et dont les peuples ne participent aux décisions du gouvernement ni directement ni par des représentants élus librement, ne peuvent prétendre être admis dans le cercle des peuples qui forment les Communautés européennes."

14. The heads of state and government who underwrote the Rome Treaty underlined their determination "to lay the foundations of an ever closer union among the peoples of Europe," the first of a series of guidelines that the preamble, solemn though not binding, enumerates. The subsequent treaties regarding the EU also mention the "ever closer union" in their preambles.

15. Two Fouchet plans, commissioned by General de Gaulle and put forth in 1961, envisaged an intergovernmental common foreign and defense policy, and a union of peoples shedding all pretense of supranationalism: "La participation à la coopération dans le domaine de la politique étrangère et de la défense supposerait cependant une attitude qui, allant au-delà d'une sympathie générale pour le monde occidental, implique un engagement très net en matière de politique étrangère et militaire."

16. Article 2 states that the Union is founded on the values of respect for "human dignity, freedom, democracy, equality, the rule of law and respect for human rights, including the rights of persons belonging to minorities. These values are common to the Member States in a society in which pluralism, non-discrimination, tolerance, justice, solidarity and equality between women and men prevail." Article 49 stipulates: "Any European State which respects the values referred to in Article 2 and is committed to promoting them may apply to become a member of the Union. The European Parliament and national Parliaments shall be notified of this application. The applicant State shall address its application to the Council, which shall act unanimously after consulting the Commission and after receiving the consent of the European Parliament, which shall act by a majority of its component members. The conditions of eligibility agreed upon by the European Council shall be taken into account. . . . The conditions of admission and the adjustments to the Treaties on which the Union is founded, which such admission entails, shall be the subject of an agreement between the Member States and the applicant State. This agreement shall be submitted for ratification by all the contracting States in accordance with their respective constitutional requirements" (Treaty on the European Union, 1992). Both articles of the Consolidated Version of the Treaty on the European Union (i.e., the Maastricht Treaty on European Union, TEU) have been incorporated in the further treaties amending the Maastricht (the Treaty of Amsterdam, the Treaty of Nice, and the Treaty of Lisbon), as well as in further accession treaties to the European Union.

17. In July 1989, the G-7 entrusted the Commission to support Poland and Hungary's transition with financial and technical help through the PHARE program. PHARE was later extended to all candidates. Further instruments were established by the Commission, for instance, Twinning and Taiex; to provide technical help, a European initiative later called the European Instrument for Democracy and Human Rights was created on the insistence of the European Parliament.

2. The Limits of Enlargement

1. I recall a meeting with some of my former students from Viadrina University, Germany. The meeting took place in Bucharest in the summer of 2006, and these young people were critical of their country's accession due a few months later, even though they had a vested, personal interest in Romania's membership, for instance, in allowing them later to work as young professionals in the EU.

2. The first Orbán government adopted a status law that grants specific rights to citizens of neighboring countries with a Hungarian background. On Orbán's "kin policies," see Waterbury 2010; Batory 2010.

3. According to Szabolcs Fazakas, Hungarian member of the European Audit Office, this resulted in a positive balance of €24 billion (MTI 2014).

4. This was epitomized probably by the unprecedented confrontation between civilians and police forces in September 2006. In the April elections of that year, the right-wing party Jobbik obtained 16 percent of the votes. For an insight into this nihilism, see *A pitbull cselekedetei* (Pitbull's Acts), a play by Péter Kárpáti.

5. Regarding the accession to the Schengen Area, however, other factors also play an important role, such as the fear of Roms, especially from Romania, coming to Western European countries.

6. In 2014, the country ranked 69 out of 175 countries evaluated by Transparency International (Index 2014, transparency.org).

7. Two years after a nationalist party, the so-called Freiheitliche Partei Österreichs (FPÖ, Austria's Liberal Party), shared power in Vienna, which triggered criticism throughout the EU, the Nice Treaty, and later the Lisbon Treaty, adopted Article 7.

8. In 2015, 56 percent of Polish citizens thought that the democracy system was in danger, while in 2011 59 percent of Hungarians were pessimistic about the future of their country (Standard Eurobarometer 2011: 88).

9. http://europa.eu/legislation_summaries/enlargement/western_balkans/r18002_en.htm. CARDS was replaced in 2007 by Instrument for Pre-accession Assistance (IPA), covering both candidate and potential candidate countries.

10. The independence of Kosovo, however, is not recognized by all the member states of the EU, let alone by the whole international community.

11. The High Representative of the Union for foreign affairs and security policy, Catherine Ashton, and some of the governments of the member states, the German chancellor Angela Merkel first and foremost, were very clear that Belgrade had to stop supporting parallel Serbian institutions in northern Kosovo and settle for a dialogue with Prishtina. In 2013, the president of Serbia, Tomislav Nikolić, consented to formalize Serbia's relations with Kosovo, short of recognition, in an agreement signed in Brussels under the aegis of the High Representative.

12. I thank my colleague Frédéric Bozo for his explanations and references regarding de Gaulle's motivations.

13. Nathalie Tocci, who carefully analyzed the Cypriot conflict, ridiculed the lack of acumen of Günter Verheugen, the enlargement commissioner, who professed he had been cheated by the Greek Cypriots when he thought they would approve the UN settlement.

14. Actually, Greek-Turkish relations had improved considerably in the late 1990s, though this rapprochement was not the first. Under Kostas Simitis's leadership, Foreign Minister George Papandreou adopted an open approach in dealing with Turkey, helped by the outpouring of sympathy on both sides of the Aegean after a twin earthquake in Turkey and Greece in the summer of 1999, and by the partial, though imperfect, Europeanization of Greek elites, who came to approve of Turkey's inclusion in the EU. However, distrust mars relations between the two countries. For instance, only a NATO mission could provide support to stem human trafficking in the Aegean.

15. This comes on top of the chapters blocked because of Turkey's refusal to include the RoC in its implementation of the Customs Union.

16. Not only do all these measures violate the EU's fundamental rights and requirements, the government has taken steps that contradict commitments made within the Customs Union or requirements of the EU, were the country to join the latter (European Commission 2010, 2014, 2015).

17. On the particular ideological synthesis of the AKP, which explains the radicalization of the party in the latter part of the first decade of the new millennium, see Hamit Bozarslan (2013: 454–463), to whom I owe valuable insights.

18. The Sèvres Treaty in 1920, subsumed, in 1923, by the Lausanne Treaty, encapsulates Turkish resentment—and echoes the resentment of the Hungarians toward the Trianon Treaty.

19. This foreign policy came to be known among officials as a "zero-problem" policy regarding neighbors, and among commentators as a "post-Ottoman" strategy to restore influence in its neighborhood.

3. Peace, War, and Confetti

1. The position of the High Representative for Foreign and Security Policy, created by the Amsterdam Treaty in 1999, became, with the Lisbon Treaty, in force in 2010, the High Representative for the Union for Foreign Affairs and Security Policy. The High Representative is in charge of CFSP and CSDP.

2. A joint peacekeeping force consisting of Georgians, Georgians from Ossetia, and Russians had been set up in South Ossetia, and the OSCE monitored the region and the Georgian-Russian border. In Abkhazia, the Commonwealth of Independent States (CIS), created in December 1991 after the dissolution of the USSR, footed peacekeeping troops, actually mainly Russian. No Georgian troops were involved. The United Nation Observer Mission in Georgia (UNOMIG) oversaw compliance. A Joint Control Commission (JCC) was to deal with South Ossetia, a lopsided structure consisting of Georgia and Russia, and both Georgian provinces of South Ossetia and North Ossetia, with OSCE representatives attending. In 1999, the EU Commission obtained an observer status in the JCC in its capacity as financial contributor, not as political player. Nor did the EU play a role in the Geneva negotiations over Abkhazia. The Georgian and Abkhaz parties, representatives of the Russian Federation and the OSCE, and the so-called Group of Friends of the Secretary-General, Germany, France, the Russian Federation, the UK, and the United States, took part in these negotiations under UN auspices. Led by the three Baltic states, Poland, Romania, and Bulgaria, the EU launched, in 2005, a New Group of Georgia's Friends.

3. A Special Representative of the EU (EUSR) for the South Caucasus was appointed in 2003. Georgia, Armenia, and Azerbaijan were included in the ENP. An EU rule of law mission, EUJUST Themis, was dispatched to Tbilisi (2004–2005).

4. Interestingly enough, the Law Library of Congress does not include the official version of this agreement (see loc.gov/law/help/russian-georgia-war.php footnote 27). One can access a Russian version on the website of the South Ossetia Control Commission's Peacekeeping Force, http://www.peacekeeper.ru.

5. The United Nations Organization Mission in Georgia (UNOMIG) was terminated in 2009, at Russia's behest.

6. Having facilitated the cease-fire, the EU cochairs the Geneva negotiations. On the ground, the EU agreed on 15 September 2008 to send an EU (civilian) Monitoring Mission (EUMM), quickly deployed on 1 October (Fischer 2009). Yet the EUMM has not been allowed to fulfill its original purpose.

7. http://eeas.europa.eu/mepp/docs/venice_declaration_1980_en.pdf. President Mitterrand had called for a Palestinian state as early as 1982, in a speech in front of the Knesset, on 4 March that year, and the French were the first to promote the notion of a viable state.

8. In 1997, the EUSR for the Middle East contributed to the Hebron Agreement, according to which Israeli troops partially withdrew from the city, and the EU provided some security assurances. The EU's High Representative, Javier Solana, was appointed to the Mitchell Committee on the unraveling of the peace process (2000–2001). Individual member states played a diplomatic role: the German minister for foreign affairs mediated between the Israelis and Palestinians in 2001, and both the German and French governments' plans provided

the blueprint for the road map to peace adopted in 2003. During the war between Israel and Hezbollah in Lebanon in 2006, several European governments were involved in the cease-fire negotiations, and several European states contributed to the renewed United Nations Interim Force in Lebanon (UNIFIL). During the Israeli war against Gaza in December 2008 and January 2009, the High Representative and the French government worked toward a cease-fire.

9. Sweden was the first to do so in 2014.

10. This does not preclude the EU's strong condemnation of violence and terrorism. The EU supported reforms of the financial and fiscal systems, of the judiciary, and of the security services. At the EU's insistence, the PNA adopted a Basic Law in 2002, and instituted the office of prime minister in 2003. The EU helped organize and monitor elections. Since 2005, the EU and its members have deployed two civilian missions, EUBAM Rafah, at the border between Egypt and Israel, suspended in 2007 after Hamas took over the Gaza Strip, and EUPOL COPPS, to professionalize the Palestinian police, help the PNA fight against terrorism, and cooperate with Israeli authorities.

11. This involves Israel's inclusion in the Single Market, its adoption of CFSP declarations and démarches, and when and if possible, its participation in various programs and agencies, such as EUROPOL, and in CSDP missions, or auditing Israeli experts in the Security and Defence Committee of the European Union.

12. Interview.

13. This includes the cessation of terrorist operations, the recognition of the state of Israel, and an acknowledgment of all the agreements signed by the PNA.

14. Interview. The EU has also been unable to follow a coherent policy concerning the regime that applies to goods produced in the Palestinian territories. Concerning the products produced in Palestinian territories controlled by the PNA, the EU-PLO Interim Association Agreement of 1997, which granted Palestinian goods duty-free access to the European market, should apply. Yet Israel contends that the EU-Israeli Association Agreement prevails, and the EU has not pressed its point. In the case of products produced in Israeli settlements on the West Bank, the preferential treatment that Israel enjoys following the EU-Israeli Association Agreement should not apply, a position upheld by the Court of Justice of the European Union. However, Israel does not distinguish between Israeli territory and settlements in its definition of origin. Members are divided, and no agreement has been reached yet (APRODEV et al. 2012).

15. Sinn Féin is a nationalist Irish Republican party, founded in 1905, that is present in both the Republic of Ireland and Northern Ireland.

16. The 1994 PEACE program covered the years up to 1999, followed by PEACE II (2000–2006), III (2007–2013), and IV (2014–2020). Two billion euros were disbursed during the first three phases of the program. For the latest phase, 333 million euros have been earmarked.

17. Alone or with other international donors, the EU funded the rehabilitation of infrastructures, such as the railway link between Gori and Tskhinvali, electricity and gas networks in Tskhinvali, and the Enguri power plant. It financed the construction or rehabilitation of schools, hospitals, and farming cooperatives involving the different communities. It gave assistance to IDPs, and supported reconciliation, directly or through local NGOs. Interviews.

18. http://www.enpi-info.eu/mainmed.php?id=11&id_type=10.

19. The National Intelligence Estimate published an eminently prescient US study, in October 1990, that warned about possible fatal consequences (Glaurdic 2011: 109–110).

20. In 2002, the same forces of attraction would have the same impact, albeit peaceful, on the State Union of Serbia and Montenegro that the EU tried to impose on the two states by dangling the prospect of accession, and making it difficult to dissolve. In a referendum successfully held in 2006, 55 percent of the Montenegrins would have to request it.

21. In July 1991, the French government, followed by the German government, suggested a lightly armed peacekeeping troop under the banner of the Western European Union (WEU), a small defense organization founded in 1954 to oversee Germany's rearmament, which Paris sought to revitalize to bolster a European defense. The WEU played a small military role during the Yugoslav Wars. It came to an end in 2011.

22. Europeans and Americans beefed up their forces and boosted the military mandates after the horrendous massacre of Srebrenica in July 1995, where Serbian militias murdered the Muslim male population under the eyes of so-called peacekeepers, mostly Dutch.

23. The Germans also played a diplomatic role in both 1999, to bring an end to the war over Kosovo, and 2007, to clarify Kosovo's status.

24. CSDP kept being revamped with each new EU treaty, the Amsterdam Treaty, the Nice Treaty, and the Lisbon Treaty, under which it is now ESCD.

25. As of January 2012, the Commission and EU member states had committed 158 million euros to both humanitarian aid and civil protection (European Commission 2012a).

26. In Buzzati's novel, the attack takes place, yet far too late for the hero, who has been waiting for his whole life.

27. Besides France and the UK, Belgium, Bulgaria, Denmark, Greece, Italy, the Netherlands, Romania, Spain, and Sweden took part in the campaign. The operation also included Canada, Jordan, Norway, Qatar, Turkey, the United Arab Emirates (UAE), and the United States.

28. On Tunisia, see chapter 4. Concerning Libya, the French president may have had his own, very personal reasons for removing Colonel Gaddafi from the scene, as the latter is said to have financially contributed to Nicolas Sarkozy's electoral campaign in 2007.

29. In an interview with the *Atlantic*, President Obama laid the blame at the feet of British prime minister Cameron and French president Hollande (http://www.theatlantic.com/personal/archive/2016/03/the-obama-doctrine-the-atlantics-exclusive-report-on-presidents-hardest-foreign-policy-decisions/473151/).

4. Boundaries and Borderlands

1. However, the question of Europe's borders does not arise in the East only. Where does Europe end in the West? Is Greenland included? Regarding the South, see below.

2. There is a huge body of literature on the identity of Europe and what constitutes it: for the more essentialist points of view, or analyses denying cohesion because of the lack of primordial common elements, see A. Smith 1999. For studies of features that European countries share, see Therborn 1995; Kaelble 2001; Delanty 1995; on the presumption that the Communities are based on laws and "kommunikatives Handeln," see Habermas 1981; Ferry 2000, to name but a few.

3. Some of the richer and more democratic countries of Europe, Iceland, Norway, and Switzerland, as well as Liechtenstein, which depends on Switzerland for its currency and defense, stayed out of the EU to preserve their sovereignty and prosperity, and the strong economic, financial, and political niches that they had carved out for themselves. Nonetheless, they fall into the EU's web because of the latter's internal dynamics and politics, Internal Market, and Schengen Area. As a consequence, they entered elaborate agreements with the EU. Since 1994, the European Economic Area (EEA) links the EU to three of these countries, while Switzerland, which did not ratify the EEA, entered a series of bilateral agreements with the EU. Iceland, Liechtenstein, Norway and Switzerland, as well the microstates of Monaco, San Marino and the Vatican, are included in the Schengen Area, of which all EU states, apart from Ireland and the UK, are or will be members. On Schengen, see chapter 5.

4. This is no wonder in a state, Moldova, where roughly a third of the population holds a Romanian, that is, an EU passport. Around 120,000 of the 3.6 million inhabitants have Romanian passports, and 800,000 are said to be waiting for such passports. See Bidder 2010.

5. Poll organized by the Center for Social and Marketing Research, SOCIS, Kiev, and quoted in "More Than Half of Ukrainians Want to Join EU, Poll Shows," *Moscow Times*, 7 March 2014.

6. The misappropriation of approximately €1 billion by a pro-European government, that is, 12 percent of Moldova's GDP, unveiled in 2015, may, however, reverberate with regard to the country's orientation.

7. On Belarus, see the interview of Condoleezza Rice, US secretary of state, with Jill Dougherty, CNN, Moscow, 20 April 2005.

8. I owe this remark to my colleague Luis Martinez.

9. Italy and Spain demanded a CSCM (Conference on Security and Co-operation in the Mediterranean), emulating the CSCE that never came to light. A 5+5 framework, encompassing France, Italy, Spain, Portugal, and Malta, and the five southern states from Mauritania to Libya, that is, also including Morocco, Algeria and Tunisia, remained confined to more practical security cooperation issues.

10. His letter was addressed to his British counterpart, Jack Straw. He gained the support of the UK as well as Poland, Sweden, and Germany, besides the southern members of the EU.

11. The label "Wider Europe," which was coined first and might have conveyed the hope of future enlargements, was abandoned for the less ambiguous term "neighbours," in short, outsiders, albeit special ones.

12. The Union grants support thanks to those technical and financial instruments already in place in the 1990s, for example, Technical Assistance to the Community of Independent States (TACIS), designed for the ex-USSR, and Mesures d'accompagnement financières et techniques (MEDA), catering to the Mediterranean countries. They were merged in 2007 into a European Neighbourhood Policy Instrument (ENPI). Through the ENPI, €11.3 billion were disbursed for the years 2007–2013. The ENPI funding is superior to both MEDA and TACIS, especially if one takes into account the fact that the ENPI covers fewer countries than the former instruments: Mongolia and the five Central Asian countries, former recipient of TACIS, now have their own program and financial instrument. In 2011, after the start of the Arab uprisings, it was agreed that a new European Neighbourhood Instrument (ENI), taking effect in 2014, would ratchet up the offer, with €15 billion provided till 2020 to reward good governance, involving more programs. See below.

13. For more on the Association Agreement, and the DCFTA with Ukraine, see chapter 6.

14. The mobility partnership that was agreed upon in 2013 entails temporary-entry visa facilitation, temporary migration schemes, and the fight against illegal migration.

15. On the respective advantages and disadvantages of a DCFTA vs. membership in the ECU for Ukraine, see chapter 6.

16. Independence of the judiciary remains a major source of concern, and the introduction of plea bargaining has done little to alleviate concern. It has certainly hastened the pace of criminal proceedings, but raises questions concerning a system where the prosecutor is more powerful than the judge, and fines may nurture corruption.

17. See note 17.

18. Poland was then holding the rotating presidency of the European Union. Thus the commissioner for enlargement and neighbourhood policy, Štefan Füle, opposed the suspension of Belarus from the EaP and favored its inclusion in the multilateral dimension.

19. The Slovenian government tried to prevent a Belarusian oligarch, with which it was dubiously linked, from being included on the EU's blacklist.

20. The shortsightedness of the French government is well documented in a number of declarations by various French presidents, Jacques Chirac and Nicolas Sarkozy in particular. When visiting Tunisia in 2003, Chirac declared that "the first of all human rights, is to eat," while the human rights advocate Radhia Nasraoui was on hunger strike (liberation.fr 5/12/2003). In 2008, Sarkozy hailed the "increasing space given to human rights" in Tunisia (france24 28/4/2008). On 12 January 2011, in the midst of the upheavals against Ben Ali, the

French foreign minister, Michèle Alliot-Marie, offered to share with the Tunisian police the French know-how to "deal with security questions." France is Tunisia's major trading partner, and a number of major French enterprises have invested in the country, including Total, Air Liquide, Veolia, BNP, Société Générale, AGF, and Groupama.

21. The Association Agreement between the EU and Tunisia was signed in 1998, and the subcommittee met for the first time in 2007, though the principle of such a subcommittee for the neighborhood had already been adopted in 2005. The subcommittee's lack of traction confirms suspicions that human rights dialogues pursued by the EU may be of little avail, similar to a drawer, which is closed once the topic has been raised.

22. The European Commission funds radio programs, albeit with limited coverage, for example, a consortium of Russian, German, Polish, Lithuanian, and Belarusian partners, the European Radio for Belarus, and a Deutsche Welle program. Poland supports the Polish radio station Racija, targeting, among others, a Belarusian public since 1999. Belsat TV, the first independent TV channel also based in Warsaw, started broadcasting in 2007.

23. The Belarusian Journalists' Association received the prize in 2004, and Aleksandr Milinkevitch, a main critic of the regime, in 2006.

24. Named after the Polish king Stefan Báthory, voivod of Transylvania and king of the Lithuanian-Polish Commonwealth, the Batory Foundation was created in 1988 in Poland, with the backing of George Soros, the American financier and philanthropist of Hungarian origin. The foundation started supporting programs in Poland itself, and increasingly extended its help to neighboring countries such as Belarus and Ukraine. Among other things, it funds "Citizens in Action" and "Memoria" in Belarus.

25. Interview.

5. A Crisis in the Making?

1. The Schengen Agreement, which aimed at the gradual abolition of border checks, was signed in 1985 by five of the ten member states of the European Economic Community. In 1990 the Schengen Convention foresaw the abolition of internal borders and a common visa policy. It encompasses twenty-three EU member states and three non-EU members (Iceland, Norway, and Switzerland, to which Liechtenstein must be added). Since the erection of EU borders redirects migratory flows, these non EU-countries have had to adopt EU regulations on that matter, and join the Schengen Area for fear of bearing the brunt of migratory flows after the EU strengthened its outer borders (Lavenex and Uçarer 2004; Bigo and Guild 2005; Rijpma and Cremona 2007).

2. These definitions are provided by the United Nations High Commissioner for Refugees (UNHCR). The dividing lines between economic migrants, on the one hand, and refugees and asylum seekers, on the other, as well as between those who are individually persecuted and those who flee a conflict, are somewhat blurred (UNCHR 2015).

3. Hence, national borders are never tightly closed to so-called economic migrants. Thus, according to European statistics, between 2010 and 2013, about 1.4 million non-EU migrants a year legally settled in the EU—this number leaves refugees aside (European Commission 2015a). Besides family reunification, other legal means exist. Thus, a sixth or a fifth of Moldovans retain a Romanian passport and can travel to the Schengen Area. Last, illegal migrants also settle in the EU.

4. http://frontex.europa.eu/about-frontex/mission-and-tasks/. The concept of Integrated Border Management, which is not proper to the EU alone, refers to a policy involving all the activities of a country or group of countries to protect the external borders.

5. Turkish Bodrum is 167 miles from the Greek island of Lesbos, the Italian island of Lampedusa lies 88 miles off the Tunisian coast, and 60 miles off the African coast. The Canary Islands are 60 miles from the African coast.

6. Spain has been working with the Senegalese and Mauritanian governments over the past years, bringing down the number of migrants that have landed on the Canary Islands from over 30,000 to a couple of hundred, a case hailed as a success and an example.

7. Indeed Prussia was the first state to invent such agreements in the nineteenth century (Coleman 2009).

8. In some cases, the EU also set up CSDP missions to control borders: the EU Border Mission (EUBAM) at the border of the Transnistrian region of Moldova and Ukraine and EUBAM Rafah at the Egypt-Palestine border are such examples.

9. Krajina and Ukraine literally mean "border" or "on the border," and Brandenburg was formerly called Mark Brandenburg, the march of Brandenburg. I am not comparing the EU to an empire, in contrast to political scientists who do so (see Waever 1997; Zielonka 2006; Chandler 2006; Posener 2007, to name but a few). I am rather drawing an analogy to clarify the policy of the EU vis-à-vis its neighborhood.

10. *Hic sunt leones*, "Here are the lions" (or alternatively, *dracones*, the "dragons") labeled uncharted territories on medieval maps.

11. The erection of this fence at the border of an EU member state and a candidate country, Turkey, was to be completed at the end of 2015. It did not attract the same amount of attention, let alone criticism, that Hungary's fence toward the candidate country Serbia raised in 2015. Greece erected a similar barrier on its border with Turkey, at the river Evros/Mériç, in 2011 (see above).

12. It is difficult to estimate exactly how many migrants enter the EU, since they may be counted twice, when entering Greece and later reentering the EU after crossing the Balkans. They may also evade registration, either because the country they enter does not register them or does not register them properly, or because they want to settle in another EU country (see below). Applications may refer to first-time application, or to applications after rejection.

13. In 2014, men represented 70 percent of all asylum seekers in the EU-28, proportions that changed later when women and children constituted a majority (Eurostat 2015). In the first few months of 2016, 60 percent of the refugees were women and children (Council of Europe, Commissioner for Human Rights 2016). In November 2015, the Swedish government raised concern over the question of gender equality. That same month, the head of the Jewish community in Germany expressed his worries over Jewish-Muslim relations in the future.

14. In September 2015, President Gauck had already issued such a call.

15. Interviews.

16. As a whole, however, ECHO grants €4.4 billion for relief and recovery to IDPs and refugees in Lebanon, Jordan, Turkey, and Iraq. According to a former European civil servant, the EU had not previously distributed much aid, as the Turkish authorities rejected the conditions linked to disbursement. On the problem of EU disbursements to Turkey, see below on the lack of willingness on the part of Ankara to comply with EU specifications.

17. I thank Hamit Bozarslan, EHESS Paris, for this information.

18. Interview.

19. Before being voted into power in Greece, in January 2015, Syriza (i.e., the Radical Left Coalition) had promised to open the country's borders to refugees and abolish controls over the refugee camps that had so far been guarded in order to enforce registration, and also to improve the security of migrants who had previously often been harassed. When the new government was constituted, the maverick defense minister, Panos Kammenos, from the right-wing ANEL, asserted that if "Europe hits Greece, we send the migrants to Berlin" (http://www.skai.gr/news/politics/article/276903/kammenos-an-i-europi-htupisei-tin-ellada-stelnoume-tous-metanastes-verolino/). I thank my student Aris Lefakis for his help. I also thank Angeliki Dimitriadi from ECFR for her very illuminating and detailed explanations.

20. On 4 September, the Hungarian authorities let refugees leave the country for Austria and Germany after the Orbán government had first pretended to keep borders closed to allow registrations according to EU regulation.

21. For instance, sending Syrian children to schools that harbor a majority of Turkish pupils does not facilitate integration.

22. This runs counter to the Convention Relating to the Status of Refugees, which, as mentioned above, states that refugees have to respect the constitutional order of the country they enter and, thus, have to register.

23. Viktor Orbán accused Angela Merkel of "moral imperialism" (quoted in *Zeit Online* 23 September 2015).

24. For instance, on 1 January 2016, the BAMF restored stringent procedures to vet refugees.

25. In Estonia and Latvia, which have reluctantly accepted refugees, hesitation is often explained by the fact that these countries already harbor important (Russian) minorities. In France, the glaring failure to integrate parts of the second generation, migrants' children, repercussions of terrorist actions, and the overwhelming presence of the right-wing, xenophobic Front National account for limited acceptance of refugees in the past few years.

26. In 1979, France opened its doors to 120,000 boat people from Vietnam.

27. An EU member state facing urgent and exceptional pressures at its external borders, due to large numbers of third-country nationals trying to enter its territory illegally, may request support of Frontex's Rapid Border Intervention Teams mechanism (RABIT), created in 2007. Greece, in particular, has used this facility. Fabrice Leggeri became director of Frontex in 2015.

28. EU's help came from the European Asylum Support Office (EASO), Frontex, the EU Police Cooperation Agency (EUROPOL), and the EU Judicial Cooperation Agency (EUROJUST).

29. The European think tank ESI is also said to have inspired the blueprint.

6. Competitive Decadence?

1. The formula "competitive decadence" was coined by Leopold Labedz (1920–1993), the editor of *Survey* and head of the London office of the Polish Committee for the Defense of Workers (KOR). Pierre Hassner helped to make it known. Labedz wondered whether the USSR or the West would collapse first under its contradictions.

2. EU member states and Russia had to sign new border treaties. The ratification of the border treaty between Estonia and Russia, signed at long last in 2014, is still pending at the time of this writing. The EU harbors a sizable Russian minority, hovering above 500,000, mostly in the Baltic states; some of them are not fully integrated for many different reasons. Moreover, a considerable number of German Russians immigrated from the USSR and its "successor states" to Germany. Their number is difficult to determine for various reasons. Some of them carry a Russian passport.

3. In 1991, a North-Atlantic Cooperation Council, later Euro-Atlantic Partnership Council, was created to formalize Russia's relations with NATO. Russia participated in the Partnership for Peace, which it joined in June 1994, and in May 1997 a Founding Act on Mutual Relations, Cooperation and Security was signed. A Russia-NATO council was created in 2002 to examine security issues and conduct joint projects on a basis where Russia was supposed to play a more equal role than previously.

4. One may regret that Russia joined the Council of Europe. The Russian delegation has been able to intimidate the Council into subservience over the question of Chechnya and the war between Russia and Georgia.

5. Between 1991 and 2006, the Commission disbursed €2.7 billion to Russia, funded 1,500 projects in fifty-eight regions, and, in addition, moneys came from other programs, such as TACIS multicountry programs, including the Regional Program and the Cross-Border Cooperation Program (Delegation of the European Union to Russia). Over €100 million have gone to Kaliningrad since 1991 through TACIS and other EU instruments. https://eeas.europa.eu/headquarters/headquarters-homepage_en/720/The%20Russian%20Federation%20and%20the%20European%20Union%20(EU). Since Russia is not a member of the ENP, it has to cofinance these instruments.

6. Yevgeny Primakov (1996–1998) was followed by Igor Ivanov (1998–2004) and Sergei Lavrov (2004–).

7. The European answer to Russia's woes was petty, at most: the Commission merely offered food aid.

8. Besides the Common Economic Space, the three other spaces cover Freedom, Security, and Justice; External Security; Research and Education.

9. Kaliningrad was to become a Russian exclave in the EU after 2004.

10. Vladimir Putin was president from 2000 to 2008 and from 2012 to the present; he was prime minister between 2008 and 2012.

11. NATO members had refused to ratify the adapted version of this treaty, agreed upon at the OSCE summit in Istanbul in 1999 after the breakup of the USSR, because Russia did not comply with its commitment to withdraw its troops from Moldova and Georgia. Russia argued that the enlargement of NATO and the deployment of bases in Romania and Bulgaria modified the balance in Europe.

12. In 2007, the former head of the policy planning staff in the German Ministry of Defense, Ulrich Weisser, wrote: "After all that Germany inflicted upon Russia during World War II, we, Germans, have the duty to conduct a policy of reconciliation, compensation and cooperation with Russia." He added: "This policy vis-à-vis Russia, which has been pursued for decades, is threatened by the negative influence of the new member states from Central Europe, which perceive Russia differently from the way we do, due to their own experience" (Weisser 2007: 49).

13. Interview.

14. Conversely, 31 percent of East Germans support Germany's membership in transatlantic and European institutions, while 46 percent of West Germans favor a policy of neutrality or equidistance.

15. Interview.

16. The figures for Hungary and Austria were respectively 80 percent and 60 percent, for France 16 percent, while the UK did not buy any Russian gas at all.

17. Strangely enough, Claude Mandil, a former director of the International Energy Agency (IEA), did not take asymmetries into consideration, stressing only interdependence.

18. Only gas is being considered here as a case study, because the fixed transportation system through pipelines ties the EU to Russia, creating a particular kind of market and of interrelations, even though the gas market is changing through diversification (exploitation of shale gas, transportation of liquefied natural gas by tankers).

19. Nabucco, which would have linked the Caspian basin to European consumers, died of many causes, market uncertainties, limited funding, overcapacities of transportation, and scarcity of supply, all weaknesses that Gazprom astutely reinforced.

20. The Polish government sent a letter to the German chancellery in May 2005 to raise its concerns about the project, and contended that no reply was given until July that year (confirmed by a former Polish high official).

21. Leonid Kravchuk (1991–1994), Leonid Kuchma (1994–2005), Viktor Yushschenko (2005–2010) and his prime minister Yulia Tymoshenko (2005 and 2007–2010), and Viktor Yanukovych (2010–2014).

22. So did the Moldovan and Georgian governments which both agreed to a political association and DCFTA with the EU, in June 2014.

23. The Commissioner for Enlargement and Neighborhood Policy, Štefan Füle, dismissed, however, the need for a strategy, bizarrely equating the latter with a zero-sum game.

24. Among these are the Helsinki Final Act (1975), the CSCE's high mark, the Paris Charter for a New Europe (1990), which turned the CSCE into the OSCE, and the NATO-Russia agreement of 1997, all of which banned the use of force and called for the respect of sovereignty; two major arms-control treaties, the CFE, signed in 1990 and denounced by Moscow in 2007, which put a ceiling on conventional troops on the continent, and the 1987 treaty eliminating Intermediary Nuclear Forces; as well as a series of agreements specific to Ukraine: the Budapest Memorandum on Security Assurances of 1994, whereby the parties to the treaty, Russia, the United States, and the UK, provided security assurances to Ukraine and guaranteed its security as it relinquished the nuclear weapons that had been stationed on its soil at the time of the USSR; the 1997 Russian-Ukrainian Treaty of Friendship, Cooperation and Partnership, which pledged to respect sovereignty and borders; the 1997 Partition Treaty on the Status and Conditions of the Black Sea Fleet, and the 2010 Kharkiv Treaty, which specified the conditions under which the Russian Black Sea Fleet used facilities on Ukraine's Crimean peninsula, both denounced by the Duma in 2014.

25. The representatives of the secessionist entities of Donetsk and Luhansk also signed them.

26. The text of the "Protocol on the Results of Consultations of the Trilateral Contact Group," i.e., Minsk I (Minsk, 05/09/2014), is to be found on mfa.gov.ua. The full text of the Minsk agreement, i.e., Minsk II, is on ft.com.

27. Despite ratification in Parliament, the DCFTA was rejected by a majority of Dutch voters in a referendum held in April 2016.

Conclusion

1. Quoted in Hassner 2015: 36.

2. Remarks delivered on 8 May 2015 at the Brzezinski Institute.

3. In his 2014 article, published in *Foreign Affairs*, Walter Russell Mead spoke of "the return of geopolitics," which G. John Ikenberry denounced as an illusion in the same issue (Mead 2014; Ikenberry 2014).

4. In his famous book *The Great Illusion: A Study of the Relation of Military Power in Nations to Their Economic and Social Advantages*, Norman Angell did not announce the end of all wars, as often surmised, but rather contended that war did bring the easy catch that it was supposed to. One might add that it is not always the same individuals who acquire wealth through peace and those who grab resources in times of war—even though wealth through peace may sometimes be equated with resource grab.

Bibliography

Adomeit, Hannes. 2014. "Collapse of Russia's Image in Germany: Who Is to Blame?" *Outlook* (blog of the Carnegie Moscow Center), 18 February. http://carnegie.ru/commentary/?fa=54540.

Ahren, Raphael. 2009. "Solana: EU Has Closer Ties to Israel Than Potential Member Croatia." *Haaretz*, 7 April.

AIDA (Asylum Information Database). 2015. "Germany: Halt on Dublin Procedures for Syrians." 24 August. asylumineurope.org.

Almond, Gabriel, and Sidney Verba. 1963. *The Civic Culture: Political Attitudes and Democracy in Five Nations*. Thousand Oaks, CA: Sage Publications.

Amato, Giuliano. 2005. *The Balkans in Europe's Future*. International Commission on the Balkans. Sofia: Centre for Liberal Strategies.

Amnesty International. 2015. "Syria's Refugee Crisis in Numbers." 4 September. www.amnesty.org.

——. 2016. "Turkey: Illegal Mass Returns of Syrian Refugees Expose Fatal Flaws in EU-Turkey Deal." 1 April. www.amnesty.org.

Andréani, Gilles. 2010. "Answering Medvedev." *Survival* 52, no. 1: 236–244.

Andréani, Jacques. 2005. *Le piège: Helsinki et la chute du communisme*. Paris: Odile Jacob.

Angell, Norman. 1910. *The Great Illusion: A Study of the Relation of Military Power in Nations to Their Economic and Social Advantages*. New York: G. P. Putnam's Sons.

APRODEV et al. 2012. "La paix au rabais: Comment l'Union européenne renforce les colonies israéliennes." http://www.fidh.org/IMG/pdf/lapaix.pdf.

Arbitration Commission. 1992. "The Opinions of the Arbitration Commission 4–10." *European Journal of International Law* 4, no. 1: 74.

Arendt, Hannah. [1943] 1994. "We Refugees." In Marc Robinson, ed., *Altogether Elsewhere: Writers on Exile*. Boston: Faber and Faber.

——. 1949. "The Rights of Man? What Are They?" *Modern Review* 3, no. 1.

Aron, Raymond. 1951. *Guerres en chaîne*. Paris: Gallimard.

——. 1959. *La société industrielle et la guerre*. Paris: Plon.

Ash, Timothy Garton. 2014. "Putin's Deadly Doctrine." *New York Times*, 18 July.

Åslund, Anders. 2013. "Ukraine's Choice: European Association Agreement or Eurasian Union?" Policy Brief, PB 13–22, Peterson Institute for International Economics, Washington, DC, September.

Asmus, Ronald D. 2010. *A Little War That Shook the World: Georgia, Russia, and the Future of the West*. New York: Palgrave Macmillan.

Baker, James A., III. 2002. "Russia in NATO?" *Washington Quarterly* 25, no. 1: 95–103.

Balleix, Corinne. 2010. *L'aide européenne au développement*. Paris: La Documentation française.

BAMF (Bundesamt für Migration und Flüchtlinge). 2015. "Aktuelle Zahlen zu Asyl." December. bamf.de.

Bánffy, Miklós. 2002. *Vos jours sont comptés*. Paris: Phébus. Translation of the 1934 Hungarian edition.

Barnett, Michael, and Raymond Duvall, eds. 2003. *Power in Global Governance*. Cambridge: Cambridge University Press.

——. 2005. "Power in International Politics." *International Organization* 59 (Winter): 39–75.

Batory, Agnes. 2010. "Kin-State Identity in the European Context: Citizenship, Nationalism, and Constitutionalism in Hungary." *Nations and Nationalism* 16, no. 1: 31–48.

BDI (Bundesverband der deutschen Industrie). 2014. BDI Aussenwirtschaftsreport, 2. Berlin.

Behr, Timo. 2010. *Regional Integration in the Mediterranean: Moving out of the Deadlock?* Paris: Notre Europe.

Bernardt, Rudolf, et al. 1994. "Report on the Conformity of the Legal Order of the Russian Federation with Council of Europe Standards." *Human Rights Law Journal* 15, no. 7.

Bertrand-Sanz, Agnès. 2010. "The Conflict and the EU's Assistance to the Palestinians." In Bulut Aymat Esra, ed., *European Involvement in the Arab-Israeli Conflict*, 43–53. Chaillot Papers 124. Paris: Institute of Security Studies of the European Union.

Bērziņš, Jānis. 2014. "Russia's New Generation Warfare in Ukraine." Policy Paper 02, National Defence Academy of Latvia's Center for Security and Strategic Research, Riga, April.

Bibó, István. 1986. *Misère des petits états d'Europe de l'est*. Paris: L'Harmattan.

Bicchi, Federica. 2007. *European Foreign Policy Making towards the Mediterranean*. New York: Palgrave Macmillan.

Bidder, Benjamin. 2010. "Entering the EU through the Backdoor." *Spiegel Online*, 13 July.

Biehl, Heiko, Bastian Giegerich, and Alexandra Jonas. 2013. *Strategic Cultures in Europe: Security and Defence Policies across the Continent*. Potsdam: Springer.

Bigo, Didier, and Elspeth Guild. 2005. *Controlling Frontiers: Free Movement into and within Europe*. Aldershot: Ashgate.

Bildt, Carl. 1998. *Peace Journey: The Struggle for Peace in Bosnia*. London: Weidenfeld and Nicolson.

Bildt, Carl, Karel Schwarzenberg, Radek Sikorski, and Guido Westerwelle. 2010. "Lukashenko the Loser." *International Herald Tribune*, 24–26 December.

Blanke, Hermann-Josef, and Stelio Mangiameli. 2013. *The Treaty on European Union (TEU): A Commentary*. Heidelberg: Springer.

Boidevaix, Francine. 2005. "L'Europe gère les Balkans: La responsabilité reste au concert des puissances." *Relations Internationales* 1, no. 121: 91–107. doi: 10.3917/ri.121.0091.

Bordachev, Timofei V. 2003. "Strategy and Strategies." In Arkady Moshes, ed., *Rethinking the Respective Strategies of Russia and the European Union*, 31–61. Helsinki and Moscow: Special FIIA and Carnegie Moscow Center.

Bossuat, Gérard. 2011. *Emile Noël, premier secrétaire général de la Commission européenne*. Brussels: Bruylant.

Bozarslan, Hamit. 2013. *Histoire de la Turquie: De l'empire à nos jours*. Paris: Éditions Tallandier.

Briedis, Laimonas. 2009. *Vilnius: City of Strangers*. Budapest: CEU Press, Baltos Lankos.

Bull, Hedley. 1982. "Civilian Power Europe: A Contradiction in Terms?" *Journal of Common Market Studies* 21, no. 2: 149–164.

Bundesregierung. 2015a. Pressekonferenz Pressestatements von Bundeskanzlerin Merkel und dem französischen Staatspräsidenten Hollande vor ihrem Gespräch am 24. August 2015.

——. 2015b. Pressekonferenz von Bundeskanzlerin Merkel, dem österreichischen Bundeskanzler Faymann, dem serbischen Ministerpräsidenten Vučić, und der Hohen Vertreterin der Union für Außen- und Sicherheitspolitik und Vizepräsidentin der Europäischen Kommission Mogherini anl. der Konferenz zum westlichen Balkan am 27. August 2015.

Buzan, Barry, and Ole Waever. 2003. *Regions and Powers: The Structure of International Security*. Cambridge: Cambridge University Press.

Buzzati, Dino. [1945] 1989. *Il deserto dei Tartari*. Milan: Mondadori.

Byrne, Andrew, and Duncan Robinson. 2016. "Athens Hits Back at EU Plan to Isolate Greece over Migrants." *Financial Times*, 25 January.

Cadman, Emily, and Henry Mance. 2016. "Michael Gove Says Leaving EU Would Mean Quitting Single Market." *Financial Times*, 8 May.

Cameron, Alastair. 2012. "The Channel Axis: France, the UK and NATO." In Adrian Johnson and Saqeb Mueen, eds., *Short War, Long Shadow: The Political and Military Legacies of the 2011 Libya Campaign*, 15–24. Whitehall Report 1–12. London: Royal United Services Institutes.

Cameron, David. 2013. *EU Speech at Bloomberg*. London. 23 January. www.gov.uk/government/speeches/eu-speech-at-bloomberg.

Capelle-Pogàcean, Antonela. 2011. "*Hybris* et incertitude dans la Hongrie de Viktor Orbàn." November. http://www.ceri-sciences-po.org.

Cassarino, Jean-Pierre. 2010. "Informalising Readmission Agreements in the EU Neighbourhood." *International Spectator* 42, no. 2: 179–196.

———. 2015. "Nouveaux enjeux du système de la readmission." In Camille Schmoll, Hélène Thiollet, and Catherine Withol de Wenden, eds., *Migrations en Méditerranée*, 73–88. Paris: CNRS Éditions.

Chandler, David. 2006. *Empire in Denial: The Politics of State-Building*. London: Pluto Press.

———. 2007. "EU Statebuilding: Securing the Liberal Peace through Enlargement." *Global Society* 21, no. 4: 593–607.

Chopin, Thierry, and Christian Lequesne. 2016. "Differentiation as a Double-Edged Sword: Member States' Practices and Brexit." *International Affairs* 92, no. 3: 531–545.

Christiansen, Thomas, Fabio Petito, and Ben Tonra. 2002. "Fuzzy Politics around Fuzzy Borders: The European Union's Near Abroad." *Cooperation and Conflict* 35, no. 4: 389–417.

Clark, Christopher. 2012. *The Sleepwalkers: How Europe Went to War in 1914*. London: Penguin.

Coakley, John. 2008. "Has the Northern Ireland Problem Been Solved?" *Journal of Democracy* 19, no. 3: 98–112.

Coleman, Nils. 2009. *European Readmission Policy: Third Country Interests and Refugee Rights*. Leiden: Martinus Nijhoff.

Coman, Ramona. 2006. "Les défis de l'européanisation dans la réforme du système judiciaire." *Revue Française de Sciences Politiques* 6: 999–1027.

Commission of the European Communities. 1989. *Commission Opinion on Turkey's Request for Accession to the Community*, SEC(89) 2290, final/2, Brussels, 20 December.

———. 2003. "Wider Europe—Neighbourhood—A New Framework for Relations with Our Eastern and Southern Neighbours." Communication from the Commission to the Council and the European Parliament, COM(2003) 104 final, Brussels, 11 March.

———. 2004. "European Neighborhood Policy, Strategy Paper." Communication from the Commission, COM(2004) 373 final, 12 May.

Committee to Protect Journalists. 2013. *2013 Prison Census: 211 Journalists Jailed Worldwide, December*. cpj.org.

Cooper, Robert. 2005. "Imperial Liberalism." *National Interest* 79: 25–34.

Cottey, Andrew. 2009. "Sub-regional Cooperation in Europe: An Assessment." Bruges Regional Integration and Global Governance Papers, 3/2009.

Council of Europe. 2011. *Opinion of the Commissioner for Human Rights on Hungary's Media Legislation in Light of Council of Europe Standards on Freedom of the Media*. CommDH (2011) 10, Strasbourg, 25 February.

Council of Europe, Commissioner for Human Rights. 2016. "Human Rights of Refugee and Migrant Women and Girls Need to Be Better Protected." The Commissioner's Human Rights Comments, 7 March.

Council of the European Union. 1993. "Presidency Conclusions." Brussels, 10–11 December.

———. 1994. "Presidency Conclusions." Essen, 9 and 10 December.

———. 2000. "Presidency Conclusions." Santa Maria de Feira, 19–20 June.

———. 2003. "Presidency Conclusions, 11638/03." Thessaloniki, 19 and 20 June; Brussels, 1 October.

———. 2004. "Presidency Conclusions, 16238/04." Brussels, 14–15 December, 17 December.

———. 2011a. "Council Conclusions on Libya." 3076th Foreign Affairs Council Meeting. Brussels, 21 March.

———. 2011b. "European Union Military Operation in Support of Humanitarian Assistance Operations in Response to the Crisis Situation in Libya (EUFOR Libya) DECISION 2011/210/CFSP." 1 April.

Court of Justice of the European Union. 2013. "Judgment in Case C-4/11 Bundesrepublik Deutschland v Kaveh Puid." Press Release, No. 147/13, Luxembourg, 14 November.

Crawford, Beverly. 1995. "German Foreign Policy and European Political Cooperation: The Diplomatic Recognition of Croatia." *German Politics and Society* 13, no. 2: 1–34.

———. 1996. "Explaining Defection from International Cooperation: Germany's Unilateral Recognition of Croatia." *World Politics* 48, no. 4: 482–521.

Crines, Andrew S., Timothy Heppell, and Peter Dorey. 2016. *The Political Rhetoric and Oratory of Margaret Thatcher*. Basingstoke: Palgrave Macmillan.

CSCE (Commission on Security and Cooperation in Europe). 1975. Final Act.

Danner, David. 1997. "The U.S. and the Yugoslav Catastrophe." *New York Review of Books*, 20 November, 64.

Davies, Will. 2016. "Thoughts on the Sociology of Brexit." *PERCblog*, 24 June. www.perc.org.uk//project_posts/thoughts-on-the-sociology-of-brexit/.

Delanty, Gerard. 1995. *Inventing Europe: Idea, Identity, Reality*. New York: St. Martin's.

Delanty, Gerard, and Chris Rumford. 2005. *Rethinking Europe: Social Theory and the Implications of Europeanization*. London: Routledge.

Delcour, Laure. 2002. *La politique de l'Union européenne en Russie (1990–2000): De l'assistance au partenariat?* Paris: L'Harmattan.

Del Sarto, Rafaella, and Tobias Schumacher. 2005. "From EMP to ENP: What's at Stake with the European Neighbourhood Policy towards the Southern Mediterranean?" *European Foreign Affairs Review* 10: 17–38.

De Souza, Lúcio Vinhas. 2011. *An Initial Estimation of the Economic Effects of the Creation of the EurAsEC Customs Union on Its Members*. Economic Premise, no. 47. Washington, DC: The World Bank.

Deutsch, Karl W., et al. 1957. *Political Community and the North Atlantic Area: International Organization in the Light of Historical Experience*. Princeton, NJ: Princeton University Press.

Diez, Thomas, Mathias Albert, and Stephan Stetter. 2008. *The European Union and Border Conflicts: The Power of Integration and Association*. Cambridge: Cambridge University Press.

Dosenrode, Soren, and Anders Stubkjaers. 2002. *The European Union and the Middle East*. Contemporary European Studies 12. London: Bloomsbury.

Duchêne, François. 1972. "The European Community and the Uncertainties of Inter-dependence." In Max Kohnstamm and Wolfgang Hager, eds., *A Nation Writ Large? Foreign Policy Problems before the European Community.* London: Macmillan.

ECtHR (European Court of Human Rights). 2011. "ECtHR—MSS v. Belgium and Greece (GC)." 30696/09, 21/01.

EIA (US Energy Information Administration). 2014. Russia Country Brief, rev. 12 March.

Eldridge, Justin L. C. 2007. "Playing at Peace: Western Politics, Diplomacy, and the Sta-bilization of Macedonia." *European Security* 11, no. 3: 46–90.

Eltchaninoff, Michel. 2015. *Dans la tête de Vladimir Poutine.* Solin: Actes Sud.

Emerson, Michael, and Gergana Noutcheva. 2004. "Europeanisation as a Gravity Model of Democratisation." CEPS Working Document 214, Brussels, November.

Energy Charter Secretariat. 2004. "The Energy Charter Treaty and Related Documents: A Legal Framework for International Energy Cooperation." Brussels.

EPF (Eurasia Partnership Foundation). 2013. "Knowledge and Attitudes towards the EU in Georgia: Changes and Trends 2009–2013."

ESI (European Stability Initiative). 2005. *Islamic Calvinists: Change and Conservatism in Central Anatolia.* Report, Berlin-Istanbul, 19 September. www.esiweb.org.

Euro-Mediterranean Human Rights Network. 2010. Financial Statement, 2010. 8 December. Copenhagen.

European Commission. 2006a. "Attitudes towards European Union Enlargement." *Special Eurobarometer*, July.

——. 2006b. *Communication of the Commission to the European Parliament and the Council, Enlargement Strategy and Main Challenges, 2006–2009, Including Annexed Special Report on the EU's Capacity to Integrate New Members.* SEC(2006) 1383–1390, COM(2006) 649 final, Brussels, 8.11.

——. 2009a. Concept Note on Libya—Country Strategy Paper and National Indicative Programme 2011–2013, Brussels, April.

——. 2009b. "Views on European Union Enlargement: Analytical Report." *Flash Euro-barometer*, February.

——. 2010a. "European Commission and Libya Agree on a Migration Cooperation Agenda during High-Level Visit to Boost EU-Libya Relations." MEMO/10/472, Brussels, 5 October.

——. 2010b. *Report of the Commission to the European Parliament and the Coun-cil on Progress in Romania under the Co-operation and Verification Mechanism.* SEC(2010) 949, Brussels.

——. 2011. "EU Response to the Arab Spring." The SPRING programme, Brussels, 27/09/2011.

——. 2012a. "Antitrust: Commission Opens Proceedings against Gazprom." IP/12/937, 04/09/2012.

——. 2012b. "EU-Ukraine Deep and Comprehensive Free Trade Area."

——. 2012c. "The Cooperation and Verification Mechanism for Bulgaria and Roma-nia." *Flash Eurobarometer* 351, Brussels.

——. 2013. "Development and Cooperation." EuropeAid, Morocco.

——. 2014a. "European Commission Presents a Framework to Safeguard the Rule of Law in the European Union." 11 March.

——. 2014b. "Myths about the EU-Ukraine Association Agreement: Setting the Facts Straight." 22 January.

——. 2014c. *Report from the Commission to the Council and the European Parliament, EU Anti-Corruption Report.* COM(2014) 38 final, Brussels, 3 February.

——. 2015a. "Asylum Statistics." Eurostat.

——. 2015b. "Immigration in the EU Based on Eurostat." 10 June.

——. 2016. "Communication from the European Commission to the European Parliament, the European Council and the Council: First Report on Relocation and Resettlement." COM(2016) 165 final, Brussels, 16.3.

European Commission, DGs Migration and Home Affairs. 2015. "Funding in the Areas of Migration and Border Management." http://ec.europa.eu/dgs/home-affairs/what-we-do/policies/european-agenda-migration/background-information/docs/funding_country_sheet_bg_en.pdf.

European Commission, Directorate-General for Trade, Export Helpdesk. 2013. Statistics.

European Commission, High Representative of the European Union for Foreign Affairs and Security Policy. 2013. "Implementation of the European Neighbourhood Policy in Georgia: Progress in 2012 and Recommendations for Action." SWD(2013) 90 final, Brussels, 20.3.

European Commission, Humanitarian and Civil Protection. 2012. "The Libyan Crisis, Facts and Figures, as of 11 January 2012."

——. 2015. Turkey. "Syria Crisis June."

European Council. 1980. "Venice Declaration." 13 June. http://eeas.europa.eu/mepp/docs/venice_declaration_1980_en.pdf.

——. 1999a. "Common Strategy of the European Union of 4 June 1999 on Russia." 1999/414/CFSP.

——. 1999b. "Presidency Conclusion." 24–25 March.

——. 2003. "A Secure Europe in a Better World." European Security Strategy, Brussels, 12 December.

——. 2011. (Extraordinary) EUCO 7/1/11 REV 1, CO EUR 5, CONCL 2, 11 March.

——. 2015. "Meeting of Heads of State or Government with Turkey." EU-Turkey statement, 29/11/2015.

——. 2016. "Schengen Evaluation of Greece: Council Adopts Recommendation to Address Deficiencies in External Borders." Brussels, 12 February.

European Council Decision. 2015a. (EU) 2015/1523 of 14 September 2015 Establishing Provisional Measures in the Area of International Protection for the Benefit of Italy and of Greece.

——. 2015b. (EU) 2015/1601 of 22 September 2015 Establishing Provisional Measures in the Area of International Protection for the Benefit of Italy and Greece.

European Court of Auditors. 2003a. *PHARE and ISPA Funding of Environmental Projects in Candidate Countries.*

——. 2003b. *Twinning as the Main Instrument to Support Institution-Building in Candidate Countries.*

——. 2012. *European Union Assistance to Kosovo Related to the Rule of Law.* Special Report 18/2012.

——. 2013. Annual Report.

European Economic and Social Committee. 2008. "Opinion of the European Economic and Social Committee on the Role of the EU in the Northern Ireland Peace Process." SC/029, Brussels, 23 October.

European External Action Service and European Commission Directorate-General for Development and Cooperation—EuropeAid. 2014. "Programming of the European Neighbourhood Instrument (ENI—2014–2020): Strategic Priorities 2014–2020 and Multi-annual Indicative Programme 2014–2017; European Neighbourhood-Wide Measures."

European Parliament. 1961. *Rapport de Willi Birkelbach sur les aspects politiques et institutionnels de l'adhésion ou de l'association à la Communauté.* 19 December.

——. 2012. *European Parliament Resolution of 16 February 2012 on the Recent Political Developments in Hungary.* 2012/2511(RSP).

Eurostat. 2015. "Asylum Statistics." ec.europa.eu/eurostat/statistics-explained.

Eyl-Mazzega, Marc-Antoine. 2010. "L'Ukraine, les relations Ukraine-UE et la sécurité énergétique de l'Europe: Coopérations? transformations? européanisation? risque? ajustements et convergences." PhD diss., Paris, Institut d'études politiques.

Faye, Jean-Pierre. 1992. *L'Europe une: Les philosophes et l'Europe.* With a preface by Jacques Delors. Paris: Gallimard.

Featherstone, Kevin, and Dimitris Papadimitriou. 2008. *The Limits of Europeanization: Reform Capacity and Policy Conflict in Greece.* London: Palgrave.

Ferry, Jean-Marc. 2000. *La question de l'état européen.* Paris: Gallimard.

Fischer, Sabine. 2009. "The European Union Monitoring Mission in Georgian (EUMM)." In Grevi Giovanni, Damien Helly, and Daniel Keohane, eds., *European Security and Defence Policy: The First 10 Years (1999–2009),* 379–390. Paris: EU Institute for Security Studies.

Fischer, Severin, and Oliver Geden. 2015. "Die Grenzen der 'Energieunion': Auch in absehbarer Zukunft werden lediglich pragmatische Fortschritte bei der Energiemarktregulierung im Zentrum der EU-Energie- und -Klimapolitik stehen." Berlin, SWP Aktuell 36, April.

Foreign and Commonwealth Office. 2002. Letter from Jack Straw to Josep Piqué, London, 28 January.

Foucher, Michel. 1991. *Fronts et frontiers: Un tour du monde géopolitique.* Paris: Fayard.

France, Olivier de, and Nick Witney. 2013. "Europe's Strategic Cacophony (Policy Brief, 77)." Brussels: European Council on Foreign Relations.

Frontex. 2015. "Annual Risk Analysis." frontex.europa.eu.

Gallagher, Tom. 2009. *Romania and the European Union: How the Weak Vanquished the Strong.* Manchester: Manchester University Press.

Galtung, Johan. 1973. *The European Community: A Superpower in the Making.* Oslo: Universitetsforlaget; London: George Allen & Unwin.

Garde, Paul. 1991. *Vie et mort de la Yougoslavie.* Paris: Fayard.

Gauck, Joachim. 2015. "Unsere Möglichkeiten sind endlich: Bundespräsident Gauck hat für Mitgefühl gegenüber Flüchtlingen plädiert; Die Aufnahmefähigkeit Deutschlands sei aber begrenzt und die Grenzen müssten sicher bleiben." *Die Zeit* online, 27 September.

——. 2016. "Über die Hoffnung auf Wohlstand—Anmerkungen zu Einwanderung und Flucht nach Europa." Weltwirtschaftsforum in Davos, 20 January. www.bunde spraesident.de.

Gawęda, Marcin. 2013. "Kto płacił więcej od Polski za gaz?" *Onet.pl*, 7 February.

Gehler, Michael. 2004. "A Newcomer Experienced in European Integration: Austria." In Wolfram Kaiser and Jürgen Elvert, eds., *European Union Enlargement: A Comparative History*, 131–149. London: Routledge.

George, Stephen. 1998. *An Awkward Partner: Britain in the European Community*. 3rd ed. Oxford: Oxford University Press.

Gillspie, Richard, and Richard Youngs. 2002. *The European Union and Democracy Promotion: The Case of North Africa*. Portland, OR: Frank Cass.

Glaurdic, Josip. 2011. *The Hour of Europe: Western Powers and the Breakup of Yugoslavia*. New Haven, CT: Yale University Press.

Gloriant, Frédéric. 2014. "Le grand schisme: La France, la Grande-Bretagne et les problèmes euro-atlantiques, 1957–1963." Thesis, Université de Paris-3 Sorbonne Nouvelle.

Gnesotto, Nicole. 1994. *Leçons de la Yougoslavie*. Chaillot Papers 14. Paris: Institute of Security Studies of the European Union.

Gökalp, Ziya. [1915] 2008. *Kizil elma* (The Red Apple). Ankara: Elips Kitap.

Goldgeier, James M., and Michael McFaul. 2003. *Power and Purpose: U.S. Policy toward Russia after the Cold War*. Washington, DC: Brookings Institution.

Gorbachev, Mikhail. 1996. *Memoirs*. New York: Doubleday.

——. 2014. "'I Am against All Walls': Interview with Maxim Korshunov." *Russia beyond the Headlines*, 16 October.

Gordadze, Thornike. 2009. "Georgian-Russian Relations in the 1990s." In Svante E. Cornell and S. Frederick Starr, eds., *The Guns of August 2008: Russia's War in Georgia*, 28–48. London: M. E. Sharpe.

Gower, Jackie. 1999. "EU Policy to Central and Eastern Europe." In Karen Henderson, ed., *Back to Europe: Central and Eastern Europe and the European Union*. London: UCL.

Grabbe, Heather. 2001. "How Does Europeanization Affect CEE Governance? Conditionality, Diffusion, and Diversity." *Journal of European Public Policy* 8, no. 6.

——. 2002. "European Union Conditionality and the Acquis Communautaire." *International Political Science Review* 23, no. 3: 249–268.

——. 2006. *The EU's Transformative Power: Europeanization through Conditionality in Central and Eastern Europe*. Basingstoke: Palgrave Macmillan.

Grardel, Alice. 2009. *Le "Programme spécial de soutien pour la paix et la réconciliation en Irlande du Nord" de l'Union européenne, et ce qu'il révèle du processus d'intégration d'une région en conflit à ses institutions, mémoire de sciences politiques*. Paris: Sciences Po (Politiques et sociétés en Europe).

Gros, Daniel, and Alfred Steinherr. 2004. *Economic Transition in Central and Eastern Europe*. Cambridge: Cambridge University Press.

Guiraudon, Virginie. 2003. "Before the EU Border: Remote Control of the 'Huddled Masses.'" In K. Groenendijk, E. Guild, and P. Minderhout, eds., *In Search of Europe's Borders*, 191–214. The Hague: Kluwer Law International.

Gussarsson, Maria. 2004. "Combining Dependence with Distance: Sweden." In Wolfram Kaiser and Jürgen Elvert, eds., *European Union Enlargement: A Comparative History*, 170–188. London: Routledge.

Guzzini, Stefano. 1993. "Structural Power: The Limits of Neorealist Power Analysis." *International Organization* 47, no. 3: 443–478.

Habermas, Jürgen. 1981. *Theorie des kommunikativen Handelns*. Frankfurt am Main: Suhrkamp.

Hacke, Christian. 1993. *Weltmacht wider Willen: Die Außenpolitik der Bundesrepublik Deutschland*. Frankfurt am Main: Ullstein.

Hanioğlu, M. Sükrü. 2008. *A Brief History of the Late Ottoman Empire*. Princeton, NJ: Princeton University Press.

Hassner, Pierre. 2014. "Feu (sur) l'ordre international?" *Esprit*, August–September.

———. 2015. *La revanche des passions*. Paris: Fayard.

Haukkala, Hiski, and Sergei Medvedev, eds. 2001. *The EU Common Strategy on Russia: Learning the Grammar of the CFSP*. Helsinki: Ulkopoliittinen instituutti and Institut für Europäische Politik.

Havel, Václav. 1991. "Don't Make Us Europe's Second-Class Citizens." *The European*, 14 June.

Hayward, Katy. 2006. "Reiterating National Identities: The European Union Conception of Conflict Resolution in Northern Ireland." *Cooperation and Conflict* 41, no. 3: 261–284.

———. 2007. "Mediating the European Ideal: Cross-Border Programmes and Conflict Resolution on the Island of Ireland." *Journal of Common Market Studies* 45, no. 3: 675–693.

Hayward, Katy, and Antje Wiener. 2008. "The Influence of the EU towards Conflict Transformation on the Island of Ireland." In Thomas Diez et al., eds., *The European Union and Border Conflicts: The Power of Integration and Association*, 33–63. Cambridge: Cambridge University Press.

Hibou, Béatrice. 2006. *La force de l'obéissance: Économie politique de la répression en Tunisie*. Paris: Éditions la Découverte.

Hillion, Christophe. 2011. "EU Enlargement." In Paul Craig and Gráinne de Búrca, eds., *The Evolution of EU Law*, 188–216. Oxford: Oxford University Press.

Hirschman, Albert O. 1977. *The Passions and the Interests: Political Arguments for Capitalism before Its Triumph*. Princeton, NJ: Princeton University Press.

Holbrooke, Richard. 1998. *To End a War*. New York: Random House.

House of Lords, European Union Committee. 2006. *The Further Enlargement of the EU: Threat of Opportunity? Report with Evidence*. London: The Stationery Office Limited, 23 November.

———. 2008. *The European Union and Russia*. London: The Stationery Office Limited, May.

———. 2015. *The European Union and Russia: Before and Beyond the Crisis in Ukraine*. London: The Stationery Office Limited, February.

Howorth, Jolyon. 2007. *The Security and Defence Policy in the European Union*. Basingstoke: Palgrave Macmillan.

Human Rights Watch. 2009. "Italy/Libya: Gaddafi Visit Celebrates Dirty Deal." 9 June. hrw.org.

———. 2013. *Hungary: Constitution Changes Warrant EU Action*. 12 March. hrw.org.

Hurrelmann, Klaus, and Michael Weichert, eds. 2015. *Lost in Democratic Transition: Political Challenges and Perspectives for Young People in South East Europe; Result of Representative Surveys in Eight Countries*. Sarajevo: Friedrich Ebert Stiftung Regional Dialogue SEE.

Hyndle-Hussein, Joanna. 2014. "Russia-Lithuania: Towards a Normalisation of Gas Relations?" *OSW Analyses*, 4 June. https://www.osw.waw.pl/en/publikacje/analyses/2014-06-04/russia-lithuania-towards-a-normalisation-gas-relations.

Ikenberry, G. John. 2014. "The Illusion of Geopolitics." *Foreign Affairs* 93, no. 3: 89–90.

Ilievski, Zoran, and Dane Taleski. 2009. "Was the EU's Role in Conflict Management in Macedonia a Success?" *Ethnopolitics* 8, nos. 3–4: 355–367.

Independent International Fact-Finding Mission on the Conflict in Georgia. 2009. Report.

Institute for Regional and International Studies. 2012. *The Western Balkans in 2010/11: Departures in Democratisation and European Integration in Europe's Southeast*. Sofia, January.

Ioffe, Grigory. 2008. *Understanding Belarus and How Western Policy Misses the Mark*. Lanham, MD: Rowman and Littlefield.

IOM (International Organization for Migration). 2014. "Fatal Journeys: Tracking Lives Lost during Migration." iom.int.

———. 2015. "Missing Migrants Project Newsdesk." 27 November. iom.int.

Ipsos MORI. 2016. *Half of People in Nine European Countries Believe UK Will Vote to Leave the EU*, 9 May. www.ipsos-mori.com.

Ischinger, Wolfgang. 2015. "Eine Aufgabe für Generationen: Der Westen muss gegenüber Deutschland auf eine neue Doppelstrategie setzen." *Internationale Politik*, January–February, 30–35.

Jaidi, Larabi, and Ivan Martin. 2010. "Comment faire avancer le statut avancé UE-Maroc." Institut Européen de la Méditerranée. www.iemed.org.

Jeandesboz, Julien. 2007. "Définir le voisin: La genèse de la Politique européenne de voisinage." In "Construire le voisin: La genèse de la Politique européenne de voisinage." *Cultures et Conflits* 66 (Summer): 11–12.

Joffe, Josef. 1984. "Europe's American Pacifier." *Foreign Policy* 54 (Spring): 64–82.

Johansson, Elisabeth. 2001. "EU and Its Near Neighbourhood: Subregionalization in the Baltic Sea and in the Mediterranean." In Nicolas Levrat and Pierre Willa, eds., *EU's Influence and Capability in International Relations*, 188–211. EUROPA, Graduate Institute of European Studies, University of Geneva.

Jones, Dorian. 2015. "EU's Delayed Report on Turkey Fuels Human Rights Concerns." *Voice of America*, 21 October.

Jones, Sam. 2016. "Sea Gives Terrorists 'Back Door into Europe,' Experts Warn." *Financial Times*, 5 February.

Jorry, Hélène. 2007. "Construction of a European Institutional Model for Managing Operational Cooperation at the EU's External Borders: Is the FRONTEX Agency a Decisive Step Forward?" Research Paper 6, CEPS: Challenge Liberty and Security, March.

Juncker, Jean-Claude. 2014a. "My Priorities." http://juncker.epp.eu/my-priorities.

———. 2014b. "A New Start for Europe." Commission Européenne, Communiqué de Presse, Base de données, 15 July.

Jungholt, Thorsten. 2014. "Die Deutschen gehen auf Distanz zum Westen." *Die Welt*, 3 April.

Kaelble, Hartmut. 2001. *Europäer über Europa: Die Entstehung des europäischen Selbstverständnisses im 19. und 20. Jahrhundert*. Frankfurt am Main: Campus.

Kaiser, Wolfram. 2004. "'What Alternative Is Open to Us?': Britain." In Wolfram Kaiser and Jürgen Elverts, eds., *European Union Enlargement: A Comparative History*, 10–33. London: Routledge.

Kalaitzidis, Akis. 2009. *Europe's Greece*. New York: Palgrave Macmillan

Karagül, Ibrahim. 2015. "Açın kapıları, milyonlar Avrupa'ya aksın!" 7 September. http://www.yenisafak.com/yazarlar/ibrahimkaragul/acin-kapilari-milyonlar-avrupaya-aksin-2021647.

Kardaś, Szymon. 2014. "The Creeping 'de-Gazpromisation' of Russian Exports." Warsaw: OSW, 11 June, online.

Kausch, Kristina. 2010. "Morocco's 'Advanced Status': Model or Muddle." Fride: Policy Brief, 43, March.

Keil, Soeren, and Zeynep Arkan, eds. 2014. *The EU and Member State Building: European Foreign Policy in the Western Balkans*. London: Routledge.

Kelley, Judith. 2006. "New Wine in Old Wineskins: Promoting Political Reforms through the New European Policy." *JCMS* 44, no. 1: 29–55.

Kerber, Markus. 2015. "Flüchtllinge: Kritik an 'Euphorie' der Industrie." *Die Zeit* online, 18 October.

Ker-Lindsay, James, and Spyros Economides. 2012. "Standards before Status before Accession: Kosovo's EU Perspective." *Journal of Balkan and Near Eastern Studies* 14, no. 1: 77–92.

Keyman, Fuat, and Ziya Öniş. 2007. *Turkish Politics in a Changing World*. Istanbul: Bilgi University Press.

Klimentyev, Mikhail. 2014. "DPA, Ria-Novosti: Umfrage zu Russland; Deutsche befürworten härtere Sanktionen gegen Putin." *Spiegel Online*, 27 July.

Knaus, Gerald, and Felix Martin. 2003. "Lessons from Bosnia and Herzegovina: Travails of the European Raj." *Journal of Democracy* 14, no. 3: 60–74.

Kneuer, Marianne. 2007. *Demokratisierung durch die EU: Süd- und Ostmitteleuropa im Vergleich*. Wiesbaden: VS Verlag für Sozialwissenschaften.

Köcher, Renate. 2014. "Allensbach-Umfrage: Ein gefährliches Land." *Frankfurter Allgemeine Zeitung*, 15 April.

Kohl, Helmut. 1989. *Zehn-Punkte-Programm Kohls zur Überwindung der Teilung Deutschlands und Europas*. Bundeskanzler Dr. Helmut Kohl vor dem Deutschen Bundestag am 28.11.

Kometer, Michael W., and Stephen E. Wright. 2013. *Winning in Libya: By Design or Default?* Focus stratégique 41. Paris: Ifri, Laboratoire de Recherche sur la Défense.

Kornai, János. 2015. "Hungary's U-Turn: Retreating from Democracy." *Journal of Democracy* 26, no. 3: 34–48.

Kouchner, Bernard. 2008. "Declaration." *Associated Press*, 25 August.

Koutrakos, Panos. 2013. *The EU Common Security and Defence Policy*. Oxford: Oxford University Press.

Krastev, Ivan. 2005. "Russia's Post-Orange Empire." https://www.opendemocracy.net/democracy-europe_constitution/postorange_2947.jsp.

———. 2007. "Russia as the 'Other Europe.'" *Russia in Global Affairs* 4 (October–December).

———. 2008. "Russia and the European Order: Sovereign Democracy Explained." *American Interest*, November/December, 16–24.

Kundera, Milan. 1983. "Un Occident kidnappé ou la tragédie de l'Europe central." *Le Débat*, 27 November.

———. 1984. "The Tragedy of Central Europe." *New York Review of Books*, 26 April, 33–38.

Kurowska, Xymena, and Benjamin Tallis. 2009. "EU Border Assistance Mission: Beyond Border Monitoring?" *European Foreign Affairs Review* 14: 47–64.

Kutter, Barbara, and Vera Trappmann, eds. 2006. *Das Erbe des Beitritts: Europäisierung in Mittel- und Osteuropa*. Baden-Baden: Nomos.

Lannon, Erwan, and Peter van Elsuwege. 2004. "The EU's Northern Dimension and the EMP-ENP: Institutional Framework and Decision-Making Processes Compared." www.fscpo.unict.it/EuropMed/EDRC5/euneighbours01.pdf.

Larionova, Marina, and Vitaly Nagornov. 2010. "Making the Most of the Partnership for Modernisation." The EURUssia Center: The EU-Russia Modernisation Partnership, Brussels, *The EURussia Centre Review*, October, 33–54.

Lavenex, Sandra. 2004. "EU External Governance in 'Wider Europe.'" *Journal of European Public Policy* 11, no. 4: 680–700.

———. 2006. "Shifting Up and Out: The Foreign Policy of European Immigration Control." *West European Politics* 29, no. 2: 329–350.

Lavenex, Sandra, and Emek M. Uçarer. 2004. "The External Dimension of Europeanization: The Case of Immigration Policies." *Cooperation and Conflict: Journal of the Nordic International Studies Association* 39, no. 4: 417–443.

Leggeri, Fabrice. 2015. "Crise migratoire: Frontex a vu son budget tripler pour les opérations en Méditerranée." Interview with Europe1, 1 September.

Le Gloannec, Anne Marie. 2007. *Berlin et le monde*. Paris: Autrement.

———. 2008. "Marcus Aurelius' Foot: Looking for Turkey's Project in the EU; An Interpretation of the French Debate on Turkey." In Nathalie Tocci, ed., *Talking Turkey in Europe: Towards a Differentiated Communication Strategy*, Talking Turkey II, IAI-TEPAV Project, Istituto Affari Internazionali: Quaderni IAI, 119–134.

Le Gloannec, Anne Marie, and Jacques Rupnik. 2008. "Democratization by Extension: Searching for Re-insurance." In Zaki Laïdi, ed., *The Reception of Europe: EU Preferences in a Globalized World*. London: Routledge.

Le More, Anne. 2008. *International Assistance to the Palestinians after Oslo: Political Guilt, Wasted Money*. London: Routledge.

Lendvai, Paul. 2010. *Mein verspieltes Land: Ungarn im Umbruch*. Salzburg: Ecowin.

Lequesne, Christian. 2008. *La France dans la nouvelle Europe: Assumer le changement d'échelle*. Nouveaux Débats. Paris: Presses de Sciences Po.

Les Echos. 2016. "Un Européen sur trois veut que son pays quitte l'Union européene." 9 December.

Lippert, Barbara. 2006. "Erfolge und Grenzen der technokratischen EU-Erweiterungspolitik." In Barbara Kutter and Vera Trappmann, eds., *Das Erbe des Beitritts: Europäisierung in Mittel- und Osteuropa*, 59–74. Baden-Baden: Nomos.

Łoskot-Strachota, Agata. 2009. *Gazprom's Expansion in the EU: Co-operation or Domination?* Warsaw: OSW, Ośrodek Studiów Wschodnich, Centre for Eastern Studies.

Lucarelli, Sonia. 2000. *Europe and the Breakup of Yugoslavia: A Political Failure in Search of a Scholarly Explanation.* The Hague: Kluwer Law International.

Ludlow, N. Piers. 1997. *Dealing with Britain: The Six and the First UK Application to the EEC.* Cambridge: Cambridge University Press.

——. 2012. "Problematic Partners: De Gaulle, Thatcher, and Their Impact." In Erik Jones, Anand Menon, and Stephen Weatherill, eds., *The Oxford Handbook of the European Union*, 206–218. Oxford: Oxford University Press.

Lundestad, Geir. 1986. "Empire by Invitation? The United States and Western Europe, 1945–52." *Journal of Peace Research* 23, no. 3: 263–277.

Maier, Charles S. 2006. *Among Empires: American Ascendancy and Its Predecessors.* Cambridge: Harvard University Press.

Mandil, Claude. 2008. "Sécurité énergétique et Union européenne: Propositions pour la présidence française." Report of the Premier Ministre.

Mankoff, Jeffrey. 2009. *Russian Foreign Policy: The Return of Great Power Politics.* Lanham, MD: Rowman and Littlefield.

Manners, Ian. 2002. "Normative Power Europe: A Contradiction in Terms?" *Journal of Common Market Studies* 40, no. 2: 235–258.

——. 2006. "Normative Power Europe Reconsidered: Beyond the Crossroads." *Journal of European Public Policy* 13, no. 2: 182–199.

——. 2011. "Symbolism in European Integration." *Comparative European Politics* 9, no. 2: 243–268.

Mardin, Şerif. 1972. "Centre-Periphery Relations: A Key to Turkish Politics." *Daedalus*, Winter, 169–190.

——. 2006. *Religion, Society, and Modernity in Turkey.* Syracuse, NY: Syracuse University Press.

Maresceau, Marc, and Erwan Lannon, eds. 2001. *The EU's Enlargement and Mediterranean Strategies: A Comparative Analysis.* Basingstoke: Palgrave Macmillan.

Martín de la Guardia, Ricardo. 2004. "In Search of Lost Europe: Spain." In Wolfram Kaiser and Jürgen Elvert, eds., *European Union Enlargement: A Comparative History*, 93–111. London: Routledge.

Martinez, Luis. 2009. *Maghreb: Vaincre la peur de la démocratie.* Cahiers de Chaillot 115. Paris: Institut d'études de sécurité, Union européenne.

Matlock, Jack. 1995. *Autopsy on an Empire: The American Ambassador's Account of the Collapse of the Soviet Union.* New York: Random House.

Mattli, Walter. 1999. *The Logic of Regional Integration: Europe and Beyond.* Cambridge: Cambridge University Press.

Maull, Hanns W. 1990. "Germany and Japan: The New Civilian Powers." *Foreign Affairs* 69, no. 5: 91–106.

McLoughlin, P. J. 2009. "The SDLP and the Europeanization of the Northern Ireland Problem." *Irish Political Studies* 24, no. 4: 603–619.

Mead, Walter Russell. 2014. "The Return of Geopolitics." *Foreign Affairs* 93, no. 3: 67–79.

Medvedev, Dmitri. 2008. Interview with the Television Channels Rossiya, the First Channel, and NTV, August 31. www.kremlin.ru.

Mendras, Marie. 2008. *Russie: L'envers du pouvoir.* Paris: Odile Jacob.

———. 2012. *Russian Politics. The Paradox of a Weak State.* London: Hurst.

Mertes, Michael. 2001. *The Role of the Federal Chancellery during the Process of German Unification, 1989–90.* Washington, DC: Konrad-Adenauer Stiftung.

Meyer, Christoph O. 2006. *The Quest for a European Strategic Culture.* London: Palgrave Macmillan.

Milov, Vladimir. 2008. *Russia and the West: The Energy Factor, Europe, Russia, and the United States; Finding a New Balance.* Washington, DC: Ifri, Center for Strategic & International Studies.

Moisseron, Jean-Yves. 2005. *Le partenariat euro-méditerranéen: L'échec d'une ambition régionale.* Grenoble: Presses Universitaires de Grenoble.

Monar, Jörg. 2002. "The CFSP and the Leila/Perejil Island Incident: The Nemesis of Solidarity and Leadership." *European Foreign Affairs Review* 7, no. 3: 251–255.

Monnet, Jean. 1955. *Les États-Unis d'Europe ont commencé.* Paris: Robert Laffont.

Montalbano, Pierluigi. 2007. "The ENP: Toward a New EU-Med Partnership?" In Marise Cremona and Gabriella Meloni, eds., *The European Neighbourhood Policy: A Framework for Modernisation?* EUI Working Papers, LAW 21. Florence: European University Institute.

Movchan, Veronika, and Ricardo Giucci. 2011. "Quantitative Assessment of Ukraine's Regional Integration Options: DCFTA with European Union vs. Customs Union with Russia, Belarus and Kazakhstan." Berlin/Kyiv: German Advisory Group, Institute for Economic Research and Policy Consulting, November.

Movchan, Veronika, and Volodymyr Shportyuk. 2012. "EU-Ukraine DCFTA: The Model for Eastern Partnership Regional Trade Cooperation." CASE Network Studies & Analyses 445. Warsaw: CASE.

Mudde, Cas. 2011. *Sussex vs. North Carolina: The Comparative Study of Party-Based Euroscepticism.* SEI Working Paper No. 121, EPERN Working Paper No. 23. Greencastle, IN: De Pauw University.

Müller, Jan-Werner. 2011. "The Hungarian Tragedy." *Dissent,* Spring, 5–9.

Mungiu-Pippidi, Alina. 2007a. "Hijacked Modernization: Romanian Political Culture in the 20th Century." *Südost Europa,* 55, no. 1: 118–144.

———. 2007b. "Is East-Central Europe Backsliding? EU Accession Is No 'End of History.'" *Journal of Democracy* 18, no. 4: 8–16.

———. 2015. *The Quest for Good Governance: How Societies Develop Control of Corruption.* Cambridge: Cambridge University Press.

Musu, Costanza. 2010. *European Union Policy towards the Arab-Israeli Peace Process.* Basingstoke: Palgrave Macmillan.

NATO. 2016. "Standing NATO Maritime Group Two Conducts Drill in the Aegean Sea." 27 February. www.nato.int.

Nemtsov, Boris, and Vladimir Milov. 2008. "Putin and Gazprom." Translated by David Essel. http://www.europeanenergyreview.eu/data/docs/Viewpoints/Putin%20and%20Gazprom_Nemtsov%20en%20Milov.pdf.

NISEPI. 2010–2011. "Reports on Public Opinion." *Belarus Digest.*

Nossiter, Adam. 2016. " 'That Ignoramus': 2 French Scholars of Radical Islam Turn Bitter Rivals." *New York Times,* 12 July.

Nouzille, Jean. 1991. *Histoire de frontiers: L'Autriche et l'Empire ottoman.* Paris: Berg International.

Nye, Joseph S. 1990. *Bound to Lead: The Changing Nature of American Power.* New York: Basic Books.

———. 2004. *Soft Power: The Means to Success in World Politics.* New York: Public Affairs.

Nyiri, Zsolt, and Joshua Raisher. 2012. "Public Opinion and NATO Transatlantic Trends." 16 May.

Obama, Barack, David Cameron, and Nicolas Sarkozy. 2011. "Libya's Pathway to Peace." *New York Times,* 14 April.

Office for a Democratic Belarus. 2013. "EU Neighbourhood Barometer: What Belarusians Think about Belarus and the EU." 11 June. *Belarus Digest.*

Ojanen, Hanna. 2004. "If in 'Europe,' Then in Its 'Core'?" In Wolfram Kaiser and Jürgen Elvert, eds., *European Union Enlargement: A Comparative History,* 150–169. London: Routledge.

Oliver, Tim. 2015. "Europe's British Question: The UK-EU Relationship in a Changing Europe and Multipolar World." *Global Society* 29, no. 3: 409–426.

Onar, Nora. 2009. "The Lure of Europe: Reconciling the European Other and Turkish/ Greek Selves." In Othon Anastasakis, Kalypso Aude Nicolaidis, and Kerem Öktem, eds., *In the Long Shadow of Europe: Greeks and Turks in the Era of Postnationalism,* 47–72. Leiden: Martinus Nijhoff Publishers.

Öniş, Ziya. 2001. "An Awkward Partnership: Turkey's Relations with the European Union in Comparative-Historical Perspective." *Journal of European Integration History* 7, no. 1: 105–119.

———. 2007. "Conservative Globalists versus Defensive Nationalists: Political Parties and Paradoxes of Europeanization in Turkey?" *Journal of Southern Europe and the Balkans* 9, no. 3: 247–261.

Orbán, Viktor. 2012. "Weekly Interview." *MR1-Kossuth Rádió,* 13 April.

———. 2014. Full text of speech at Băile Tuşnad (Tusnádfürdő), 26 July 2014. *The Budapest Beacon,* 29 July.

Ould Aoudia, Jacques. 2008. *Croissance et réformes dans les pays arabes méditerranéens.* Paris: Karthala.

Pamuk, Orhan. 2006. *Nobel Lecture.* 7 December. Nobelprize.org.

———. 2010. "The Fading Dream of Europe." *New York Review of Books,* 25 December. http://www.nybooks.com/articles/archives/2011/feb/10/fading-dream-europe/.

Pardo, Sharon, and Joel Peters. 2010. *Uneasy Neighbors: Israel and the European Union.* Lanham, MD: Lexington Books.

Paszyc, Ewa. 2011. *Sektor gazowy: Ekspansja Gazpromu na regionalnym rynku.* Warsaw: OSW.

Perroux, François. 1955. *L'Europe sans rivages.* Paris: Presses Universitaires de France.

Pew Research Center. 2014. "Despite Concerns about Governance, Ukrainians Want to Remain One Country." *Global Attitudes Project,* 8 May.

Phinnemore, David. 2006. "Beyond 25—the Changing Face of EU Enlargement: Commitment, Conditionality, and the Constitutional Treaty." *Journal of Southern Europe and the Balkans* 8, no. 1: 7–26.

———. 2009. "From Negotiations to Accession: Lessons from the 2007 Enlargement." *Perspectives on European Politics and Society* 10, no. 2: 240–252.

Pollard, Sidney. 1981. *Peaceful Conquest: The Industrialization of Europe, 1760–1970.* Oxford: Oxford University Press.

Pope Francis. 2013. "Visit to Lampedusa." Homily of Holy Father Francis, 8 July. w2.vatican.va.

Popescu, Nicu. 2007. "Europe's Unrecognised Neighbours: The EU in Abkhazia and South Ossetia." CEPS Working Document 260, Brussels, March.

——. 2011. *EU Foreign Policy and Post-Soviet Conflicts: Stealth Intervention.* London: Routledge.

Popescu, Nicu, and Andrew Wilson. 2009. "The Limits of Enlargement-Lite: European and Russian Power in the Troubled Neighbourhood." London: European Council on Foreign Relations.

Posener, Alan. 2007. *Imperium der Zukunft.* Munich: Pantheon.

Powell, Charles. 2001. "International Aspect of Democratization: The Case of Spain." In Laurence Whitehead, ed., *The International Dimensions of Democratization: Europe and the Americas*, 285–315. Rev. and expanded ed. Oxford: Oxford University Press.

Pridham, Geoffrey. 2005. *Designing Democracy: EU Enlargement and Regime Change in Post-Communist Europe.* Basingstoke: Palgrave Macmillan.

——. 2007. "The Scope and Limits of Political Conditionality: Romania's Accession to the European Union." *Comparative European Politics* 5: 347–376.

——. 2008. "The EU's Political Conditionality and Post-Accession Tendencies: Comparison from Slovakia and Latvia." *Journal of Common Market Studies* 46: 365–387.

Prifti, Eviola, ed. 2013. *The European Future of the Western Balkans: Thessaloniki@10 (2003–2013).* Paris: EUISS.

Prodi, Romano. 2002. "A Wider Europe—a Proximity Policy as the Key to Stability." Peace, Security, and Stability International Dialogue and the Role of the EU, Sixth ECSA-World Conference, Jean Monnet Project, Brussels, 5–6 December.

Putin, Vladimir. 2000. "Direct Line with the Readers." *Komsomolskaya Pravda*, 9 February. http://www.kremlin.ru/text/appears/2000/02/135717.shtml.

——. 2005. Annual Address to the Federal Assembly of the Russian Federation, 25 April. www. kremlin.ru.

Radaelli, Claudio. 2000. "Whither Europeanization: Concept Stretching and Substantive Change." *European Integration Online Papers* 4, no. 8.

Razumkov Centre. 2010. "EU Will Not Condemn the Local Elections in Ukraine." 3 November.

——. 2013a. "Customs Union or Europe? The Public Opinion," 4–5, 104–132. Kiev: National Security and Defence.

——. 2013b. "How Citizens See Ukraine's Integration in the EU or the Customs Union: Focus Group Results," 4–5, 98–103. Kiev: National Security and Defence.

——. 2014. "Public Opinion Survey: Citizens Attitude towards Different Types of Territorial Organization." 10 March.

Reitschuster, Boris. 2016. *Putins verdeckter Krieg: Wie Moskau den Westen destabilisiert.* Berlin: Ullstein.

RIA Novosti. 2013. "Putin, Yanukovych Review Joint Naval Parade in Sevastopol." 28 July.

Riding, Alan. 1991. "Conflict in Yugoslavia: Europeans Send High-Level Team." *New York Times*, 29 June.

Rijpma, Jorrit J., and Marise Cremona. 2007. "The Extra-Territorialisation of EU Migration Policies and the Rule of Law." EUI Working Papers, LAW 2007/01. Florence: European University Institute.

Rokkan, Stein, and Derek W. Urwin. 1983. *Economy, Territory, Identity: Politics of West European Peripheries*. London: Sage Publications.

Rupnik, Jacques, ed. 1992. *De Sarajevo à Sarajevo: L'échec yougoslave*. Brussels: Editions Complexe.

——. 2007. "From Democracy Fatigue to Populist Backlash." *Journal of Democracy* 18, no. 4: 17–25.

——, ed. 2011. *The Western Balkans and the EU: "The Hour of Europe."* Chaillot Papers 126. Paris: Institute for Security Studies of the European Union.

Rusi. 2011. "Accidental Heroes: Britain, France, and the Libya Operation." An Interim RUSI Campaign Report, September.

Sampedro, José Luis, and Juan Antonio Payno, eds. 1983. *The Enlargement of the European Community: Case-Studies of Greece, Portugal, and Spain*, London: Macmillan.

Sarotte, Mary Elise. 2009. *1989: The Struggle to Create Post–Cold War Europe*. Princeton, NJ: Princeton University Press.

Schimmelfennig, Frank. 2001. "The Community Trap: Liberal Norms, Rhetorical Action, and the Eastern Enlargement of the European Union." *International Organization 5*, no. 1: 47–80.

——. 2008. "EU Political Accession Conditionality after the 2004 Enlargement: Consistency and Effectiveness." *Journal of European Public Policy*, September.

Schimmelfennig, Frank, and Ulrich Sedelmeier. 2004. "Governance by Conditionality: EU Rule Transfer to the Candidate Countries of Central and Eastern Europe." *Journal of European Public Policy* 10, no. 4: 661–679.

——, eds. 2005a. *The Europeanization of Central and Eastern Europe*. Ithaca, NY: Cornell University Press.

——. 2005b. *The Politics of European Union Enlargement: Theoretical Approaches*. London: Routledge.

Schlögel, Karl. 2014. "Dieser Russland-Aufruf ist ein peinliches Dokument." *Die Welt*, 8 December.

Schmid, Dorothée, and Fares Braizat. 2006. "The Adaptation of EU and US Democracy Promotion Programmes to the Local Political Context in Jordan and Palestine and Their Relevance to Grand Geopolitical Designs." EuroMesco Paper 50, October.

Schuman, Robert. [1963] 2010. *Pour l'Europe*. Paris: Les Éditions Nagel; Geneva: Marika Torrione.

Schwegmann, Christoph. 2000. *The Contact Group and Its Impact on European Institutional Structure*. Occasional Paper 16. Paris: Institute for Security Studies, WEU.

Sedelmeier, Ulrich, and Helen Wallace. 2000. "Eastern Enlargement: Strategy of Second Thoughts?" In Helen Wallace and William Wallace, *Policy-Making in the European Union*, 427–460. 4th ed. Oxford: Oxford University Press.

Seers, Dudley, Bernard Schaffer, and Marja-Liisa Kiljunen, eds. 1979. *Underdeveloped Europe: Studies in Core-Periphery Relations*. Hassocks: The Harvester Press.

Serviciul Independent de Sociologie și Informații, "Opinia." 2013. "Widening the European Dialogue in Moldova." Sociological Survey, Prepared for the Slovak Atlantic Commission, 19 November.

Shevtsova, Lilia. 2007. *Russia: Lost in Transition; The Yeltsin and Putin Legacies.* Washington, DC: Carnegie Endowment for International Peace.

——. 2010. *Lonely Power: Why Russia Has Failed to Become the West and the West Is Weary of Russia.* Washington, DC: Carnegie Endowment for International Peace.

Shumylo-Tapiola, Olga. 2012. "Ukraine at the Crossroads: Between the EC DCFTA & Customs Union." Paris: Ifri, Russia/NIS Center.

Smith, Anthony D. 1999. *Myths and Memories of the Nation.* Oxford: Oxford University Press.

Smith, Karen E. 2004. *The Making of EU Foreign Policy: The Case of Eastern Europe.* 2nd ed. Basingstoke: Palgrave Macmillan.

Smith, Michael. 1996. "The European Union and Changing Europe: Establishing the Boundaries of Order." *Journal of Common Market Studies* 34, no. 1: 5–28.

Snyder, Timothy. 2011. *Bloodlands: Europe between Hitler and Stalin.* London: Vintage Books.

Socor, Vladimir. 2005. "France Leads the EU's Nyet to Georgia Border Monitoring." *Eurasia Daily Monitor*, 19 April. www.jamestown.org.

——. 2009. "Russia Seeks Control of Ukraine's Gas Transit System through a Consortium." *Eurasia Daily Monitor*, 15 January.

Sonne, Werner. 2013. *Staatsräson? Wie Deutschland für Israels Sicherheit haftet.* Berlin: Propyläen.

Spendzharova, Aneta B., and Milada Vachudova. 2012. "Catching Up? Consolidated Liberal Democracy in Bulgaria and Romania after EU Accession." *West European Politics* 35, no. 1: 39–58.

Stelzenmüller, Constanze. 2009. "Germany's Russia Question: A New Ostpolitik for Europe." *Foreign Affairs* 88, no. 2: 89–100.

Stent, Angela. 2014. *The Limits of Partnership: U.S.-Russian Relations in the Twenty-First Century.* Princeton, NJ: Princeton University Press.

Stern, Jonathan P. 2005. *The Future of Russian Gas and Gazprom.* Oxford: Oxford University Press for the Oxford Institute for Energy Studies.

Stolz, Joëlle. 2013. "L'Europe met Viktor Orban sous surveillance." *Le Monde*, 18 July.

Strange, Susan. 1988. *States and Markets.* 2nd ed. London: Pinter Publishers.

Szűcs, Jenő. 1985. *Les trois Europes.* Paris: L'Harmattan.

Tagliapietra, Simone, and Georg Zachmann. 2015. "The Gazprom Case: Good Timing or Bad Timing?" *Bruegel*, 23 April. bruegel.org.

Tavares, Rui [reporter]. 2013. *Report on the Situation of Fundamental Rights: Standards and Practices in Hungary (Pursuant to the European Parliament Resolution of 16 February 2012) (2012/2130 (INI)).* European Parliament, Committee of Civil Liberties, Justice and Home Affairs, A7-0229/2013, 24 June.

Thatcher, Margaret. 1988. *Address Given by Margaret Thatcher.* 20 September.

Therborn, Göran. 1995. *European Modernity and Beyond: The Trajectory of European Societies, 1945–2000.* London: Sage.

Tocci, Nathalie. 2004. *EU Accession Dynamics and Conflict Resolution: Catalysing Peace or Consolidating Partition in Cyprus?* Aldershot: Ashgate.

——. 2005. "Does the EU Promote Democracy in Palestine?" In Michael Emerson, ed., *Democratisation in the European Neighbourhood*, 131–152. Brussels: CEPS.

Todorova, Maria. 1997. *Imagining the Balkans.* New York: Oxford University Press.

Toje, Asle. 2010. *The EU as a Small Power: After the Post–Cold War*. Basingstoke: Palgrave Macmillan.

Tsingos, Basilios. 2001. "Underwriting Democracy: The European Community and Greece." In Laurence Whitehead, ed., *The International Dimensions of Democratization: Europe and the Americas*. Rev. and expanded ed. Oxford: Oxford University Press.

Tsoukalis, Loukas. 1981. *The European Community and Its Mediterranean Enlargement*. London: George Allen & Unwin.

——. 2002. "Greece in the European Union: Political and Economic Aspects." In Panayotis C. Ioakimidis, ed., *Greece in the European Union: The New Role and the New Agenda*, 37–45. Athens: MPMM.

Tulmets, Elsa. 2005. "New Modes of Governance in EU's External Relations: Explaining the Transfer of Ideas and Cooperation Methods from the Enlargement to the Neighbourhood Policy." In Sarunas Liekis et al., eds., *European Union and Its New Neighbourhood: Different Countries, Common Interests*. Vilnius: Mykolas Romeris University.

Türkmen, Buket. 2014. "The New Islamist Domination in Turkey: Occidentalism Toppled." In Riva Kastoryano, ed., *Turkey between Nationalism and Globalization*, 107–122. London: Routledge.

Ulusoy, Orçun. 2016. "Turkey as a Safe Third Country?" *Border Criminologies* (blog), University of Oxford, 29 March. https://www.law.ox.ac.uk/research-subject-groups/centre-criminology/centreborder-criminologies/blog/2016/03/turkey-safe-third.

UNHCR (United Nations High Commissioner for Refugees). 2015. "World At War: Global Trend Report 2014: Forced Displacement." June. unhcr.org.

United Nations Human Rights Office, Office of the High Commissioner. 2016. "Greece: Europe's Lack of Political Will Creates Serious Suffering for Thousands of Migrants in Greece; UN Rights Expert." http://www.ohchr.org/.

UNSC (United Nations Security Council). 2011. "Security Council Approves 'No-Fly Zone' over Libya Authorizing 'All Necessary Measures' to Protect Civilians, by Vote of 10 in Favour with 5 Abstentions." SC/10200, 6498th Meeting (Night), 17 March.

Vachudova, Milada. 2005. *Europe Undivided: Democracy, Leverage, and Integration after Communism*. Oxford: Oxford University Press.

Verney, Susannah. 2007. "The Dynamics of EU Accession: Turkish Travails in Comparative Perspective." *Journal of Balkan and Near Eastern Studies* 9, no. 3: 307–322.

Waever, Ole. 1997. "Imperial Metaphors: Emerging European Analogies to Pre-Nation-State Imperial Systems." In Ola Tunander, Pavel Baev, and Victoria Ingrid Einagel, eds., *Geopolitics in Post-Wall Europe: Security, Territory, and Identity*, 59–93. Oslo: International Peace Research Institute.

Waterbury, Myra A. 2010. *Between State and Nation: Diaspora Politics and Kin-State Nationalism in Hungary*. Basingstoke: Palgrave Macmillan.

Weisser, Ulrich. 2007. "Wir brauchen Russland." *Internationale Politik*, March, 48–55.

Whitney, Nick, and Anthony Dworkin. 2012. "A Power Audit of EU–North Africa Relations." European Council on Foreign Relations, September. ecfr.eu.

Wijkman, Per Magnus. 1990. "Patterns of Production and Trade." In William Wallace, ed., *The Dynamics of European Integration*, 89–105. London: Pinter Publishers for the RIIA.

Winkler, Heinrich August. 2015. "Auslaufmodell Westen? Demokratien sind gefährdet." DeutschlandFunk, 4 February.

Woodward, Susan. 1995. *Balkan Tragedy: Chaos and Dissolution after the Cold War.* Washington, DC: Brookings.

World Bank. 2014. *World Development Report 2015.* Washington, DC: World Bank.

Wynaendts, Henry. 1993. *L'engrenage: Chroniques yougoslaves juillet 1991–août 1992.* Paris: Denoël.

Yacobi, Haim, and David Newman. 2008. "The EU and the Israel-Palestine Conflict." In Thomas Diez, Mathias Albert, and Stephan Stetter, *The European Union and Border Conflicts: The Power of Integration and Association*, 173–202. Cambridge: Cambridge University Press.

Yeltsin, Boris. 1997. "Declaration." Associated Press, 22 March.

Yılmaz, Bahri. 2008. "The Relations of Turkey with the European Union: Candidate Forever." Working Paper Series 167. Harvard University, Center for European Studies.

Younge, Gary. 2016. "Brexit: A Disaster Decades in the Making." *The Guardian*, 30 June.

Youngs, Richard. 2005. "Engagement: Sharpening European Influence." In Richard Youngs, ed., *Global Europe,* Report 2, *New Terms of Engagement*, 1–14. London: The Foreign Policy Center.

——, ed. 2008. *Is the European Union Supporting Democracy in Its Neighbourhood?* Madrid: FRIDE and European Council on Foreign Relations.

——. 2010. *Europe's Decline and Fall: The Struggle against Global Irrelevance.* London: Profile Books.

Zarakol, Ayşe. 2011. *After Defeat: How the East Learned to Live with the West.* Cambridge: Cambridge University Press.

Zielonka, Jan. 2006. *Europe as Empire: The Nature of the Enlarged European Union.* Oxford: Oxford University Press.

Zoellick, Robert. 2015a. "Lessons of German Unification." *Huffington Post*, 10 January.

——. 2015b. "A World in Flux." http://www.aicgs.org/events/a-world-in-flux-german-american-relations-and-a-changing-global-order/.

Zweig, Stefan. [1942] 2013. *Die Welt von Gestern.* Frankfurt: Fischer.

INDEX